A CULTURAL HISTORY OF LAW

VOLUME 1

A Cultural History of Law
General Editor: Gary Watt

Volume 1
A Cultural History of Law in Antiquity
Edited by Julen Etxabe

Volume 2
A Cultural History of Law in the Middle Ages
Edited by Emanuele Conte and Laurent'Mayali

Volume 3
A Cultural History of Law in the Early Modern Age
Edited by Peter Goodrich

Volume 4
A Cultural History of Law in the Age of Enlightenment
Edited by Rebecca Probert and John Snape

Volume 5
A Cultural History of Law in the Age of Reform
Edited by Ian Ward

Volume 6
A Cultural History of Law in the Modern Age
Edited by Richard K. Sherwin and Danielle Celermajer

A CULTURAL HISTORY OF LAW
IN ANTIQUITY

Edited by Julen Etxabe

BLOOMSBURY ACADEMIC
LONDON • NEW YORK • OXFORD • NEW DELHI • SYDNEY

BLOOMSBURY ACADEMIC
Bloomsbury Publishing Plc
50 Bedford Square, London, WC1B 3DP, UK
1385 Broadway, New York, NY 10018, USA
29 Earlsfort Terrace, Dublin 2, Ireland

BLOOMSBURY, BLOOMSBURY ACADEMIC and the Diana logo
are trademarks of Bloomsbury Publishing Plc

First published in Great Britain 2019
Paperback edition published in 2023

Copyright © Bloomsbury Publishing Plc, 2019

Julen Etxabe has asserted his right under the Copyright, Designs
and Patents Act, 1988, to be identified as Editor of this work.

Cover image © Ivy Close Images/Alamy Stock Photo

All rights reserved. No part of this publication may be reproduced or transmitted
in any form or by any means, electronic or mechanical, including photocopying,
recording, or any information storage or retrieval system, without prior permission in writing
from the publishers.

Bloomsbury Publishing Plc does not have any control over, or responsibility
for, any third-party websites referred to or in this book. All internet addresses given
in this book were correct at the time of going to press. The editor and publisher
regret any inconvenience caused if addresses have changed or sites have ceased to
exist, but can accept no responsibility for any such changes.

A catalogue record for this book is available from the British Library.

A catalog record for this book is available from the Library of Congress.

ISBN:		
	PB set:	978-1-3503-6891-0
	HB:	978-1-4742-1229-8
	PB:	978-1-3503-6826-2
	ePDF:	978-1-3500-7923-6
	eBook:	978-1-3500-7924-3

Series: The Cultural Histories Series

Typeset by Integra Software Services Pvt. Ltd.
Printed and bound in Great Britain

To find out more about our editors and books visit www.bloomsbury.com
and sign up for our newsletters.

CONTENTS

LIST OF FIGURES	VI
NOTES ON CONTRIBUTORS	IX
SERIES PREFACE	XI

Introduction: Writing a Cultural History of Law in Antiquity 1
Julen Etxabe

1 Justice 21
   Kathryn Slanski

2 Constitution 41
   Jill Frank

3 Codes 59
   Barry Wimpfheimer

4 Agreements 75
   Roberto Fiori

5 Arguments 91
   David Mirhady

6 Property and Possession 109
   Paul J. du Plessis

7 Wrongs 125
   Jacob Giltaij

8 Legal Profession 143
   Kaius Tuori

NOTES	158
BIBLIOGRAPHY	172
INDEX	193

LIST OF FIGURES

INTRODUCTION

0.1	Fragment of an Athenian decree concerning the collection of the tribute from members of the Delian League, probably passed in the spring of 447 BCE.	4
0.2	The shield of Achilles, Homer's *Iliad* (translated by Pope).	7
0.3	Ishtar Gate.	8
0.4	Augustus coin found in the Pudukottai Hoard, India.	8
0.5	Ara pacis relief.	9
0.6	Roman Road at Timgad, Algeria.	9

JUSTICE

1.1	*Law Stele of Hammurabi*.	28
1.2	Impression of third millennium cylinder seal.	29
1.3	Mixing bowl (calyx krater) with the killing of Agamemnon (face depicting the murder of Aigisthos by Orestes).	36
1.4	Mixing bowl (calyx krater) with the killing of Agamemnon (face depicting the murder of Agamemnon by Aigisthos).	37
1.5	Mixing bowl (calyx krater) with the killing of Agamemnon (side view).	38

CONSTITUTION

2.1	Democracy crowning Dēmos (the Athenian People).	45
2.2	Portrait statue of Solon along the balustrade.	46
2.3	Athenian decree. Detail of a marble stele inscribed with a decree of the Athenian boulē, *c.* 440–425 BCE.	56

CODES

3.1	Portions of the temple scroll, labeled 11Q19, Second century BCE.	61
3.2	Babylonian Talmud, 1522.	62
3.3	Law Code of Gortyn, Louvre.	63

LIST OF FIGURES vii

3.4 Justinian's Digest. 64
3.5 Detail of Hammurabi's Stele, showing the cuneiform writing style in legible form. 68

AGREEMENTS

4.1 Reliefs on a sarcophagus depicting farmers gathering legumes and milking sheep. 80
4.2 Roman marble sarcophagus with relief depicting nuptial rite. 82
4.3 The goddess Pudicitia. 83
4.4 Roman merchant ship. 85
4.5 Stipulation of a contract or will. 87

ARGUMENTS

5.1 Bronze juror's identification ticket (*pinakion*), inscribed with name, patronymic, and deme, fourth century BCE. 91
5.2 Fragment of the inscribed lid of a cooking pot with dipinto, fourth century BCE. 94
5.3 A Klepsydra (waterclock) used to time speeches in the Athenian courts. 97
5.4 Inscribed jurors' ballots, fourth century BCE. One ballot has a solid axle, the other a hollow axle. 102

PROPERTY AND POSSESSION

6.1 A military diploma granting its holder Roman citizenship. 114
6.2 A *groma* [surveying equipment]. 117
6.3 Cadastre D'Arausio. 122
6.4 *Forma Urbis Romae*. 122

WRONGS

7.1 Fresco from the Sala di Grande Dipinto, Scene II in the Villa de Misteri (Pompeii). 127
7.2 Fresco from the Sala di Grande Dipinto, Scene VI in the Villa de Misteri (Pompeii). 130
7.3 Fresco from the Sala di Grande Dipinto, Scene VIII in the Villa de Misteri (Pompeii). 133
7.4 Roman fresco showing a dancing menad from the Villa dei Misteri in Pompeii (Sala del Grande Dipinto, scene V). 136
7.5 Full fresco in the Villa dei Misteri at Pompeii, triclinium wall. 137

7.6 Dancing satyr (second style) from the cubiculum next to the Sala del Grande Dipinto in the Villa de Misteri (Pompeii). 140

LEGAL PROFESSION

8.1 The Roman Forum and the Comitium on 44BC, a reconstruction. 145

8.2 Cicero, from the bust at the Capitoline Museum, Rome. 147

8.3 Fresco representing Terentius Neo and his wife discovered in Pompeii, Italy. 148

8.4 Scaevola confronts Porsenna. Rubbens and Van Dyck (before 1628). 150

8.5 A scene from the Forum, from the Plutei of Trajan, a stone balustrade built by Emperor Trajan, now at Curia Julia in Rome. 157

NOTES ON CONTRIBUTORS

Julen Etxabe is docent in legal theory from the University of Helsinki. He teaches and writes in the areas of legal and political theory, law and humanities, and comparative human rights. He published *The Experience of Tragic Judgment* (2013) and co-edited several other books, most recently *Rancière and Law* (2018). He was also co-editor in chief of *No-Foundations: An Interdisciplinary Journal of Law and Justice* from 2012 to 2017.

Roberto Fiori is Professor of Roman Law at the University of Rome "Tor Vergata." His research interests range from archaic Roman law to classical contract law, civil and criminal procedure, the law of persons, the relationship between Roman law and Greek philosophy, and the legacy of Roman law to the modern systems of civil and common law. His most recent book is *Bonus vir. Politica filosofia retorica e diritto nel de officiis di Cicerone* (2011).

Jill Frank is Professor of Government at Cornell University. Author of *A Democracy of Distinction: Aristotle and the Work of Politics* (2005) and *Poetic Justice: Rereading Plato's* Republic (2018), and founding director of the Classics in Contemporary Perspectives Initiative at the University of South Carolina, Columbia (2008–2014), she writes about power, human nature, desire, lying, poetry, friendship, property, persuasion, and law.

Jacob Giltaij wrote his dissertation on the problem of human rights in Roman law. (*Mensenrechten in het Romeinse recht* (Nijmegen: Wolff, 2011)). Since then, he has published on political theory, philosophy, and law in ancient Rome. He is a university researcher at the Academy of Finland Centre of Excellence in Law, Identity and the European Narratives (EUROSTORIE), at the Faculty of Social Sciences of the University of Helsinki.

David Mirhady is Professor of Humanities at Simon Fraser University, Vancouver. He has published on ancient Greek law and rhetorical theory, and on the school of Aristotle.

Paul J. du Plessis is Professor of Roman law at the School of Law, the University of Edinburgh. His main field of research is Roman law (with specific reference to property, obligations and, to a lesser extent, persons and family). In the context of his interest in "law and society," his research also focuses on a further period where Roman legal principles were used to create law, namely the period of the European *iuscommune* in the late Middle Ages. Here, his research explores themes such as structure, doctrine and legitimacy with a view to challenging the accepted "macro-narratives" of European legal history.

Kathryn Slanski is an Assyriologist who studied at Johns Hopkins, Munich, and Harvard. She is Senior Lecturer in Humanities and in Near Eastern Languages and Civilizations at Yale, where she has led the Directed Studies Program since 2013.

Kaius Tuori is Associate Professor of European Intellectual History at the University of Helsinki. He has published widely on matters of legal culture and Roman law. His latest book is *Emperor of Law: The Emergence of Roman Imperial Jurisdiction* (Oxford University Press, 2016).

Barry Wimpfheimer is Associate Professor of Religious Studies and Law at Northwestern University. His most recent book is *The Talmud: A Biography* (Princeton: Princeton University Press, 2018).

SERIES PREFACE

The six volumes in *A Cultural History of Law* present a panorama of law's cultural significance over the span of several centuries, especially as it relates to the place of law in the arts and humanities. Each volume focuses on a distinct time period from antiquity to modernity and in each volume a chapter is devoted to one of eight legally significant themes: "Justice," "Constitution," "Codes," "Agreements," "Arguments," "Property and Possession," "Wrongs," and "The Legal Profession." The collection does not seek to provide encyclopedic coverage, but rather to present cultural case studies that highlight how particular cultural artifacts express and explore the key legal—and inevitably the key political and social—concerns of their time. The authors have picked flowers from their field of expertise—a play, a painting, a mosaic, a book, a film—which bring into close focus the cultural and legal flourishing of the time. The volume editors are internationally distinguished scholars with a passion and deep appreciation for the law and culture of their chosen period. Together with the experts that they have assembled to contribute chapters on the eight themes, they are reliable guides not merely to the facts about each period but to the feel of each period. Every volume has an ethos and a style that immerses the reader in the distinctive quality of its era. The series is indebted to the archivist's concern to discover and catalog historical materials, but what sets it apart is its concern to show how the materials of history are materially meaningful. In this way, our retrospective of more than 2,000 years continues to have relevance for lawyers and for all culturally concerned citizens today.

Sometimes we find that artifacts have lost the cultural meanings that first produced them. Likewise, we sometimes we find that artifacts are culturally meaningful today in ways that they were not at the time of their creation. Take the example of Magna Carta—The Great Charter of King John of England sealed at Runnymede on the Thames in 1215. Today, in the United States in particular, Magna Carta has been hoisted to totemic heights in the cultural imagination. It might therefore seem strange to us that William Shakespeare's play *King John* makes no reference at all to this great artifact. The reason for its omission is that for Shakespeare and his early modern contemporaries, the most dramatic historical event in the reign of King John was his surrender of the crown to the papal legate and his receiving it again as a papal vassal. The modern significance of Magna Carta is largely a post-Enlightenment invention and its principal promoters were the great myth-makers who framed the American Constitution and created the idea of the United States. It is some proof of this that the Magna Carta memorial which stands at Runnymede today was erected by the American Bar Association. The small-scale temple, like the much larger Jefferson Memorial in Washington DC, has become a place of secular pilgrimage; a sanctuary to the values of political freedom and human rights under law.

In 2015, to mark the 800th anniversary of the sealing of Magna Carta, sculptor Hew Locke's "The Jurors" was installed at Runnymede. It comprises twelve bronze chairs, each of which (according to the official narrative) "incorporates symbols and imagery representing concepts of law and key moments in the struggle for freedom, rule of law and equal rights." In this respect, it performs a similar function to the eight bas-relief panels by sculptor John Donnelly Jnr that adorn the great bronze doors of the United States Supreme Court in Washington DC. Shakespeare would have appreciated the performative purpose of these "solemn temples" but he would surely be surprised to see today how much has been made of Magna Carta. The rise of Magna Carta as an artifact of cultural history would certainly have amazed the landed aristocrats who first compelled King John to set his seal to the charter in the culturally Christian, monarchal and feudal context of the High Middle Ages. The narrative accompanying "The Jurors" alerts us to the license that the sculptor has taken with the history of law. We are told that it is "not a memorial, but rather an artwork that aims to examine the changing and ongoing significance and influences of Magna Carta." It is, in short, a cultural reworking of an artifact that owes its great status to creative cultural appropriation. The actual provisions of Magna Carta that survive in law are impressively few, but the three survivors are perhaps all the more significant for their small number. Much is still made of the survival of the right to trial by jury. Rather less is made, nowadays, of the provisions that preserve the "liberties of the English Church" and the "privileges of the City of London." One of the most important contributions we can make to the appreciation of history is to show where cultures are selective in what they present as fact. The artifacts of history are always presented in the cabinets of culture.

The word "fact" comes, in fact, from the Latin *facere* ("to make") and it can be helpful to think of historical facts as things that are produced by the action of culture and as things which, in turn, produce cultures. Even where a society is collectively in error in its understanding of historical fact, a commonly held mistake inevitably becomes part of the cultural history of that society. The story becomes the history. One of the mistakes we often make, as the shifting status of Magna Carta indicates, is to suppose that the modern commentator can claim a monopoly in the present moment to determine "true" history from "false." Today's official history is only ever the history of the present. The past had its own histories. Cultural history allows an appreciation of the cultural stories that give meaning to societies in time and across time. From a cultural perspective, myths can be more meaningful, and in that cultural sense more "true," than many a cold matter of fact.

Another great and oft-repeated mistake that this book series seeks to remedy is the supposition that law can be meaningfully separated from the culture in which it exists. In *Law as Culture*, Lawrence Rosen observes that law:

> never stands apart from life—some refined essence of professional inquiry or arcane speech. Rather, it forms the conscious attention we give to our relationships. Like art and literature, through law we attempt to order our ties to one another ... However it is displayed, however it is applied, we can no more comprehend the roles of legal institutions without seeing them as part of their culture than we can fully understand each culture without attending to its form of law.[1]

There is an historical aspect to this understanding of law as culture. Pierre Legrand writes, for example, that:

> French law is, first and foremost, a cultural phenomenon, not unlike singing or weaving. The reason why the French have the *chanteurs* they have lies somewhere in their history, their Frenchness, in their identity. Similarly, the reason why the French have the legislative texts or the judicial decisions they have, say, on a matter of sales law, lies somewhere in their history, their Frenchness, in their identity.[2]

There are obvious limits to the mechanistic metaphor by which we talk of cultural history as something manufactured or fabricated. Human hands fashion historical artifacts, but legal artifacts grow out of a culture in a way that makes it hard to know where the artifact starts and the culture ends. It might be better to take the "culture" metaphor seriously and to suggest that laws grow out of a society organically and that the artificial intervention of human hands are like those of the gardener—taming, tending, and ordering wild growth. Thus the cultural history of law becomes something like a horticultural history. This is not such a strange thought when one considers that the English word for the "court" of law is derived from the Latin *hortus* (garden). Malcolm Andrews has suggested that "one could write an illuminating, if oblique, history of a nation's cultural development by examining its changing conception of the garden's scope, design and function."[3] The gardening metaphor may be especially useful in helping us to understand the cultural history of law, given the complex relation between natural justice and artificial laws in human society. Dress is another artificial creation of human craft which, as a cultural outworking of the complex relation between nature and human ordering, serves well as a way to understand the artificial and creative nature of law's contribution to culture. Laws are produced in society in much the same way that gardens, dress, and other products of complex cultural systems are produced in society. When we have completed our journey through the six volumes of this series we may conclude that the chief legislator across the ages has been no parliament nor any body of the people politically represented, but that the great lawmaker has always been the deep, rich, and creative power of human culture.

Gary Watt, Professor of Law, University of Warwick, UK

Introduction

Writing a Cultural History of Law in Antiquity

JULEN ETXABE

As I begin to write the introduction for this volume, I want to share with the reader the initial sense of unease that came with the invitation: Antiquity (as the term came to be known in the Renaissance) covers a huge span of time and space, with societies as diverse as the ancient Near Eastern cities of Assyria and Babylon in Mesopotamia, the Hittites in Anatolia, the Kingdoms of Egypt,[1] the land of Canaan and Ancient Israel, as well as the Greece of archaic, classical, and Hellenistic periods. It also includes the thousand-year expansion of a seven-hilled city of Rome, which grew to become the most enduring empire the world has ever known, even extending its contacts in the east towards India and China.[2]

All these societies have left us imposing legal documents: the Code of Hammurabi (c. 1750 BCE), the Hebrew Bible (eighth—fifth centuries BCE), the Twelve Tables (c. 450 BCE); Athenian law court speeches and oratory (fourth century BCE), Justinian's *Corpus Iuris Civilis* (529–534 CE), among an immense amount of epigraphic, literary, and iconographic material in inscriptions, vase-painting, sculpture, architecture, as well as more prosaic notary documents, contracts, sales, inheritances, and adoptions preserved in clay-tablet and papyri. These materials are not easy to read, let alone master, for any scholar: some are written in extinct languages like Akkadian, Sumerian, Hittite, Aramaic ... and forms of inscription predating the Phoenician alphabet (cuneiform script, Linear-B), which require years of "initiation."[3] Among the additional difficulties we face are the massive holes in knowledge: important legal sources have been lost entirely or exist only in fragmentary or unreliable citation; even when the texts of law are known, like the Twelve Tables, either their context is not known or is known only as a speculative reconstruction (Beard 2015). But for all the gaps of information, the main difficulty is one of *meaning*.

This is what one of the leading experts of Near Eastern law, after years of study and translation of all the law collections of ancient Mesopotamia (Roth 1997), has to say about the simple question "What are the Mesopotamian Law collections?" or, more generally, "What is Mesopotamian Law?" Her opening statement deserves citation in full:

> I now confess that I do not "know" what the law collections (or "codes") meant for the ancient scribes, for the judicial authorities, and for the contemporary and mostly illiterate populations; nor do I any longer think that there is a single "answer" that we will ever "know" Rather, I have become more and more convinced that the "law" and the "law collections" through Mesopotamia, considering the variety of social, linguistic, political, economic, and ethnic changes over three millennia, contain a rich multitude of layers of meaning. Although there are shared traditions,

> there is no single "common law" throughout the ancient Near East, from the Mediterranean to the Zagros Mountains, from Anatolia to the Sinai, from the third millennium to the conquest of Alexander. There is no uniform "law" of any specific legal category ("law of adultery" or "law of homicide," for example), any more than there is a single procedure for animal sacrifice, or a single form of letter address. More specifically, the formal collections of legal cases (the often-called "law codes") cannot be viewed as reifications of the abstractions, devoid of intentions and the reinterpretative readings of their drafters, of their royal sponsors, and especially their audiences ... For the "law collections" are not simply collections of laws; the laws of Hammurabi, in particular, is a historical artifact, operating in and trough time and space in distinctive and measured ways. (Roth 1995: 13–14, footnotes omitted)

That a scholar as knowledgeable as Martha Roth feels the need to "confess" that she does not know what the law meant for the judicial authorities and the populations in question, and doubts that there is actually an answer to this question that we will ever know, should give us some pause.

Any attempt to write a cultural history of law in antiquity must begin from the recognition that, concerning societies separated from ours by millennia, an abyss opens before us: there is simply too much we do not know, and will never know, about what the law was, what it meant, and how it worked; it is hard to tell how far law was enforced, how wide was its transmission and how it affected the ordinary lives of people.[4] Scholars may hope to construct impressive edifices to collect and amass all the data, but at the end of the day these constructions remain vulnerable: new evidence, a revolutionary find analogous to the Rosetta stone or the decipherment of the cuneiform, or the development of hypotheses and general theories that reorient the field can make the edifice crumble, making us doubt even the things we thought we knew.[5]

Yet this is not a call to despair. Despite Roth's cautionary warning, she mentions ancient scribes, judicial authorities, and general populations; practices of writing and literacy; the distinction between drafters and sponsors of the law; institutions like animal sacrifice; legal categories such as adultery and homicide; and a diversity of social, linguistic, ethnic, political, and economic practices to be considered towards the formation of legal cultures. Furthermore, Roth makes two important points for a cultural perspective of law, as we shall see: first, the importance of viewing law not only as abstraction or reification, but also to seek for the aims, purposes, goals, and significations it may have had for the people themselves. Second, an emphasis on the process of historical mediation between the past and the present.

And thus with the challenge came also the excitement. To someone who views law as ubiquitous and deeply embedded in culture—in fact itself as a certain kind of culture—it offers an opportunity to reflect anew. So, firstly, how does one go about writing a cultural history of law in antiquity—and what, in fact, does the term "cultural" add to a history of law? Secondly, is any category of law capacious enough to comprehend these diverse contexts—and their internal differentiation? Thirdly, can we even compare between them all—and how? Fourthly, how do we engage meaningfully from our own present with the texts and contexts of law in antiquity? Before I go on to say something about each of these four questions (cultural-historical, jurisprudential, comparative, and hermeneutic) in turn, I want to zero in on their challenges in more detail.

* * *

First, some of the materials inherited in the catalog of laws are not laws in the modern "statutory" sense of the term: the Mesopotamic "laws" are not meant to regulate general behavior, nor is the Code of Hammurabi a "code" in the systematic and comprehensive sense of Napoleon's (or Justinian's).[6] Likewise, what has been transmitted to us as the Athenian Constitution is not a constitution,[7] nor are the Roman emperor's *constitutiones* anything like a set of fundamental principles for the organization of the state. The Roman *ius civile*, out of which we have inherited the term civil law, was not intended to regulate the relations of private individuals generally (like modern civil law); rather it was the law that applied exclusively to Roman citizens, different from that applicable to non-citizens. Terminological problems aside, the real difficulty is, as Roth reminds us, that the *cultural* context in which all these laws came to mean anything is long gone.

Secondly, nowadays we seem to know what we mean when we say "the Roman law of contract" or "the Greek laws of homicide" and we readily think of discrete areas of scholars working on Greek, Roman, Jewish, Near Eastern laws. But the alleged unity of some of these legal corpora is questionable. In a famous series of articles, Moses Finley argued that never in Antiquity was there a unified Greece in the sense in which there was a Rome, as Greece was never under a unified political and jurisdictional control (1951 and 1966). Finley alluded further to the lack of a "close-knit corps of professionals (bureaucrats, professors, guildsmen, judges) at any time or place in the Greek city-states before the Roman era" (1966: 89) who would have provided the conceptual glue to the divergent legal practices. In conclusion, Finley questioned the pertinence of the heading "Greek law," and suggested that the focus should be on particular city-states (Figure I.1). Whatever side we take in this debate,[8] the answer is connected to the prior *jurisprudential* question of what we think law to be.[9]

Thirdly, even if we could somehow identify a concept of law sufficient to enable us to speak of Mesopotamic, Hebrew, Greek, and Roman law (in their multiple instantiations), on what basis can we establish valid comparisons between them? What would we be comparing—legal rules and institutions, social functions, or something more culturally ingrained? Fourth and finally, how do the modern perceptual filters and categories of analysis, and our own situatedness in the world, mediate our understanding of past societies and their cultural creations? What kind of relationship or processes of historical mediation do we hope to establish with the texts and contexts of law in antiquity? I plan to treat these four issues—cultural-historical, jurisprudential, comparative, and hermeneutic—one at a time, drawing from scholars faced with similar questions and providing illustrations from diverse legal contexts in antiquity.

CULTURAL HISTORY AND A "CULTURAL" APPROACH TO LAW

What are the aims, methods, and presuppositions of cultural history? What does the term "cultural" add to history generally—and to the history of law in particular? One way to begin is to bring back one of the precursors of cultural history, Jacob Burckhardt, who taught at the University of Basel when a young Nietzsche was named professor of classical philology. Burckhardt conceived his cultural approach to history mostly as a reaction to the positivist conception then prevalent in Germany—in turn a reaction against the Hegelian conception of history as the development of Spirit.[10] Against the empirical ethos of the era (or perhaps guessing its inherent limitations), Burckhardt approached history not as

FIGURE 0.1. Fragment of an Athenian decree concerning the collection of the tribute from members of the Delian League, probably passed in the spring of 447 BCE. Elgin collection. © The Trustees of the British Museum.

a concatenation of facts and events and their causal relationships. Instead, Burckhardt aimed "at describing what manner of people these were, what they wished for, thought, perceived and were capable of" ([1872] 1998: 5). In so doing, he sought to find the underlying core meanings, habits of thoughts, attitudes, and constants of culture.

A significant aspect was the study of whatever source could grant him access to the era. He thought that a first-hand engagement with primary sources was preferable to any second-hand commentary (even at the peril of occasional misunderstanding). Thus, he recommended

> everyone must reread the works which have been exploited a thousand times, because they present a peculiar aspect, not only to every reader and every century, but also to every time of life. It may be, for instance, that there is in Thucydides a fact of capital importance which somebody will note in a hundred year's time. ([1902] 1979: 52)

Crucially, Burckhardt emphasized the capacity of cultural artifacts to "betray their secrets unconsciously and even, paradoxically, through fictitious elaborations, quite apart from the material details they may set out to record and glorify" ([1872] 1998: 5). Burckhardt thought, as the Greek historian Herodotus before him, that a story could have something to reveal, even though its veracity might be doubted. Furthermore, by claiming that no historical account is free from a point of view, Burckhardt foreshadowed the arguments of historians such as Hayden White (1973) and Paul Veyne (1984) who emphasized the role of narrative emplotment, metaphor, and imagination in every historical account. Thus, Burckhardt recognized that, while his attempt at understanding the historical period was genuine, a different historian could have woven a different story out of exactly the same threads ([1860] 2004: 19).

Perhaps our modern era remains reasonably suspicious about claims to being able to grasp core cultural constants or the underlying spirit of an era, but modern cultural history owes a profound debt to works such as Burckhardt's (Burke 2004a and b; Arcangeli 2012). As a thriving field of study between intellectual history or history of ideas on the one hand, and social history or the study of socio-economic and political structures on the other, cultural history includes aspects of culture both material (art, literature, iconography, clothing, dance, performance) and immaterial, such as leisure, inherited privilege, knowledge, memory (Connerton 1989; Green 2008) and emotional landscapes and repertoires (Rosenwein 2010). In addition to high or elite culture, cultural history is interested in popular culture and has been enriched by cross-cutting categories like class, race, and gender (Scott 1986). The focus is not only on core meanings, but also on those that are marginal and capable of rewriting the norm (Davis 1983; Surkis 2014).

The concept of "culture" too has undergone significant variation. Cultural anthropologists warn against a reified notion of culture that could be apprehended in its totality and transported to the modern world like the marbles of the Parthenon (Geertz 1973; Turner 1982; Geertz 1983). One problem of such view is that it deprives individuals of agency, who are imagined as trapped within patterns they cannot escape—be they a set of structures, the prevailing notions of the times, or a collective mentality. "Instead of a reified notion of a fixed and stable set of beliefs, values, and institutions, culture is being redefined as a flexible repertoire of practices and discourses created through historical processes of contestation over signs and meanings" (Merry 1998: 577). In this view, a culture is never a closed, entirely coherent system that would serve to explain people's behavior, but exists as permanent contestation as to what culture entails and what its central meanings and values are.

The same goes for the concept of *legal* culture (Freedman 1990; Nelken 2004).[11] Trying to develop an "interpretive" rather than as an "explanatory" concept of culture (Geertz 1973; Nelken 2004), Jeremy Webber explains that "a culture is not defined by a single, constant, and bounded content—by, for example, a specific set of beliefs that all members of that culture hold in common" (2004: 31). Still, and to the extent that individuals engage in intensive interaction, they will likely share many reference points (terms of controversies, formulation of questions, vocabulary for expressing praise or blame, language of commendation or reproach), even though participants may disagree or offer different interpretations about them. In this conception, the term culture is not "a tightly bound unit of analysis" (33), but "a lens through which to perceive, evaluate, and further reflect about normative phenomena" (Webber 2004: 33).

However fuzzy the definition, this volume adopts an adjectival use of the term culture, where the object to be explained is not culture as such (if such a thing can be said without contradiction), but a *cultural* way to approach legal phenomena (still to be defined). Thus the term "cultural" is the mark of a distinctive manner to approach the subject matter differently from, say, an economic, sociological, or political standpoint. So what does a cultural approach bring to law? First, an expansion of relevant sources: for example, a cultural approach to law may focus upon the engravings on the stelae of Hammurabi (Chapter 1); on the shield of Achilles in Homer's *Iliad* (Figure I.2) as an everyday scene of legal dispute (Gagarin 2005c); on sculpture and pictorial representations; on architecture and monuments (e.g., the Jewish Temple, the Ishtar Gate (Figure I.3), the Greek Parthenon as embodiment of Athenian hegemony, or the *Ara Pacis* of Roman peace (Figure I.4)); on literature and drama (e.g., the Greek theater as a legal-political institution) (Vernant and Vidal-Naquet 1988; Goldhill 2000; Etxabe 2013); on objects of clothing and certain garments denoting status e.g., the Roman toga (Watt 2013); on fine pieces of jewelry, coinage, effigies, and emblems (Goodrich 2014 (Figure I.5)).

However, the point is not merely to amass cultural artifacts. The more ambitious goal is for these sources (and with them the law) to be *read differently*, as a much-needed correction to doctrinal and formalistic approaches that have dominated nineteenth and twentieth-century scholarship. Take, for example, the *Institutes* of Gaius, a textbook introduction to the elements of Roman law. Legal scholars are often content with the description of the tripartite analytical categories (persons, things, and actions) and the divisions and subdivisions that permit locating any given legal situation in the institutional scheme. But why stop there? While one can indeed marvel at the architectonics of the whole edifice, one could also reflect on what the apparent need for categorization says about the legal culture in question. Further, one could investigate the cultural dissemination of Gaius' Institutes in universities from Beirut to Constantinople(Figure I.6). Finally, one could also reflect on how a text conceived as a student textbook came to have such an impact, transforming a legal tradition that had grown cumulatively into a conceptually organized system, and how this conceptual equipoise helped to maintain Roman law together in the face of tremendous diversity (Birks and McLeod 1987: 16).

To reduce law and its study to the content and systematization of legal precepts not only impoverishes both law and its study, but severs law from the vital forces that make it more than a mere technique for governing or settling disputes. As Robert Cover famously put it, "once understood in the context of the narratives that give it meaning, law becomes not merely a system of rules to be observed, but a world in which we live" (1983: 4–5), and a cultural approach to law seeks to understand what *enlivens* that world. To this

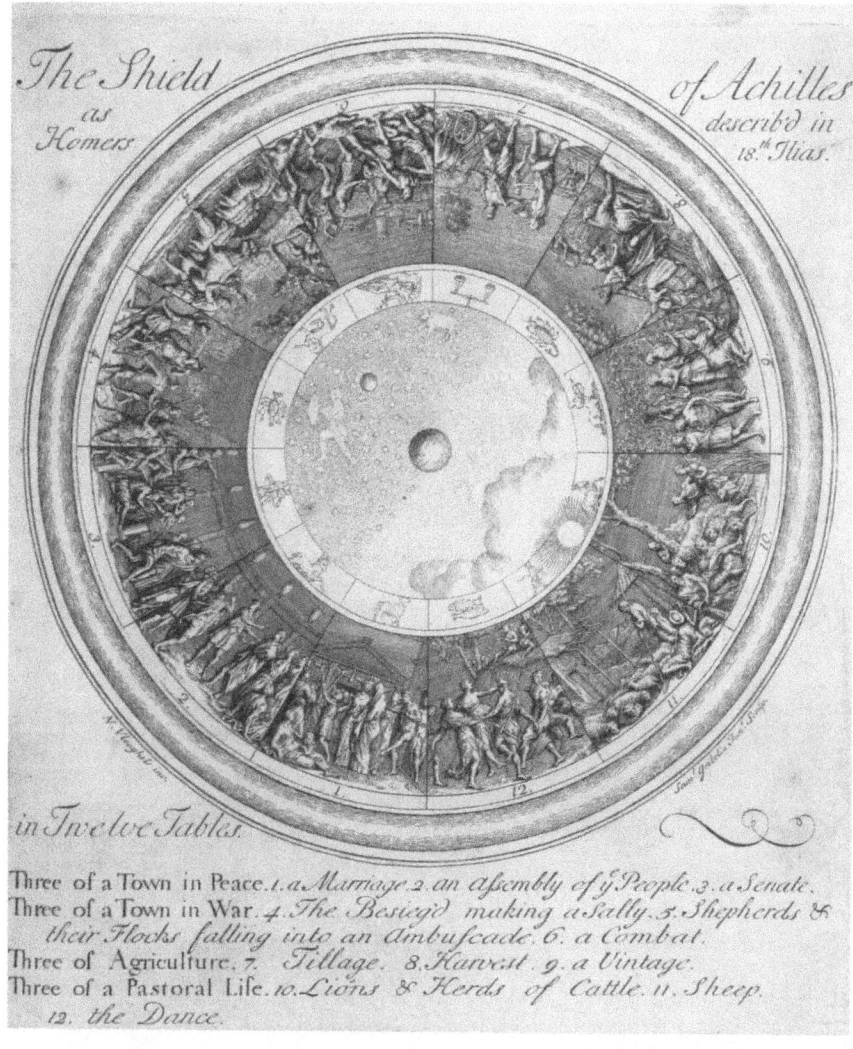

FIGURE 0.2. The shield of Achilles. From the British Library, released to Flickr commons by the British library. Images extracted from page 171 of volume 5 of *the Iliad* of Homer (translated by Pope), published in 1720.

end, the modern separation between legal and moral or social norms is less helpful, than to observe their mutual interdependence. In this vein, one could study the role of violence in the warrior culture of the *Iliad* (Weil [1940–41] 2003), or the complex web of obligations entailed by the laws of hospitality or *xenia* in the *Odyssey*, or the sophisticated repertoire of normative argument for inter-state relationships in Thucydides' history on the Peloponnesian War.[12] This is not to say that everything *is* law, but that everything can *become* legal (i.e., legally relevant) once it enters into the attention of the normative field, for the ability to see something *as* legal depends entirely on our frames of vision (Etxabe 2010).

FIGURE 0.3. Ishtar Gate. Pergamon Museum, Berlin 29 August 2010. Source: Wikimedia/Radomir Vrbovsky/CC BY-SA 4.0.

FIGURE 0.4. Augustus coin found in the Pudukottai Hoard, India. Source: Wikimedia/PHGCOM/CC BY-SA 3.0.

FIGURE 0.5. *Ara Pacis* Relief. Source: Wikimedia/Manfred Heyde/CC BY 3.0.

FIGURE 0.6. Roman road at Timgad, Algeria. Source: Wikimedia/PhR61/CC BY 2.0.

Finally, a cultural approach to law takes the role of actors and their "jurisgenetic" (Cover 1983) and "law-creating possibilities" (Kleinhans and MacDonald 1997; MacDonald 2006) seriously. In his bottom-up study of legal complaints in Roman Egypt, Ari Bryen argues that seen from the perspective of those entering the field of legal contest

> law begins to look like a rather different creature from what historians (and in particular ancient historians) often take it to be: rather than a system of rules to be applied correctly or erroneously or a simple imposition of imperial power, law emerges, paradoxically perhaps, as both a field of contested practice and a simplifying language through which individual petitioners can redefine themselves and their universe of personal relationships. (2013: 6)

Rules and institutionalized judgments are of course part of the legal field, but "any attempt to view this dynamic system as a static, coherent or rationalized whole ... is bound to be frustrated" (Bryen 2013: 44). The papyri sources reveal a fluid law, where legal decisions sit "at the vanishing point between what is narrative and rhetoric and what is law" (164). Therefore, cultural sources may help to convey a view that emphasizes agency, perception, and interpretation rather than structure (203).

In sum, a cultural approach to law suggests that law and culture are inextricably intertwined (Mezey 2001). As James Boyd White suggests, law is itself a culture that can be studied as such (White 1973; White 1985). Such a study will entail numerous sub-questions, including: How is law composed and enacted—and by whom? What are its terms of value—and condemnation? What are the set of resources for expression and argument—and their limits? How is meaning generated, debated, and settled—or destroyed? How are decisions reached, on what basis, and by whom? How is legal knowledge affirmed, acquired, transmitted—or debased? How is the experience of individuals acknowledged—or denied? These are the kind of questions that a cultural approach to law inquires. The formal institutions of law are important, but they are just a fraction of what ought to claim our attention (Cover 1983).

HISTORICIZING THE PROVINCE OF JURISPRUDENCE

Contemporary scholars of globalization attest to the inadequacy of the jurisprudential framework created in the wake of the (Western) nation-state for understanding plural normative phenomena across transnational borders (Teubner and Fischer-Lescano 2004; Menski 2006; Zumbansen 2010 and 2014). Whereas globalization tests the spatial limits of modern jurisprudence, the challenge we now face is temporal, and on an epochal scale: is there a concept of law capacious enough to guide the inquiry in ancient times? Before addressing it directly, it may be helpful once again to return to a pioneering work, this time that of Henry Sumner Maine.

As a forerunner of historical jurisprudence (which is not a jurisprudence applied to history, but a historical way to conceive of jurisprudence), Maine wanted to establish the priority of "sober" historical research over "plausible, but absolutely unverified" theories such as those predicated upon the state of nature or the social contract (Maine 1906: 3). For example, in his lectures on "The Early History of Institutions," Maine criticized the Hobbesian doctrine of sovereignty by resorting to the Homeric society in which law existed without sovereign or legislative command (Pollock 1906: 20). One methodological peculiarity was his attempt to elucidate the past of legal institutions, ideas, and customs by searching not only historical sources, but also by looking for examples that were still *present* in the world (Maine 1871: 6–7). In this way Maine aimed to grasp early forms of jural conceptions, which in his mind "contained, potentially, all the forms in which law has subsequently exhibited itself" (Maine 1906: 2). Such jural conceptions were to the jurist "what the primary crusts of the earth are the geologist" (id.)

Maine's geological metaphor exhibits the presumption of continuity, even though he also left room for some discontinuities within a general evolutionary model.[13] Likewise, he accounted for profound transformations in core jural conceptions. For example, he explains how *ius gentium*, originally a category of Roman law that indicated the law applicable to non-citizens as opposed to the *ius civile*, came to be interpreted, under the influence of Greek philosophical ideals of laws of nature, as a sort of law common to all mankind. This reinterpretation was retroactively introduced and, henceforth, the praetor's edict (i.e., the annual declaration where the praetor laid out the legal principles to guide his year in office) tried to supersede civil law so as to conform to the principle of *ius gentium*, as if this was in fact "the lost Code of Nature" and the praetor was simply "gradually restoring a type from which law had departed only to deteriorate" (Maine 1906: 59). Most importantly, and despite the teleological flavor of Maine's approach, the focus on "jural conceptions"—rather than on rules and institutions—parallels the aims of well-known comparatists, such as Rodolfo Sacco's "legal formants" (1991) or Masaji Chiba's "jural postulates" (1993).[14]

Maine was not a trained classicist, and some of his bolder claims have not been borne out by later historical research (i.e., on the origins of law in the patriarchal family) and some are contested (the evolution from status to contract), while others remain insightful in light of more recent, and unknown to him, Near Eastern evidence (e.g., that judgments precede law rather than the other way around) (Maine 1906: 7). Further, Maine's approach had the merit of extending the scope of legal research to the traditions of the East and Hindu law (1871 and 1886)[15] and of indicating the importance of religion and rituals (Parker 2005: 80). He also highlighted the significance of writing (Maine 1906: chapter 3)[16] and the capacity of legal fictions to mediate between stability and change—for legal fictions enable actors to pretend that law remains what it always was, even when the rules may have changed (Maine [1861] 1906: chapter 4).[17]

His most lasting contribution, however, is the subjection of general jurisprudence to a historical critique. Having realized that many features of ancient law differed from dominant positivist accounts, he became weary of definitions purporting to isolate essential properties of law. As a contemporary of Bentham and Austin, Maine was familiar with the command theory of law, according to which law was to be understood as a *command* of the lawgiver that generates an *obligation* on the citizen carrying the threat of *sanction* in the event of disobedience. In understated commentary, he writes:

> The results of this separation of ingredients [command, obligation, sanction] tally exactly with the facts of mature jurisprudence; and, by a little straining of language, they may be made to correspond in form with all law, of all kinds, at all epochs. It is not, however, asserted that the notion of law entertained by the generality is even now quite in conformity with this dissection; and it is curious that, the farther we penetrate into the primitive history of thought, the farther we find ourselves from a conception of law which at all resembles a compound of the elements which Bentham determined. (Maine 1906: 6–7)

Maine seems to accept in principle that this definition corresponds with a "mature jurisprudence"—though "even now [the facts are not] quite in conformity with this dissection"—and further also that "a little straining of language" would make it fit to describe "all law, of all kinds, at all epochs." Yet in the end it becomes apparent that he does not deem it appropriate for ancient societies, which do not "at all resemble … a compound of the elements Bentham determined." On a closer inspection, then, the "straining of language" by which Austin and Bentham's command theory of law could be made into a general definition of law turns out to be *a straining too far* and does not serve the purpose for which it was designed, for it fails to posit itself as constant. The result is that Bentham and Austin's theories cannot remain intact once subjected to the historicizing process Maine proposes.

Following on from Maine's historicizing critique, we may wonder about modern attempts to define law in such a general conceptual manner. For example, it is doubtful that the two most prominent concepts of law of the twentieth century, those of Hans Kelsen (as system of hierarchical norms) and of H.L.A. Hart (as the combination of primary and secondary rules) fare any better. Contemporary authors who still believe in the usefulness of devising a general concept of law are aware of the need to develop flexible and adjustable concepts (Twining 2009; Cotterrell 2014). However, a true encounter with the diversity of law(s) in antiquity may put even these in question, for the very idea of a "system of law" is historically bound. So is there a notion of law capacious enough to encapsulate legal phenomena in antiquity?

In his exploration of legal traditions of the contemporary world, Patrick Glenn does not deem it appropriate to construct a general definition of law for all times and places (2010). Instead, he tries to work with an understanding of "legal tradition," as the corpus of "normative information" reflexively transmitted from the past (2010: 42). This normative flow provides a sense of continuity over time and hence of identity, which enables us to distinguish one tradition from others. A legal tradition is markedly different from the idea of a legal system, for while it has a relatively stable core, it has no fixed or precise boundaries; further, a tradition makes no claim to completeness, has no inherent notion of closure, and need not imply hierarchy; nor does it require a clear separation of law from other aspects of social life such as religion and ethics (any such requirement would be seriously unhelpful for approaching law in antiquity). Moreover, a tradition is never static and can integrate plural (sub)traditions. Finally, a tradition always alludes to a community or collective that creates, develops, and passes on the tradition, directing our attention to the human and cultural dimension of law.

Whether or not Glenn sufficiently delineates "the legal,"[18] (which at any rate cannot be predetermined a priori) and regardless of the fact that "information" is not all the law transmits, his approach represents an advancement. What the concept of tradition captures well is the idea that law is steeped in history, which Martin Krygier calls its *pastness*, and the abstract and "time-free" staples of modern jurisprudence cannot account for (1986). Since "the past speaks with many voices" (Krygier 1986: 242), it is possible to obtain a different picture of the tradition at any given moment, for "any particular 'present' is a slice through a continuously changing diachronic quarry of deposits made by generations of people with different, often inconsistent and competing values, beliefs, and views of the world" (242).

In addition, Krygier emphasizes *authoritative presence* and *transmission*, for not every part of the past enters in a tradition. On the one hand, in oral traditions, since the only available evidence of the tradition is what the existing members of a tradition recall and choose to transmit, "[w]hat is forgotten is lost, what is currently inconvenient can be forgotten ... [a]nd just as inconvenient pasts can sink without trace, so more convenient ones can rise without independent evidence" (Krygier 1986: 252). On the other hand, in written traditions the past is more readily available to be examined by all who can read; hence it remains subject to interpretation and constant controversy. Therefore, the real or imagined continuities with the past can be activated and de-activated (i.e., discontinued) depending on circumstances, contexts, and needs—as the famous controversy about the wording of an old oracle during the Athenian plague was conveniently resolved to fit the situation.[19] Finally, a tradition consists also of the evaluative commitments about the past, and the particular values attached to its memory—or forgetting. As elaborated by Glenn and Krygier, the concept of tradition helps to distinguish various legal traditions in antiquity (Greek, Roman, Hebrew, Near Eastern ...), as fluctuating composites of (somewhat inconsistent) beliefs, decisions, practices, and a widely shared structure of political imagination (Ruskola 2012: 262). Unlike the positivist idea of the legal system, a tradition can withstand the lack of a common set of institutions, rules, or unified authority. Thus, *pace* Finley, there may be some justification to speak of a Greek legal tradition (different from the Near Eastern, Persian, Roman, or Jewish), despite the noted institutional diversity of the city-states, the absence of jurisdictional domination under a single authority, and the fact that it never formed a coherent system of rules, for Greeks themselves at least since Homer recognized their common heritage as "Hellenes" in their language, religion, and customs that separated them from non-Greeks (e.g., Persians and other "barbarians").

There are other times when the terms "legal cultures" or "legal civilizations" may be preferred (Twining 2009). Each of these terms has different connotations, strengths, and shortcomings, and can be more or less valuable depending on use (e.g., the ancient Near Eastern civilization extends geographically to Mesopotamia, Egypt, Anatolia, and the Levant and contains a number of different cultures—Akkadian, Babylonian, Assyrian, Hittite—and can be approached as a legal tradition, or various) (Westbrook 2003a: 4). But whether we think of these as legal traditions, cultures, civilizations, or, as I have proposed at length elsewhere, as *normative universes* (Etxabe 2010 and 2013), the analysis must incorporate at least three important considerations: First, a diachronic element to account for profound internal transformations (beyond usual periodizations such as archaic, classical, post-classical, and so on). Second, it must be able to encapsulate deep normative pluralism and diversity (e.g., the Jewish legal tradition contains Mosaic and Talmudic law, as well as various interpretive schools). Third, its contours must be porous to account for mutual influences and hybrid spaces (e.g., interpenetration of local and Roman law in the provinces of the Empire). Fluidity and hybridity extend to the concept of territory itself, no longer understood as fixed geographic space, but as "arenas of contest" (Merry 1998: 583; Dening 2002). Even though Rome, Athens, Babylon, or Jerusalem exercise a strong gravitational pull, what these places signify is constantly being re-created—even literally, as when the "walls of Athens" were redrawn from land to sea during the Peloponnesian War, or during the years of the Jewish exile.

COMPARING LAWS IN ANTIQUITY: COMPARISON AS TRANSLATION

Having traced the contours to navigate different legal traditions, how do we compare normative universes that are so distant not just from us, but from each other?[20] The most obvious candidate is the comparison of legal rules. For example, it has been noted that similar precepts for the killing of a lover caught in the act of adultery, and for the burglar caught at night in *flagrante delicto*, exist in Near Eastern laws (Hittite Laws 197; Middle Assyrian Laws MAL A 15; Laws of Eshnunna 13), Archaic Greece (Laws of Draco), the Hebrew Bible (Exodus 22:1) and the Twelve Tables (VIII 12–13) (Westbrook 2009d: 309 fn 22, 403–404). Is the likeness in the written precepts enough to affirm the equivalence of the laws in question? An affirmative answer need not entail a-historical doctrinarism (e.g., Watson 1974; Watson 1998; Westbrook 2009d), but it surely carries with it an understanding of law as a system of (detachable and iterable) rules.

Yet similarity in written rules tells us surprisingly little about similarity in understanding, interpretation or application. Take the example of the husband who claims to have killed his wife's lover on the spot, as depicted in Lysias' famous court-speech on the murder of Eratosthenes. Can we confidently claim that the legal precept attributed to Draco[21] represents "the law" in the case? Is it safe to conclude that the husband can legally kill the lover caught in the act? A close reading of Lysias' text renders that conclusion at least premature. The speaker is at pains to describe himself as an honest and unsuspecting husband who arrives home only to discover his wife with a lover he is led to kill on the spot. All in his speech is strictly measured: it has been done right then and there and not after the lover could escape to his house (temporal and spatial elements); there is no previous animosity between them (lack of prior motive); he had no preconceived plan or premeditation; he is, in fact, the kind of person incapable of conceiving such a plan; he had formerly a trusting relationship with his wife; he was finally executing faithfully and dispassionately what he thought the law mandated of him in the situation. All the details of the narrative circumscribe the range of situations when killing one's wife's lover may have been permitted (i.e., not punished), so much so that they determine when the rule is meant to apply and when it would not be appropriate to do so. But to say that the law, in certain restricted circumstances, absolved from the punishment for homicide is not to say that the law *prescribed* killing the culprit—which is the claim Lysias' speaker makes.

It is often claimed that Athenian litigants "manipulated" the law to their advantage—a fair enough characterization of trials in classical Athens, but nothing extraordinary in itself—which tends to obscure that law operates, in classical Athens presumably as well as today, within a contested field. Indeed, legal precepts call for broad social narratives, where all the elements triggering a potential justification would have to be demonstrated to the satisfaction of the jury during a trial for murder.[22] The case reads, in fact, as if is the killing of a wife's lover were not an ordinary, but an unusual occurrence, where the law would avail a range of possible courses of action, and much was left open to interpretation. In practice, this would mean that the husband who acted on the assumption that he could kill with impunity would be taking a huge risk, for jurors could not be counted upon to render a clear verdict to absolve. Therefore, a putative legal advisor who counseled a husband that killing his wife's lover was perfectly within his rights would *not* be doing so responsibly. If neither defendant, nor jurors, nor counselor could "know" the law unequivocally in advance, to what extent can we affirm that the rule that a husband could kill his wife's lover on the spot *was* the law in classical Athens?

While the focus on comparing rules is associated with *formalism*, a second influential method of comparative law aims to replace the rules with their social function. In fact, it has been claimed that "[t]he basic methodological principle of all comparative law is that of *functionality*" (Zweigert and Kötz 1998: 34). An important methodological commitment of functionalism is the presumption of similitude. This has been explained as the assumption that different societies face similar needs and that, to survive, any one society must have (functionally equivalent) institutions that meet these needs (Michaels 2006: 369). Since all societies face the need to settle disputes, one would compare how different societies (or the same society at different times) fulfilled it by means of private vengeance, blood payment, private settlement, arbitration, jury-system, kingly prerogative, specialized judges, de-centralized functionaries, and so forth.

A functional analysis, however, does not need to assume that all societies evolve in similar fashion, for "similar institutions can fulfill different functions ... and ... similar functional needs can be fulfilled by different institutions" (Michaels 2006: 357). The key to this mode of comparison is *functional equivalence*, namely, the idea that legal institutions are comparable only if there is a (functionally similar) relation between problems and solutions (Michaels 2006: 371). In other words, the institutions are similar only in relation to the specific variable that is selected—while remaining different in the rest. The methodological distinction of functional comparison is that "the solutions we find in the different jurisdictions must be cut loose from their conceptual context and stripped of their national doctrinal overtones so that they may be seen purely in the light of their function" (Zweigert and Kötz 1998: 44). To sort out such function requires a process of abstraction, which tend to draw a rather de-contextualized description of the legal problem.

Responding to the charge that functionalism ignores culture, Ralf Michaels argues that in order to select the appropriate social function, the researcher is forced to take the cultural context into account, so "rightly understood, functionalist comparative law assumes that legal rules are culturally embedded" (2006: 366). In other words, no obstacle exists *in theory* for taking culture seriously.[23] However, he admits "the functionalists' resistance to adopting an insider's view ... and of course their reconstruction of culture as functional (or dysfunctional) relations" (Michaels 2006: 365). Further, "functionalism must assume that 'law' can somehow be separated from 'society' because otherwise law could not fulfil a function for society" (id.)

These are precisely the premises that a *cultural* (or contextual) comparison will not accept, for it would not be satisfied with accounts that the participants themselves would not be presumed to recognize as fair interpretations of their culture (Taylor 1971; Webber 2004). In contrast, by stripping narratives of their specific life and replacing them with lean functions, some of the aspects that call the attention of the cultural historian may be lost. For instance, the latter may be interested in the myths concerning the organization and administration of justice in ancient societies, *even if there is no historical truth behind them*, as a way to get access to those telling the stories and how they understood their own past. The interest lies not on the social function of these myths—which may still be a worthwhile pursuit—but on the implications of these narratives for understanding the legal cultures in question.

Functional analysis treats law as a reified entity that could be cognitively apprehended, rather than as *constitutive* of self and culture. By contrast, for a contextual or cultural approach, law cannot be "separated from" society, for law is culturally embedded. One of the principal exponents of comparative law as "thoroughly cultural," Pierre Legrand claims that the laws of a legal culture cannot be disentangled from the meanings that arise as a result of the distinct cognitive structures he labels *mentalité* (Legrand 2016), by which he means "the framework of intangibles within which individuals operate in a given society" (1995: 263). These intangibles, at once constitutive, normative, and interpretative (id.), are formed by that which is "often left unformulated, apparently insignificant, [and] remain buried at the level of the unconscious motivation within legal cultures" (1995: 273). This also marks the orientation of the approach, for "the key to successful comparative analysis lies not in the sheer accumulation of data, but in the meticulous selection and the deft interpretation of relevant material" (1995: 266). Critics of the concept of *mentalité*—a term with its own important place in modern historiography—may object to its holistic, somewhat totalizing flavor, even though Legrand assures us that he does not wish to pursue anything like legal essentialism, where each language would be solipsistically quarantined in their own world (Legrand 2014: 209). In this sense, it is important to underline that no culture, no matter how monolithic it may appear to outsiders, is free from internal division and strife (Loraux 2002; Nelken 2004: 6; Webber 2004).

With these caveats, a culturally minded study may reflect, for instance, on the instructions that the emperor Justinian gave to his *quaestor* Tribonian for the composition of the Digest—a work that reflects Justinian's own sense of the best Roman tradition of *jurisconsulti*, what was worth preserving from the past and transmitted to the future, as well as the principles that ought to inspire the distillation—where it is immediately noticeable that the values to be uphold are coherence, non-redundancy, and non-contradiction. Consequently, he writes, "there is to be no place for any antinomy ... but there is to be total concord, total consistency, with no one raising any opposition" (Mommsen et al. 1985: xlviii). Disagreement is defined as "harmful" and once the work is completed, the law therein is to undergo no change or alteration, but to remain unchanged "not merely for [his] own age but for all time, both present and future" (Mommsen et al. 1985: lx). Perfection, completion, self-sufficiency, and eternity are arguably attributes of divinity and one can perceive how enormously Christian theology (and Platonism) had permeated the ideal attributes of Roman law.

A cultural comparison also pays attention to the language through which we, and our respective audiences, "mind the law" (Amsterdam and Bruner 2000) and hence also to the "law in the mind," which enriches the usual dichotomy between "law on the books" and "law in action" (Ewald 1998). Perhaps one way to think further about this activity of "languaging," as well as to avoid the thought of cultures as self-contained boxes, is to think of comparison as a form of translation (White 1990; Ost 2009; Glanert 2014). Translation is not merely the task of rendering an alien thought into a familiar language, or a simple linguistic or philological exercise, but "the art of ... confronting unbridgeable discontinuities between texts, between languages, and between people" (White 1990: 257). In other words, a way of acknowledging, and responding to, difference. This view of translation presupposes a non-instrumental understanding of language, rather than the more usual codification and de-codification of messages (Hendry 2014: 91).

Since the comparatist connects—mediates between—what is compared, the researcher's perspective and place in the world has first to be thematized. Therefore comparative law is to become self-reflective (Frankenberg 1985: 441, 443; Frankenberg 2014). In order to reflexively account for our own mediating influence in the object of study, we might begin by recognizing that knowledge of the law is a way to orient oneself in another legal world; not a thing, but a movement, a process of self-correction and gradual "attunement" (Dawson 2014). Comparison as translation can never accomplish a perfect correspondence between cultures. In fact, what is compared are not cultures as such, but particular expressions of, and responses to, culture, just as one never translates entire languages, but particular expressions of it—a novel, a theatrical performance, an idiom.

THE HERMENEUTICAL QUEST: TEXTS AND CONTEXT OF LAW

Comparison as translation is closely associated with the hermeneutical question of how legal texts[24] and other cultural artifacts disclose their meaning to us. How we do conceive of the historical mediation by which old texts can acquire meaning and be actualized in the present? Considering Martha Roth's initial statement that legal texts are not static pieces of writing but continue to say something through space and time, what kind of relationship do we hope to establish with the texts and contexts of law in antiquity? I want to consider, first, the particular case of reading the Hebrew Bible as central to the Jewish legal tradition, and second, the way some texts are able to transcend the confines of their original context.

Texts are historical artifacts also in the sense that layers of history are imprinted on them, as demonstrated by Bernard Levinson's fascinating readings of the Hebrew Bible (Levinson 2008). Levinson develops a critical-hermeneutic method in contrast to the poetic (and synchronic) reading of Meir Sternberg, who, like Erich Auerbach before him, emphasized the figure of the omniscient narrator whose privileged knowledge, meant to reflect the omniscience of the Creator, warranted credibility to the stories therein (Sternberg 1985).

What Levinson opposes is not poetic analysis as such—he actually performs sophisticated literary readings himself[25]—but reading strategies that try to harmonize all ambiguities and tensions into a coherent and unified whole. The synchronic method finds its roots in the ancient rabbinic school of exegesis, whose interpretive point of departure is the maxim "there's neither late nor early in the Torah." Such unity, which presents itself all at once to the reader, is further underlined by the attribution of authorship of the entire Pentateuch (the books of Genesis, Exodus, Leviticus, Numbers, and Deuteronomy) to Moses. By this mechanism, rabbinic interpretation privileges the internal coherence of the biblical narratives and the laws, and thus is led to deny the very literary history that brought the Pentateuch (and the legal corpora[26]) into being (Levinson 2008: 11).

Levinson proposes instead a diachronic critical method, which recognizes (and preserves) the history of the text—its accretions, redundancies, inconsistencies, and revisions. He finds inspiration in Spinoza's hermeneutics, for whom the many contradictions faced by the Bible's attentive reader must neither be explained away through allegorical exegesis (Maimonides), nor be used to contradict reason itself (Jehuda ibn Alfakhar), but preserved in creative tension. This method, Levinson believes, is more attuned to the compositional history or the text, and the way it was finally put together during the eighth–fifth centuries BCE.

As one among many pertinent legal examples, Levinson recalls the foundational story about the organization of the judicial body in Exodus (18:24–26), where Jethro, the Midianite father-in-law of Moses, advises him not to wear himself out by adjudicating every single issue, but instead to delegate minor issues to god-fearing, trustworthy, and incorruptible people, while retaining only the most important cases for himself. This presents the theological inconvenience that Moses receives this counsel from a non-Jew but more importantly, that the administration of justice is decided even before the law is handed down. The same story is retold in the Deuteronomy, but now conveniently placed after God had given down the law to Moses. In this retelling, the revelation of law at Sinai precedes the creation of the judicial system, and there is no recognition of any foreign influence—the cause is now in revelation. For Levinson, "the highly selective, point by point adjustment of both of the chronology and the etiology of the judicial administration can only be explained in terms of the author of Deut 1 consciously seeking to revise and correct the narrative of Exod 18" (Levinson 2008: 65).[27] In other words, "Deuteronomy's authors have 'rechronologized' the narrative sequence of Exodus in order to ensure the dignity and prestige of revelation itself" (2008: 65).

This brief methodological excursus suffices to highlight that Levinson touches on issues of great religious, legal, and political import.[28] Levinson's argument goes to the heart of the Israelite legal tradition, for "[n]either the nation nor its laws existed from the beginning of time. The election of the nation, whereby it was brought into a special relationship with God, derives from history, not from cosmological destiny" (2008: 49). No less importantly, Levinson illustrates that texts, and our readings of them, are products of history.

However, while the historical–critical method serves well to situate texts in history,[29] the meaning of texts is not exhausted by their historical context. In fact, due to their capacity to mean something different even "after a thousand readings" as Burckhardt puts it, texts themselves problematize the relationship with the historical context in which they were produced. I want to introduce this final idea with the help of Dominick LaCapra, who sought to reorient (intellectual) history away from what he called a "documentary conception" towards a view of historical understanding as a conversation with the past which owed much to Martin Heidegger (LaCapra 1983). While LaCapra emphasizes literary texts, the implications extend actually to oral communication and to any text or cultural artifact of substantial complexity, whether or not inscribed with letters. (In LaCapra's view music, dance, performance, gesture, imagery, iconography raise the problem of translation from medium to medium and hence of *textuality* writ large.)

LaCapra begins by distinguishing the "documentary" and the "worklike" aspects of texts. The documentary aspect situates the text in terms of factual dimensions that convey information about it (e.g., Egyptian papyri in the Roman provinces tell us about judicial organization, or inscriptions found in a gravesite inform us about societal structure). In contrast, the *worklike* brings to the world something that did not exist before in that significant variation (e.g., the Sophoclean tragedy about Oedipus brings something that did not exist in earlier mythical accounts of the same legend). Whereas the documentary approach treats texts as evidence of an era (i.e., as signs of the times), the worklike calls that same era, its values, and ideology into question—like tragedy might question the democratic ideology of the *polis* (Vernant and Vidal-Naquet 1988; Goldhill 2000; Etxabe 2013).

Cultural artifacts may display these two aspects to a different degree, but LaCapra challenges the dominant tendency to read them merely as a document of their time, leaving aside their worklike character. Texts of the richness, say, of Cicero's letters, Tacitus' descriptions, Thucydides' speeches, Platonic dialogues, or the book of Job, call for an engagement that goes beyond their evidentiary value as tokens, illustrations, or symptoms of the society that produced them.[30]

It is in their worklike dimension in fact that texts of law call upon us as readers of the future. The task of historical interpretation often begins with the sensible admonition that things must be put "in context"— advice I have myself heeded a few times—but the relationship between text and context is not that between content and container, as if the context were a sort of holistic envelope (Gordon 2014). First, because we never have *the* context—rather "a set of interacting contexts whose relations to one another are variable and problematic and whose relation with the text being investigated raises difficult issues in interpretation" (LaCapra 35)—and second, because complex texts make use of, and respond to, those original contexts to generate new, and often unpredictable, contexts.

LaCapra argues that the "ability to pose the right questions" distinguishes productive from unproductive research, but those questions are themselves situated in a context that cannot be entirely objectified or fully known (1983: 31). By asking what a particular text presents as "question-worthy," a conversation with the past enters into dimensions which bear most forcefully on the present and future (id.). "Here anachronism is an obvious danger," warns LaCapra, "but an imaginative and self-reflective kind of comparative history inquiring into the unrealized or even resisted possibilities of the past is nonetheless an important supplement to more empirical kinds of comparisons in the dialogue between past and present" (1983: 31).[31]

Here is the paradox: while legal texts bear traces of the historical context in which they appear, they offer the opportunity to enhance our understanding of those context(s), and in fact can constitute new contexts for themselves (White 1984). Thus, we begin by situating texts in concrete space and time, but their ability to reach across a spectrum of contexts engages not only the contemporary moment, but larger conversations across time (White 1985: 88). In such productive engagement with the past we seek not only a reconstruction of ancient legal cultures—to render them objects of knowledge—but also to engage in dialogue with them. In other words, our epistemology does not follow the model of explanation, but of *participation* (Gadamer 1960; Pfau 2013).

This is the central aspect of what a cultural history of law in antiquity brings to history in general, and to the history of *law* in particular, which is not independent from the accounts (descriptive, interpretative, and evaluative) we are capable of giving in each case. As a world in which to live, and not as an object detached from the commitments of participants, law is not a thing that can be studied apart from the *jurisgenerative* capacities of actors and interpreters. Understanding law not as an abstraction separated from society but from within, we jump right in to confront the materials and primary sources directly, hoping to translate the "unbridgeable discontinuities" with the past into our own language, for our own audience, and from our own experience—while there can never be perfect correspondence between them. This task is always mediated by our own perceptual filters (or in our case *keywords*[32]), and yet we hope in the process to expand our frames of vision, to include dimensions of "the legal" that may go unperceived by modern concepts and categories. Learning the law in antiquity, and to have knowledge about it, is never complete: there can be only more or less satisfactory renderings.

The aim is not to close the gap between the past and the present, but to acknowledge its existence as we reflexively traverse it in our writing. A guiding question might be this: what would you need to understand—what terms of value, forms of reasoning, underlying assumptions, cosmologies, and institutional arrangements—to be able to navigate the normative universe with a relative sense of familiarity and/or confidence? As we seek the "reference points" of normative discussion, in particular cultural contexts, participation can thus be literal as I have tried to illustrate in the case of the murder of Eratosthenes, and ideally would be able to tell (not perfectly of course, but to some degree) what arguments to expect in a new case. In other words, we are really beginning to learn law as a legal participant would—in small fragments, but fragments in which you can have (qualified) confidence. Participation is crucial in a different sense too, for in a way it disposes of the problem of incomplete knowledge, gaps in the record, uncertainty about the relation between law and other spheres of life, etc. For if you have sufficient resources to participate intellectually and even inventively in a legal culture, you are learning something important that is not only in the past, but present.

CHAPTER ONE

Justice

KATHRYN SLANSKI

In order that the mighty not wrong the weak,
to provide just ways for the orphan and widow,
  in Babylon—city that the gods Anu and Enlil have elevated,
  in Esagila—temple whose foundations are fixed as are heaven and earth:
    to judge the judgments of the land,
    to decide the decisions of the land,
    to provide just ways for the wronged,
I inscribed my precious words upon my stela
and set it up in the presence of my image, the just king.[1]
  —*Law Stele of Hammurabi, King of Babylon* (xlvii 59–78)

INVESTIGATING JUSTICE IN ANTIQUITY: CHALLENGES, APPROACH, SOURCES

Justice in the ancient world is notoriously difficult to pin down. Plato's *Republic* (*Politeia*, literally, "Of the Polis"), perhaps the most familiar and culturally influential of the fifth century Athenian philosopher's dialogs, had in antiquity already acquired the subtitle: *Dikaiosune* "Concerning Justice." At the work's center are the joint inquiries: "What is justice?" and "Is its value instrumental or for its own sake?" Yet, like the young men participating in the discussion led by Socrates, students of the *Republic* today seeking "the answer" or even "an answer" to those questions are left frustrated and unsatisfied. Is justice "giving what is one's due?" "Helping friends and harming enemies?" "Each doing his own job?" By the time Socrates has described a transmigration of souls through the parable of Ur in the *Republic*'s tenth and concluding book, each of these proposals has been considered and rejected. Taken singly or even together, they fail to capture what any reader, ancient or modern, would consider the full meaning and value of justice.

A quick survey of the very words most commonly rendered in English as "justice" hint at the complexity with which the ancient world approached the idea. For ancient Mesopotamia, which bequeathed us the earliest evidence for our engagement with the subject, the usual Akkadian word for "justice" is *misharu*. In the last line of the passage cited above, Hammurabi refers to himself as *shar mishari* "king of justice," that is, "just king." Etymologically, *misharu* means "something made straight," and implies, then, restoration to a previous state that had become "crooked" or "out of line." In Akkadian inscriptions, *misharu* is regularly written with its Sumerian language equivalent, NÍG.

SI.SÁ, literally, "thing made straight," which likewise implies a restoration to a prior—and more just—condition.

Akkadian *kittu* "truth" is often paired with *misharu*; taken together they describe "two facets" of justice: the upholding of traditional law (*kittum*, "truth") and the tempering of the "harsh letter of the law with equity (*misharu*, 'justice')" (Westbrook 2003b: 364). Both words sometimes appear deified, thus "the god truth" and "the god justice"—suggesting a dimension of agency not easily transposed to the twenty-first century.

In the Hebrew Bible, *tsedeq* usually translated by "justice" or "righteousness," also connotes "normal" or "normative," while *mishpat*, also translated "justice," refers more specifically to "judgment," "ordinance" and "right" or "rectitude." *Tsedeq* may be understood as primary "justice," maintaining correct relationships with God and others, that results in a right life, in contrast to *mishpat* "rectifying justice," that is, "punishing wrongdoers and caring for victims of wrongdoing"[2]—a distinction that echoes Hammurabi's commitment to prevent the strong from wronging the weak, to providing "just ways for the widow and the orphan."

In ancient Greek, the term usually rendered as "justice" is *dike*, also conceptualized as a divinity. Mythologically, the goddess *Dike*—together with her sisters: Eunomia ("right laws"), Eirene ("peace"), and the four seasons—was born of a union between Olympian Zeus and the titan Themis, whose name means "right." According to Hesiod's *Theogony*:

> Next he [Zeus] married gleaming Themis, who bore the Seasons,
> And Eunomia, Dike, and blooming Eirene,
> Who attend to mortal men's works for them ... (906–908)

Greek *dike* circumscribes even more meanings than Akkadian *misharu*, and could connote revenge, a trial, or legal action, as well as an abstract notion of justice. While English translations render *dike* differently according to specific contexts, all these interrelated meanings would have been relevant for an ancient audience.[3]

This chapter draws on a selection of written works from two cultural traditions that exemplify some of the most prevalent, provocative, and enduring ancient ideas about justice: the cuneiform tradition of the ancient Near East and the Greek tradition of the ancient Mediterranean. It would be impossible to treat comprehensively all the works from antiquity that deal with justice, and in order to achieve some depth over superficiality, the works considered in this chapter address core questions or problems of justice in ways that have had lasting impact, and that were aimed at broad—in some cases explicitly public—audiences in antiquity. These are also works that we know to have been studied in antiquity, to have belonged, to greater and lesser degrees, to the body of written texts that formed the curricula of ancient education in their respective regions. Consequently, these are works that played a role in the intellectual formation of educated individuals who went on to become bureaucrats, magistrates, judges, court advisors, rulers, and, of course, writers who authored subsequent works.

Inquiry into the cultural ramifications of justice in ancient Mesopotamia and ancient Greece yields a number of points that the chapter will explore in closer examination of selected works of literature and art. These are:

- that in antiquity, justice is—and must be—continually debated and evaluated, and scenes of discussion and debate are characteristic of presentations of justice in ancient literary works;
- that visual imagery used to convey the execution and maintenance of justice make use of instruments to enable accurate *perception*; these include symbols

for weighing and for measuring, for separating truth from falsehood/relevant from irrelevant, and for illumination and vision (as opposed to opacity and blindness);

- that for both the ancient Near East and Greece, justice vs injustice is commonly expressed as "straight" vs "crooked," a structural conceptualization also manifest in the idea of a divinely ordered universe;
- that justice originates fundamentally with the gods, and is manifest in the gods' creation and ordering of the universe, evidenced in creation myths;
- that, consequently, justice is inherent in the very structure of the universe, for example, the Greek concept of *kosmos* (see below);
- that the divinely ordered structure of the universe includes a hierarchy in which man is subordinate to the divine, and, consequently, man can only ever have an imperfect and incomplete, that is, non-divine knowledge of justice (this is made clearer in the ancient Near East than in the Greek-speaking world);
- that in ancient Near Eastern mythology, man's trespassing on the divine realm results in a re-creation followed by a re-calibration of the cosmic hierarchy, one that firmly re-establishes man's station subordinate to the divine;
- that in the Greek-speaking world, we see man's challenges to the divine executed on a smaller, individual scale. Such challenges are rectified by the gods, again, with an idea of re-establishing the (necessarily prior) just order; and
- that rulers are responsible—charged by the gods—with maintaining and restoring just order in human society, analogous to the gods' doing so on a cosmic scale.

This chapter considers a selection of some of the best-known and best-attested works of ancient Near Eastern and Greek literature, those that would have formed part of the cultural background shaping the assumptions and values behind legal processes. In addition to the classical world, our Western tradition of justice also has roots in the ancient Near East, whose approaches to law and justice come down to us chiefly through the Bible.[4] Like the classical tradition, the Near Eastern tradition emphasizes a divine origin for justice, and a divine mandate charging rulers—the state—with the obligation to execute and maintain lasting just ways for their people.

The chapter takes as its starting point an explication of the way justice is portrayed by *Law Stele of Hammurabi*, popularly known as the *Code of Hammurabi*, our earliest surviving monumental source for the cultural history of justice. From ancient Greece, the chapter will explore justice in works that achieved panhellenic status during the archaic period, those that, in contrast to local myths and traditions, were known widely throughout the Greek-speaking world. Works considered include Hesiod's *Works and Days*, with reference to scenes from Homeric epic. From the fifth century "classical" or "golden age" of Athens, the chapter takes a close look at Aeschylus's *Oresteia* trilogy before concluding with the *Melian Dialogue* from Thucydides' *History of the Peloponnesian Wars*.

Utilizing both verbal and visual expression, Hammurabi's *Stele* evokes an element of performance, which, along with other works surveyed in this chapter, suggests that in both the Near East and the classical world, justice is regularly expressed through some type of performance before an audience, be it dialog, debate, disputation, or a formal theatrical performance upon a stage. Together with its very resistance to easy definition, the element of performance suggests that in antiquity justice was regarded as neither "fixed" nor "fixable," and rather as productively and necessarily a subject for discussion and debate.

LAYING SOCIAL FOUNDATIONS FOR JUSTICE: THE *LAW STELE OF HAMMURABI*

Hammurabi's[5] almost complete stele, housed today in the Louvre, stands 2¼ meters tall, some 70 centimeters wide. The inscription is partnered by a compelling sculpture in low relief that crowns the 2-meter high stone monument. Descriptive rather than prescriptive, the *Stele* is not, properly speaking, a code, and is more readily classified today as an example of the ancient Near Eastern genre of royal inscriptions called "law collections." Of the several cuneiform law collections known to us, Hammurabi's inscription is the longest and most developed. The inscription of the *Law Stele of Hammurabi* is not the earliest law collection from ancient Mesopotamia, but, without a doubt, it is the best known and most studied.[6]

There is strong evidence that King Hammurabi was personally and intensively invested in the adjudication of legal disputes throughout his realm. He conducted extensive correspondence with officials and judges throughout his kingdom, keeping informed and offering opinions on a wide range of judicial proceedings, at times ratifying and at times questioning decisions by "lower" judges. Many of these letters from the king have survived, and they suggest that actual law cases and judgments executed during Hammurabi's reign, together with theoretically driven expansions of such cases, may have been the primary sources for the legal decisions, the so-called "laws" assembled and inscribed on his monumental *Stele*. Thus, while not a law "code" in the sense of proscribing laws in a comprehensive and systematic fashion, the decisions collected and preserved on the stele do represent the legal rules and prescriptions established by a sovereign authority. Although very few actual trial records refer to the stele, the consensus among scholars is that the decisions inscribed "do not conflict with legal practice as evidenced in actual contracts from everyday life" (Greengus 1995: 472).[7]

The Louvre stele was most likely originally erected in the Esagila, the temple of the god Marduk in Hammurabi's capital city of Babylon, or possibly in the Ebabbar, temple of the god Shamash in the city of Sippar. A French expedition discovered Hammurabi's Stele in excavations undertaken in 1901–02, not in Babylon or Sippar but in Susa, the capital city of Elam, a rival power to the east, where it had been taken and displayed by a twelfth-century Elamite king.[8] Additional stone fragments found at Susa suggest that there were two, possibly even three such stelae of Hammurabi, which presumably he had set up in other cities throughout his realm (Roth 1997: 73). We know that even centuries after the stele's removal to Susa, Mesopotamian scribes traveled to the Elamite capital to study and copy its inscription.

The *Stele* is arguably the single most recognizable artifact from the ancient Near East, and there is good evidence that it was widely known in antiquity. More importantly for consideration of the cultural history of justice, the *Stele*'s inscription played a role in the intellectual and ideological formation of generations of educated Babylonians. Excerpts of the inscription, made by students learning to read and write, have been found in cities throughout Mesopotamia, some dated to as many as 1,000 years after Hammurabi reigned (Roth 1997: 74). A small number of those who learned to read and write went on to occupy high positions at court, and a similarly small number went on to advanced training in composing liturgical works in the service of religious institutions. A larger number of students were those who, having completed the requisite training in reading and writing, went on to become bureaucrats, office holders, magistrates, and judges.

In this way, the ideological prologue and epilogue, as well as the legal "decisions" recorded on the stele, can be said to have been widely and lastingly "published." We can conjecture with confidence that the *Stele*'s ideas about justice were transmitted to the larger public not trained in the scribal tradition by the literate individuals who composed, transcribed, and adapted literary and liturgical texts, as well as by those responsible for maintaining law and order through civic structures and procedures.[9]

But the *Stele* was more than just the vehicle for its inscription: its text and imagery were designed, quite deliberately, to incorporate culturally conditioned elements of performativity and memorialization, which by resonating powerfully with its ancient audience, helped perpetuate its conceptualization of justice.

A CLOSER LOOK AT *HAMMURABI'S STELE* WITHIN ITS CULTURAL CONTEXT

In addition to the law collections, thousands of clay tablets documenting legal transactions have survived from ancient Mesopotamia. Inscribed with cuneiform writing, these tablets inform us about private and state legal activity for more than two and one-half millennia. These legal documents also show that legal procedures took place in *public* spaces, before a city gate, within a temple, even, perhaps, in public portions of the palace. Local courts handled matters of property, but offenses involving loss of life or meriting capital punishment would be heard either by royal judges appointed by the king or by the king himself. Complaints of judicial malfeasance similarly were referred to the king, underscoring the gravity of such offenses according to Mesopotamian standards of justice. Penalties for trying to undermine the legal process—making a false accusation, bearing false witness and for a judge to reverse his decision—constitute prominently the very first five "laws" of the *Stele* inscription (see below) and indicate the gravity with which king and kingdom regarded legal procedure.

While of great value for illuminating legal procedure, Mesopotamian legal documents on clay tablets tell us little about the cultural understanding of justice. The *Law Stele of Hammurabi*, however, offers an integrated presentation of the meaning and image of justice through its text and iconography. As noted above, the stele's inscription is partnered by a compelling sculpture in low relief that crowns the 2-meter high stone monument. Moreover, because others survive only as later extracts copied onto clay tablets, Hammurabi's inscription is the only law collection that survives as an integral component of a royal monument whose overall sculptural and textual program can be studied holistically.

It is important to try to appreciate how Hammurabi's intended audience would have responded to the elements that composed his *Stele*. The text is the single longest continuous inscription known from the ancient Near East, and the beginning and end are written in a highly formalized poetic register of the Babylonian language.[10] The inscription is carved in archaizing cuneiform, and hearkens back to the third millennium in its sign forms and spatial orientation on the monument's surface. The sculpted image is dynamic and positioned prominently and imposingly at the top of the stele. Executed upon a single very large piece of rare, hard stone, even the material of the *Stele* itself lent weight to its integrated verbal and visual messages.[11] Moreover, the *Stele* was erected in a temple, spatially marked as sacred and thus physically and notionally separated from day-to-day mundane activity. All these elements, considered separately and in combination, are strong indications that the monument was intended to carve out a space, arguably a public space, for the contemplation of justice, even—and especially—after Hammurabi's death. As such, the monument was composed with the aim of providing its audience—citizen petitioners and future kings—with a lasting *public* resource for obtaining justice, simultaneously providing an enduring memorial to Hammurabi's rule as a divinely sanctioned just king.

THE INSCRIPTION

Assyriologists traditionally divide the *Stele*'s very long inscription into three sections: the Prologue, the "Laws," and the Epilogue. The Prologue, as noted above, is composed in a high poetic register of Babylonian. Concerned with the past, the Prologue summarizes Hammurabi's military conquests and pious building projects, achievements resulting in the gods selecting him to be king expressly to bring justice to the land:

> At that time [when the gods made Babylon great], the gods Anu and Enlil, for the enhancement of the well-being of the people, named me by name: Hammurabi, pious prince, who venerates the gods, to make justice (*misharu*) prevail in the land, to abolish the wicked and the evil, to prevent the strong from oppressing the weak, to rise like the sun-god Shamash over all mankind, to illuminate the land. (i 27–49)

The middle section, written in prose, follows the Prologue and recounts between 275 and 300 "laws" or decisions. These are all written according to the same formula: "if a man does x, then y shall be done to him." The "laws" are organized according to subject, roughly as follows:

§§1–5	false testimony
§§ 6–25	theft
§§ 26–41	labor on state-owned land
§§ 127–194	family law
§§195–214	assault and battery

As noted above, the very first "laws" deal with attempts to subvert the legal process by bringing false or un-substantiated accusation or testimony:

> § 1 If a man has accused another man and charges him with homicide but cannot bring proof against him, his accuser shall be killed.
>
> § 2 If a man has charged another man with witchcraft but cannot bring proof against him, he who is charged with witchcraft shall go to the divine River Ordeal [whereby participants were sent to be tested by immersion in the deified river].
>
> § 3 If a man has come forward to give false testimony in a case but did not bring evidence for his accusation, if that case is a capital offense, that man shall be killed. (v 26–67)

The "laws" that are probably the best known are those held up as exemplifying the principle of retributive justice often associated with the ancient world (i.e., the so-called *lex talionis*):

> § 196 If a freeman has blinded the eye of another freeman, his eye shall be blinded.
>
> § 197 If he has broken the bone of another freeman, his bone shall be broken.

§ 198 If he has blinded the eye of a dependent or broken the bone of a dependent, he shall pay 60 shekels of silver.

§ 199 If he has blinded the eye of a slave of a freeman, or broken the bone of a slave of freeman, he shall pay one-half his value [in silver] (xl 45–65).

This section strongly invites comparison to biblical precepts of justice showcased in the biblical books of Exodus, Leviticus, and Deuteronomy and referred to in Matthew 5:58.[12] It has been argued, in fact, that the biblical law collection in Exodus 20:23–23:19 used Hammurabi's very text as a model (Wright 2009). Compare, for example, Exodus 21:22: " ... If any harm follows, then you shall give life for life, eye for eye, tooth for tooth, hand for hand, foot for foot, burn for burn, wound for wound, stripe for stripe."

It is in the third section, however, the Epilogue, where we find explicit elaborations on the meaning of justice and the role of the king in establishing and maintaining justice. By returning to the poetic diction of the Prologue, the two poetic segments frame the middle section of "laws." This closing section of the inscription forges something almost like a compact between Hammurabi and his intended audience, in which the king offers in perpetuity his wise, just, decisions to any petitioner seeking justice, and simultaneously engages that petitioner to perpetuate Hammurabi's memory. Concerned with the future, and specifically with special attention to the future of the actual stele and survival of its inscription and sculpture, the Epilogue enjoins future kings to preserve and honor it; in exchange, Hammurabi will bless them with long and prosperous reigns. But to fully understand the Epilogue, we need first to consider the relief sculpture atop the monument, to which this third and closing section explicitly refers.

THE RELIEF SCULPTURE

The sculpted relief depicts Shamash, the Mesopotamian sun-god, seated, facing left, and king Hammurabi, standing, who faces right (Figure 1.1). Shamash is signified as a divinity by his stylized horned crown. He is identifiable as the sun-god by the wavy-line "rays" emanating from his shoulders and the surface detail of his footstool evoking mountainous terrain—the eastern and western locales of his rising and setting. As Sun-god, Shamash is the Mesopotamian deity of light and illumination. In contrast to Western conceptualizations of justice as blindfolded,[13] the Near Eastern god of justice illuminates the true situation. In addition to "rays," the god's frequent attribute is a saw, with which he parts the mountains for his emergence and exit at sunrise and sunset, and with which, in juridical contexts, he separates falsehood from truth (Figure 1.2).[14] Here on the *Stele*, Shamash extends or displays to Hammurabi yet another attribute: an emblem scholars have labeled the "Rod and Ring," and which occupies a prominent position in the center of the visual field.

Opposite the god, Hammurabi's headgear marks him as king. Mesopotamian art typically displays the propitious right side in order to exhibit physical perfection, often, as here, with the muscular right shoulder bared; this detail, together with the emphatic depiction of the beard, highlights Hammurabi's physical strength and masculinity.[15] Hammurabi stands, of course, in the presence of the god, whose throne evokes the façade of a temple. Differences in height also visually encode the hierarchical relationship between god and king. And, if these features of the design were too subtle, to demonstrate his humility before the god, the king is depicted unambiguously performing a ritual gesture of "touching the nose."

FIGURE 1.1. Law Stele of Hammurabi (detail of relief). Source: DEA / G. DAGLI ORTI / Getty Images.

The "Rod and Ring" emblem, which mediates visually the space between the two figures, is attested throughout the ancient Near East for almost 2,000 years. It originates in the Mesopotamian concept of justice *misharu* as "that which has been made straight" (see above) and represents surveyor's tools: a stake and line used for setting straight architectural foundations (Slanski 2007).[16] What is important here is not so much the emblem in and of itself, but its role in the entire composition: the god of justice displays to the pious king the tools for laying just foundations, an image that reflects and amplifies Hammurabi's claim in the Prologue to have "been called by the gods to establish just ways in the land."

FIGURE 1.2. Impression of third millennium cylinder seal depicting Shamash, with attributes of "rays" and saw. Source: YBC 9682, Yale Babylonian Collection.

THE PERFORMATIVE QUALITY OF THE *STELE*

It is critical to keep in mind that in Mesopotamia, three-dimensional images, even those sculpted in bas-relief such as the one crowning *Hammurabi's Stele*, were not simply representations but rather *manifestations* of the deities and persons depicted.[17] This is comparable to theology underlying biblical prohibitions *against* the worship of images.[18] For a Mesopotamian audience, each time such an image is viewed, it is as if the scene depicted is *performed*, theoretically indefinitely, or as long as the image survives and has an audience. The performative quality of images in Mesopotamia is key to understanding how Hammurabi's Stele was intended to function.

The *Stele*'s designer composed the text and sculpture of the monument with an intended audience in mind, an audience that is identified in the Epilogue. The Epilogue brings together Hammurabi's multiple and interdependent aims in erecting the monument: to ensure perpetuation of Hammurabi's memory by the living and, consequently, to improve his status in the netherworld realm of the dead; to ensure continued just ways for the land; and to ensure the maintenance of the very *Stele* itself that is the means by which those aims can be achieved.

> In order that the mighty not wrong the weak, to provide just ways for the orphan and the widow, I have inscribed my precious pronouncements upon my stele and set [them] before my image, the just king [*shar mishari*], in the city of Babylon ... By the order of [the god] Marduk, my lord, may my engraved design not be confronted by someone who would remove it. May my name always be remembered faithfully in the Esagila temple which I love. (xlvii 59–xlviii 2)

Speaking the name was believed to ensure the continued existence of the deceased, albeit in the shadowy realms of the netherworld. As long as the name was spoken—and, for those who could afford one, as long as an image of the deceased was viewed[19]—the dead were ensured of continued existence. Moreover, the more often the rituals were performed, typically by the eldest son or another family member, the better quality of afterlife the deceased would enjoy.[20] In the case of the *Law Stele*, the inscription calls not upon a living relation of Hammurabi to remember his name, but addresses instead a future litigant:

> Let any man who has a lawsuit come before my image, the just king [*shar mishari*], and have my words read out loud; let him hear my precious words, let my monument reveal to him the case. Let him see his judgment so that his heart may become soothed, [reciting the following short prayer]:[21]
>
> Hammurabi, lord, who is like a father and begetter to his people, submitted himself to the command of the god Marduk, his lord, and achieved victory everywhere. He gladdened the heart of Marduk, his lord, and he secured the eternal well-being of the people and provided just ways for the land (lit. "made the land straight") (xlviii 3– xlviii 38)

Thus, in the voice of Hammurabi, the *Stele* invites "any man who has a lawsuit" to come into the presence of Hammurabi's sculpted image. Even if the man could not read the cuneiform inscription for himself—and we understand literacy at this time to have been limited—provision is made for someone to read Hammurabi's words out loud.[22] Literate or not, the man with the lawsuit—the intended audience of the *Stele*—is called to view the performative image of Hammurabi, the just king, as he stands, marked visually by his piety, having been received into the presence of the god Shamash, who holds out before him emblematic tools for establishing justice. Simultaneously, the man with the lawsuit is instructed to invoke Hammurabi's memory both verbally through a real-time utterance of Hammurabi's name and visually through viewing the king's sculpted image.[23]

Were Hammurabi a private person, the act of viewing his image and reciting his name might have been sufficient to ensure his memory and his existence in the netherworld. But Hammurabi was a king, in which role he also promulgated justice on behalf of the state—and the *Stele*'s intended audience included more than simply a man with a lawsuit:

> Any king that might appear in the land at any time in the future, may he guard the pronouncements of justice that I inscribed upon my monument. May he not change the judgment of the land that I judged, the decision of the land that I decided. May he not remove my image … Hammurabi, the just king to whom the god Shamash granted truth, am I … If the aforementioned man [i.e., a future king] should heed my words that I inscribed upon my monument, (if) he should not overturn my decisions … (if) he should not change my words, (if) he should not damage my design—that man, like me, is a just king. May Shamash lengthen his reign! May he shepherd his people in justice! (xlviii 59–xlix 17)

Hammurabi hereby also appeals to the agent most capable of preserving his *Law Stele*, complete with his words and image—a future king. And much in the same way that Hammurabi offers justice to the man with the lawsuit in exchange for propitiation of his memory, Hammurabi, as a royal intercessory from beyond the grave, offers a future king his blessings for a long and just reign in exchange for maintaining and honoring his monument. In this way, Hammurabi draws upon the very institution of kingship to ensure his active memorialization, reflexively extending to that institution the prestige of his highly successful reign and judiciary achievements.

With text and image considered together as components of an integrated compositional program, the *Law Stele of Hammurabi* illuminates about Near Eastern justice far more than the legal principle of retribution. The gods charge the king with providing and maintaining justice for the people of his land: it is the very reason for kingship. With an emphasis on protecting the weaker members of society, the king applies rules—"laws," or decisions—that provide "straight ways" and "make the land straight." Such formulations hint that the land tends *not* to be straight or, at least, we cannot expect the land to adhere to straight ways without royal guidance, and suggest that Near Eastern justice is fundamentally *restorative* rather than *retributive*.

While the inscription tells us that the gods called Hammurabi to kingship in order to establish just ways for the land, the sculpture shows us, unambiguously, that the just ways enacted by the king originate with the gods. The "rod and ring," an emblem of surveyor's tools for laying straight foundations, is not shown in the hand of the king; rather, here—and in all other known depictions—it is firmly in the hand of a god, who *displays* or *extends* it to the king. Nonetheless, it is the king who is responsible for enacting and upholding straight ways, in accordance with principles that originate with the gods and that consequently remain fully known only to the gods.[24]

The *Law Stele of Hammurabi* is only one example of Hammurabi's ongoing commitment to justice. Ancient Near Eastern society was conceived hierarchically, a structure immediately apparent from the Akkadian term for "slave," *wardu*. The noun *wardu* gave rise to the verb *waradu* "to descend." *Wardu* was used to designate both persons who were property as well as subordinates: chattel slaves were *wardu*, but government officials could also be labeled *wardu* of the king, and the king was *wardu* of the gods. Encoded in the very word for "slave" thus is the idea of holding a position on the societal ladder that is lower relative to another.

Mandating social justice, then, was conceived not as establishing *equality*, but rather as "protecting the weaker strata of society from being unfairly deprived of their due: the legal status, property rights, and economic condition" to which they were entitled (Westbrook 2009c: 144). We see kings acting to maintain social justice at times of economic stress, when retributive laws empowering creditors to seize family land and family members of debtors unable to repay loans created the potential for widespread dispossession and enslavement of the class of small farmers. While legal, such seizures were "regarded as unjust because of their harmful economic or social consequences" (Westbrook 2009c: 147).

Where we most clearly see principles of social justice in operation are in the use of royal edicts to alleviate long-term and society-wide effects of debt and debt slavery, which undermined the social position of agrarian families and potentially threatened to destabilize the whole social order.[25] These royal edicts were, in fact, known in Akkadian as *misharu*, "justice," as in: "the king established *misharu* 'justice' in the land." The central provision of *misharu* edicts was *anduraru* "freedom" or "restoration," usually written with Sumerian logogram *amar-gi*, literally "return-to-the-mother."

Hammurabi was not the first Mesopotamian king to issue edicts to restore social justice among his subjects—there is evidence of the practice as early as 2400 BCE. Edicts of *misharu* and *anduraru* cancelling debts and debt slavery were so important to royal ideology that years of a king's reign were named according to their issuance. During his reign, Hammurabi decreed four cancellations of agrarian debts and debt slavery, first in the year of his accession (1792 BCE), and three more times during his long reign (Hudson 1993: 47). It is likely that these royal decrees, restoring weaker members of society to their "just" position, are alluded to when the *Stele*'s prologue and epilogue extol Hammurabi as being a protector of the weak.

JUSTICE AS RETRIBUTION AND RESTORATION: CULTURAL TESTIMONY FROM "GOLDEN AGE" ATHENS

Athenian authors and artists of the fifth century have bequeathed to the Western tradition a rich inheritance of literature and visual arts that continue to exert a deep and lasting impact on our conceptions of justice—one reason why we continue to value and study those works today.

As in the case of Hammurabi's *Law Stele*, some of the works that feel most relevant to audiences both ancient and modern are characterized by a performative quality. There were works in the ancient Greek-speaking world that provided a backdrop, vocabulary, and ideological framework for fifth-century Athenian explorations of justice. The most prominent of these were the epics of Homer, the *Iliad* and the *Odyssey*, which, as Bernard Knox writes in his introduction, in the fifth century were known not only "to schoolboys and scholars," but were as "familiar as household words in the mouths of ordinary Greeks" (Homer 1990: 11–12). Most people would have experienced the poems through oral performance; some would have learned them (necessarily aurally) and memorized them for oral recitation. Both poems open with invocations to the divine muses to "sing" through the poems' speakers, prominently drawing attention to their performative aspects, and alluding to the likelihood that recitation of Homer's epics were accompanied by instrumental music. The poetry of Hesiod—not as familiar today as Homer, but well-known to the educated fifth-century Athenian—was composed around the same time as the Homeric epics, probably between the eighth and sixth centuries,[26] and was also most commonly experienced as performance.

Of works composed in the fifth century, the Athenian tragedies evidence the deepest cultural engagement with justice. Plays such as *Oedipus Tyrannos, Antigone, Agamemnon,* and *The Bacchae* are part of our cultural matrix and continue to be performed today—some two-and-a-half millennia after they first premiered—precisely because the questions they provoke about justice remain as relevant now as they were then. Through public performance, the plays served in antiquity—and continue to serve—as vehicles for posing and responding to such questions on a community-wide basis.

The great Greek tragedies that come down to us were written and performed for the *Dionysia*, the annual city-wide festival in honor of the god Dionysos. The *Dionysia* was an expressly civic ritual, attended by all its citizens, regardless of wealth or status. As young men, citizens of the city performed in the chorus, and it was the responsibility of wealthy citizens to fund the productions. The great playwrights whose work survives—notably Aeschylus, Sophocles, and Euripides—were also prominent leaders: Aeschylus fought at Marathon in the Persian War, and Sophocles was a military commander in the Peloponnesian Wars. Their plays were written and performed for, and judged by an expressly public, civic audience, many of whom had served in the Athenian military.

The final work to be considered in this chapter is from Thucydides' *History of the Peloponnesian Wars*, the famous "Melian Dialogue." Formally and overtly performative, the Melian Dialogue circles back to the opening concerns of the chapter and is an appropriate place to close.

The main point to remember
Is that gods and humans go back a long way together.

(Hesiod, *Works & Days*, trans. S. Lombardo 127–128)

The early Greek poetry of Homer and Hesiod demonstrates that *dike* "justice" is both (1) justice as required and meted out by the gods, principally Zeus, and simultaneously (2) the cosmic order and consequent balance in the universe. The two aspects of *dike* are mutually interdependent, and the poet Hesiod mythologized the roots of their interdependence in the origins of *kosmos*—cosmic order. *Works and Days* explores how justice, as men know it, came to be wielded by Zeus, and that it is manifest not only in fair dealings among men, but also in the requisite regularity of honoring the gods, the regular cyclical movements of the cosmos, and in the seasons of the earth.

Over 900 lines, the long autobiographical poem is addressed by the speaker to his brother Perses, who has cheated the speaker out of his share of their father's inheritance:

Let's settle this feud right now
With the best kind of judgment, a straight one from Zeus.
We had our inheritance all divided up, then you
Made off with most of it, playing up to those
Bribe-eating lords who love cases like this. (51–54)

Right away, we recognize that the notion of justice—familiar from the ancient Near East—is conceptualized as something "straight," as opposed to "crooked." Moreover, we get a sense of expectation disappointed by the failure of earth-bound human judges to deliver "straight" justice, choosing instead personal profit, and reminiscent of the first five "laws" of Hammurabi (above).

The poem characterizes Perses as a lazy cheat, who, rather than work, supports himself through borrowing and deceit, profiting from the labors of others. Moreover, it seems that Perses has come to the speaker for money. The speaker's advice midway through the poem makes explicit that, like in the ancient Near East, the gods created humankind to work the land[27]:

Work, you fool Perses, work
The work the gods laid out for men …
What you've got to do, Perses,
Is get out of debt, and keep from starving. (447–457)

The long poem interweaves multiple aspects of justice that are hard to subsume under a single uniform definition: justice embedded in the hierarchy of the cosmos; in the straight judgments of Zeus; in honoring the ties of parents, guests, and hosts; in honest dealings and speech; in giving the gods their due; and epitomized by the speaker's advice to his brother (and us) to perform honest work. Throughout, *Works and Days* exemplifies how inseparable are these different strands of justice. About a quarter of the poem is devoted to advice for each of the seasons of the growing year, underscoring that performing the right act at the right time is a kind of justice, one that the universe rewards with human flourishing.

But when judges judge straight, for neighbors
As well as for strangers, and never turn their backs
On Justice, their city blossoms their people bloom.
You'll find peace all up and down the land

And youngsters growing tall, because broad-browed Zeus
Hasn't marked them out for war. Nor do famine or blight
Ever afflict folk who deal squarely with each other.
They feast on the fruits of their tended fields,
And the earth bears them a good living too. (261–269)

Questions of justice on multiple levels is of concern in the Homeric epics, too: both in terms of their overall story arc and in episodes narrating conflicts between individual characters, human and divine. Both the *Iliad* and the *Odyssey* present, toward their conclusions, a scene in which a form of justice is enacted in such a way that challenges easy assumption of a uniform concept of justice.

Writ large, the *Iliad* tells the story of the Achaean siege of Troy to avenge the abduction of Helen. We know—as did ancient audiences—the answer to the question of how the story will end, even though the fall of Troy takes place off stage, after the action of the poem has drawn to a close. All of Troy is destroyed to punish the home and the entire family line of Paris, who transgressed the rules of hospitality when he stole the wife of his host. On the surface, the crime is punished, justice as retribution has been mandated— demanded!—by the gods. The universe is, once again, rendered ordered and predictable.

Yet the smaller interactions that make up the poem cannot be reconciled with such a simplistic notion of justice. This tension is explored most fully in book 24, when Priam begs Achilles to return the body of his slain son, Hector, and Achilles complies. Their interaction complicates any one-dimensional understanding of justice, and belies, moreover, the reductive image of humans as pawns upon a cosmic chessboard. Similarly, if the operative question of the narrative of the *Odyssey* is "Will the gods allow Odysseus to achieve his homecoming (*nostos*)?" readers are forced to confront the justness of the discomfiting and gratuitous violence of Odysseus's slaughter of the suitors and the maids in book 22, before he is restored to his rightful place in Ithaca as father, husband, and king.

The Hesiodic and Homeric works raise questions about justice as restoration by way of retribution: are there losses that can never be made right? If not—can a cycle of retribution ever be brought to an end? While Greek literature explores these questions in greater detail than those from the ancient Near East, as in the ancient Near East, these same works resist as simplistic the notion that in antiquity there was one uniform conception of justice, and reject as artificial any claim that an earlier, more simple concept of justice evolved over time into a later, more sophisticated one.[28] What we see in the later sources, rather, is a *dialog* with the earlier ones, adding, like Socrates's interlocutors, new layers to an ongoing and increasingly nuanced debate. For two rich examples of how fifth-century Athenians approached the interrelated challenges posed by schemes of retributive and restorative justice in social and cosmic spheres, we turn to Aeschylus's *Oresteia* trilogy and Thucydides' *History of the Peloponnesian Wars*.

Drawing on the tradition of heroes returning from Troy, the *Oresteia* of Aeschylus (524– 456 BCE) explores the long-term implications of enacting justice only in terms of answering damage with damage, of viewing justice according to a model of balanced accounts. In so doing, the trilogy confronts its audience with the catastrophic consequences of such a limited view of justice, and the irreparable damage caused by an arithmetic view of righting wrongs.

The only tragic trilogy to have survived from antiquity, the *Oresteia* (*Agamemnon, Libation Bearers*, and *Eumenides*) was first performed in 458 BCE, having won for Aeschylus the annual Dionysia competition. *Agamemnon* opens with the return of Agamemnon, king of Mycenae and leader of the Achaean allies, from the victorious ten-year siege of Troy. Before the play is over, his queen Clytemnestra, together with her lover Aegisthos, have slain the king within the walls of his palace.

To tell the story of Agamemnon's return from Troy, the play reaches back into the early history of the House of Atreus: Aegisthos, who has become Clytemnestra's lover during the king's absence, is also Agamemnon's cousin. Both he and Clytemnestra justify their regicide as justice for earlier murders committed within this family: Clytemnestra citing Agamemnon's murder of their daughter, Iphigenia, infanticide committed in order to launch the expedition to Troy, and Aigisthos the horrific slaying of his siblings by his uncle Atreus, the father of Agamemnon.

Clytemnestra views her murder of Agamemnon not only as retribution fulfilling "divine law" for the killing of blood kin, but as an act that will finally end the cycle of retributive murders within the family:

> But as for me
> I gladly give my promise to
> the Spirit of the clan that I
> will bear all this, however hard,
> if only he will go from the house
>   for good and grind
> some other family out by
> bringing kin to murder. However
>   small my share
> of wealth may be, **I'll be content**
> **if I have rid our halls at last**
> **of our frenzied killing of each other.**
>   (Aeschylus 1991, *Agamemnon* 1802–13, emphasis added)

Picking up the story some ten years later at the tomb of the slain king, *Libation Bearers* centers on the children of Agamemnon, daughter Electra and son Orestes, who are compelled by a combination of divine, personal, and political motivations to kill their mother to avenge their father's murder. The play meditates on the special complications for justice when atrocities are committed upon intimates and the consequences of such crimes, and closes with the introduction of the Erinyes, the divine Furies charged since primeval times with demanding retribution for blood crimes within the family.[29] They pursue Orestes, who wielded the sword that killed Clytemnestra, to exact justice for his matricide. The play closes on the supernatural pursuit of Orestes by the Furies, demonstrating that the cycle of blood revenge is not over, an ending so unfulfilling and unfulfillable that its action intrudes into the third play.

The *Eumenides* opens on the Furies' pursuit of Orestes from Mycenae to Delphi and then to Athens, where Athena constitutes a murder court as resolution to the foregoing irresoluble, inescapable, and ultimately annihilating concept of justice. Aeschylus's trilogy concludes when Athena takes justice out of the hands of the Furies to place it instead in a civic process of the state. When the jury deadlocks, she casts the deciding vote to acquit Orestes and bring the cycle of retribution to an end. The resolution is a compromise, and neither dramatically nor morally satisfying. It is second-best justice, resolved upon to allow society to carry on through necessarily imperfect human courts and civic procedures.

The *Oresteia*, considered today one of the high peaks of the Western tradition, was referenced in other plays (see introduction in Aeschylus 1991, 3–4), suggesting that it was known widely in the fifth century. The urgency of the story it tells is also reflected in a number of depictions of

Orestes slaying Aigisthos that survive on painted ceramics. An example of these, a *krater* attributed to the Dikomasia painter and dated to about 460 BCE, is unique in depicting not only the well-attested motif of Orestes killing the murderer of his father (Figure 1.3), but on its opposite face, the only known visual rendering of Aigisthos slaying Agamemnon (Figure 1.4).[30]

Visually the two scenes are linked on the krater through their parallel designs; in fact, the artist has modelled the otherwise unattested death of Agamemnon on the well-attested scene of Aegisthos' death (Vermeule 1966: 1). But the two scenes are also linked *spatially* in the painted visual field: the artist has deployed architectural features—vertical columns—to mark "the transition in time between the two scenes, but unite them in a single hall ... allowing characters from the first murder to pass behind the barriers and intrude onto the second murder" (Vermeule 1966: 2) (Figure 1.5). While it has been claimed that the painter must have been

FIGURE 1.3. Mixing bowl (calyx krater) with the killing of Agamemnon (face depicting the murder of Aigisthos by Orestes). Obverse. Source: MFA 63.1246. Museum of Fine Arts, Boston.

FIGURE 1.4. Mixing bowl (calyx krater) with the killing of Agamemnon (face depicting the murder of Agamemnon by Aigisthos). Reverse. Source: MFA 63.1246. Museum of Fine Arts, Boston.

influenced by having viewed a performance of Aeschylus's trilogy,[31] such a direct influence is not necessary to compare the effect achieved by both the *Oresteia* and the Dikomasia krater on their respective audiences. The krater's circular form invites the viewer to read the painting as a continuous frieze—the characters from the second murder intrude into the scene of the first, and the parallel composition of the two scenes reinforces the impression that we are viewing a repeated performance. The eyes of the viewer—like the characters depicted in both the trilogy and the painted krater—are trapped in the cycle of retribution, doomed to lurch repetitively, circularly, and without end from the scene of one murder to the next.

FIGURE 1.5. Mixing bowl (calyx krater) with the killing of Agamemnon (side view). Source: MFA 63.1246. Museum of Fine Arts, Boston.

CONCLUSION

The *Oresteia* trilogy and the Boston Dikomasia painter's krater bring us back to questions of performance and audience, and a tendency in antiquity to explore the meaning and value of justice through facilitating dialog among multiple points of view. By way of conclusion, the chapter turns to its final case study, the Melian Dialogue (V.84–116) from Thucydides' (460–399 BCE) *History of the Peloponnesian Wars* (431–404).

A decade into the twenty-seven-year Peloponnesian War, Athens had compelled, through siege and surrender, a series of formerly independent islands to submit to her empire. One of the "culminating points" of the *History* (Connor 1984: 157), the Melian Dialogue is unique in its form,[32] consisting of short, blunt exchanges in which an Athenian delegation demands that the island of Melos surrender to Athens or be destroyed.

The Athenians in this dialog make no appeal to justice. On the contrary, they urge the islanders to consider instead only what best serves Melian self-interest. For the reader, the effect is akin to witnessing a play.

> **Athenians:** [W]e recommend that you should try to get what it is possible for you to get, taking into consideration what we both really do think; since you know as well as we do that, when these matters are discussed by practical people, the standard of justice depends on the quality of power to compel and that in fact the strong do what they have the power to do and the weak accept what they have to accept.
>
> **Melians:** Then in our view (since you force us to leave justice out of account and confine ourselves to self-interest)—in our view it is at any rate useful that you should not destroy a principle that is to the general good of all men—namely,

> that in the case of all who fall into danger there should be such a thing as fair play and just dealing, and that such people should be allowed to use and to profit by arguments that fall short of a mathematical accuracy. And this is a principle which affects you as much as anybody, since your own fall would be visited by the most terrible vengeance and would be an example to the world.
>
> **Athenians:** ... We do not want any trouble in bringing you into our empire, and we want you to be spared for the good both of yourselves and of ourselves.
>
> **Melians:** And how could it be just as good for us to be the slaves as for you to be the masters?
>
> **Athenians:** You, by giving in, would save yourselves from disaster; we, by not destroying you, would be able to profit from you.
>
> **Melians:** So you would not agree to our being neutral, friends instead of enemies, but allies of neither side?
>
> **Athenians:** No, because it is not so much your hostility that injures us; it is rather the case that, if we were on friendly terms with you, our subjects would regard that as a sign of weakness in us, whereas your hatred is evidence of our power.
>
> **Melians:** Is that your subjects' idea of fair play—that no distinction should be made between people who are quite unconnected with you and people who are mostly your own colonists or else rebels whom you have conquered?
>
> **Athenians:** So far as right and wrong are concerned they think that there is no difference between the two, that those who still preserve their independence do so because they are strong, and that if we fail to attack them it is because we are afraid. So that by conquering you, we shall increase not only the size but the security of our empire ... (V.89–97, trans. R. Connor 1984)

If Thucydides' history achieves its impact through authorial detachment, leaving it to the reader to draw connections and conclusions (Connor 1984: esp. 12–19), then the effect of that detachment is nowhere greater realized than in this dialog. Forced into the position of a witness to the exchange, the reader (or audience) views the Athenian and Melian representatives act out Thrasymachus' claim in the *Republic*, that "justice is nothing other than the advantage of the stronger" (*Republic* II, 338c). Thucydides' detached and understated reporting of the conclusion of the Melian episode, that: "the Melians surrendered unconditionally to the Athenians, who put to death all the men of military age whom they took, and sold the women and children as slaves," (V.116) only amplifies our horror at witnessing what the Athenians have become.

We know, of course, as did Thucydides' ancient audience, that Athens's continued expansion of her empire—connected here by Thucydides with her cold disregard for justice—will end with Athens's disastrous expedition to Sicily. But Thucydides forces us to make a direct connection between the Athenian treatment of Melos and her defeat in Sicily when he abruptly transitions from the dialogic form back to his narrative: "In the same winter the Athenians resolved to sail again against Sicily ... and, if possible, to conquer it."[33]

By connecting her defeat at Sicily with her treatment of Melos, Thucydides' text makes the case that Athens's defeat at Sicily is, somehow, justice for her having exercised the advantage of the stronger (in Plato's words), or failing, (in Hammurabi's words) "to protect the weak from the strong." Even without divine or royal authority to step in to punish Athens, Thucydides' audience—ancient and modern—is witness, nonetheless, to the operation of justice in an implicitly ordered universe.

CHAPTER TWO

Constitution

JILL FRANK

Constitution, in antiquity, refers to a set of practices, norms, or rules under two aspects: the rule of a city's governing body, on the one hand; and the established rule, custom, or way of life of a city, on the other. Herodotus' *History* offers an example of the first aspect of constitution in the debate it stages featuring three Persian aristocrats discussing the form their new government should take: Otanes advocates for rule by the many and favors democracy; Megabyxos speaks for rule by the few and opts for oligarchy; Darius endorses rule by the one to argue on behalf of monarchy (3.80–82).[1] In the *History of the Peloponnesian War*, Thucydides, too, addresses the question of constitution by reference to a city's governing body when he describes Athens under Pericles' leadership as "government by the first citizen" (2.65.9).

The fifth-century tragic stage casts light on the second aspect of constitution, as the established rule, custom, or way of life of a city. In Sophocles' *Antigone*, for example, Antigone's betrothed, Haemon, and her sister, Ismene, stand for the position that constitutional rule must take its bearings from the ways of living of the Thebans (740–750, 90–92).[2] In Aeschylus' *Eumenides*, Athena constitutes a "deliberative assembly" (570) made up of Athens's finest citizens (487) to try Orestes for the murder of his mother Clytemnestra, describing the Areopagus as best able to decide Orestes' case, better than any single mortal man (470, 696–698), and also than any god (471). Athena allows herself a vote to tip the scales of justice in Orestes' favor (735), to be sure, and that may appear to assert the constitutive power of a god. But Athena determines that Orestes brings "no harm to [her] city" (475) only after learning that *the Athenians* opened their homes to him, thus that *they* deemed him cleansed of the pollution of Clytemnestra's murder (451–452, 284–285). This suggests that her vote may instead anticipate the position of Ismene and Haemon in the *Antigone*, namely that constitutional rule is bound with the ways of living of *polis*-beings.[3]

This chapter was supported by a 2015–2016 Brett de Bary Interdisciplinary Mellon Writing Group award from the Society for the Humanities, Cornell University. For their helpful questions and suggestions, I thank the Group's participants: Lara Fresko, Rayna Kalas, Nazli Konya, Becquer Medak-Seguin, Aziz Rana, Neil Saccamano, and Jacob Swanson. For their comments on earlier drafts of this chapter, I thank Susan Buck-Morss, Julen Etxabe, Michael Kicey, Matthew Landauer, Melissa Lane, Gerald Mara, and the audience at the 2015 meeting of the Association for Political Theory. I thank Jordan Jochim for our conversations about Plato's *Laws* and for his able research assistance, and Julen Etxabe for inviting my contribution to this volume.

The historians and tragedians actually attend to both aspects of constitution. Herodotus' Otanes prefers democracy not only because it is rule by the many but also because its *isonomia*, or equality in law, enables citizens to participate in the constitution (3.80). In the funeral oration of 431 honoring Athenian warriors killed during the first year of the Peloponnesian War, Thucydides has Pericles ask after not only "the form of government under which [Athenian] greatness grew" but also "the national habits out of which it sprang" (2.36.4). The *Antigone* and *Oresteia* refer constitutional rule to a city's way of life precisely to counter a particular form of government, namely tyranny. It is in response to Creon's treatment of law as sourced in and created by himself alone (191), a product of his art (400), and his treatment of the city as his private possession (800), that the *Antigone* offers constitutional rule as "a public or a communal or shared possession" (Allen 2005: 388–389). Insisting that "there is no city possessed by one man only" (798), Haemon claims that Creon "would be a fine dictator of a desert" (801). The prophet Tiresias alludes to Creon's tyranny as well (1050–1155).[4] Refusing to speak the law on Creon's behalf (230–240), the chorus treat him as an *auto-nomos*, one who creates the law for himself, and describe him as *apolis* (405), without a city, thus explicitly marking his relation to Thebes as extra-constitutional.[5]

Underscoring the dangers of tyrannical rule, Theseus, in Euripides' *Suppliant Women*, maintains that "nothing is worse for a city than an absolute ruler," for the laws will not be "common, *konoi*." Instead, "one man has power and makes the law his own" (430–432). Aeschylus' *Agamemnon* and *Libation Bearers* may be the first tragedies to stage the unconstitutionality of privately owned law, which, in these plays, takes the form of the law of revenge (Aeschylus 2011). The *Eumenides* presents the broad political stakes of this problematic in the trial of Orestes. For, although the Erinyes and Apollo stand on opposite sides of the question of whether Orestes deserves to be punished for murdering his mother, they, like Clytemnestra and Orestes, are depicted as acting in accordance with the laws of *their* respective *apolis* jurisdictions, the underworld and heavens. Just as the ruin of Thebes attests to the extra-constitutionality of Creon's *auto-nomos* (1398–1425), so too do the mortal and immortal *auto-nomoi* of the *Oresteia* threaten the deconstitution of Argos (*Libation Bearers* 1068–1076) and Athens (*Eumenides* 778–787, 808–817). Ancient historians and tragedians thus link constitution as the rule of a city's governing body with constitution as the rule, custom, or way of life of a city.

So, too, do the philosophers of antiquity. For example, Aristotle defines constitution, *politeia*, as both "the organization of offices" determining the political form of a city (*Politics* 1289a15–17) and also as the characteristic make-up or "life" of a city (1295a40). Describing the "true forms of government," namely, monarchy, aristocracy, and polity, *politeia*, as those "in which the one, the few, or the many govern with a view to the common interest" (1279a29–31), Aristotle offers a taxonomy of regimes that reflects the irreducible duality of governing body *and* way of life associated with constitution. Calling cities ruled with a view to the private interest of the one, few, or many, as in tyranny, oligarchy, or democracy, "perversions" (1279a33, 1279b4–10, 1289a26–30), he refuses to count these as proper constitutions. A city ruled according to the ruler's "own fancy" (1295a17), in which there is "nothing shared by the ruler and ruled" (*Nicomachean Ethics* 1161a33), which is to say, tyranny, Aristotle describes as "the very reverse of a constitution" (*Politics* 1293b31). Positing "constitutional rule" as the practice of citizens ruling and being ruled by turns (*Politics* 1259b2–5), Aristotle insists that even "the ruler must learn by obeying" (1277b9–10, 1333a1–2) for "he who has never learned to obey cannot be a good commander" (1277b14–15). For a constitution to be sustained, "all parts of the state must wish that it should exist and these arrangements be maintained" (1270b21–22). For Aristotle, then, as for the tragic poets, rule is constitutional only insofar as it is accepted by those who live under it (Frank 2015).

Plato's *politeia* dialogs attend to the duality of constitution as well. The *Laws* focuses on a city's governing body, arrangements of offices, and institutions in their own right and also with a view to how these mold citizen character and way of life (630e–631a). The *Republic* understands constitution as born "from the characters of people in the city," from which everything else follows (544e), and also, as *Republic* 5, 8–9 attest, in relation to the city's governing body and institutions. Like Aristotle's *Politics*, Plato's dialogs present as unconstitutional regimes whose laws are, in the words of the Athenian in the *Laws*, not made for the sake of the whole city (715b). Thus, the Athenian calls tyranny, oligarchy, and democracy not constitutions but "administrations where the city is under the sway of despots, with some parts enslaved to other parts of itself. Each takes its name from the authority that is the despot" (712e–713a). These regimes are unconstitutional insofar as the rulers "take over the city's affairs to such an extent that they refuse to share any of the rule with those who lost out" (715a–b). In the view of the Athenian, as for Aristotle, citizens share in the constitution by knowing "how to rule and be ruled with justice" (643e). Like Aristotle and the tragedies, *Republic* 1 and 9 make tyranny their special target.

In the texts of Plato, as in Aristotle's, the two aspects of constitutional rule are presented as interrelated. What, in the *Republic*, Socrates calls "the virtuous circle" of the constitution (424a) by way of which "like always produces like" (425c), describes the idea that a city's governing body is maintained by the way of life of the city's citizens at the same time that citizens' established customs and habits are inculcated by the city's institutions and arrangement of offices. In *Republic* 8–9, for example, Socrates explains constitutional decline as the result of institutional change alongside changes in customary attitudes towards the city's laws (548b, 550d). This "mutual conditioning between individual psychology and political environment" or "two-directional causality between soul and city" (Vegetti 2013: 13–14, n. 52) appears in the *Laws* as well, when, for example, the Athenian takes issue with the institutions and offices of the Spartan and Cretan constitutions for neglecting the virtues of moderation, wisdom, and justice by orienting to success at war and teaching military courage alone (625d–626c, 631b–632d, 688a–b, 705d).[6] Aristotle shares the Athenian's concerns about those constitutions (*Politics* 1271b1–12) and, likewise, criticizes the equalization scheme of Phaleas' constitution for failing to recognize that "it is not the possessions but the desires of mankind which require to be equalized" (1266b30).

Thus, in the texts of the philosophers, the duality of antique constitutionalism is underwritten by a dynamic and reciprocal relationship between the habits, character, and practices that sustain the way of life of a city's citizens, on the one hand, and, on the other, the collective orders and institutions that structure its governing body.[7] By binding together ethics and politics, this approach to constitutionalism positions the rule, *archē*, of constitution, its source, authority, and legitimacy, within the constitution itself. This may also be seen in the writings of Cicero, where the constitution, as *res publica*, "the public thing," belongs, as such, to the *populus*. This is an "associational conception" of community, which is to say, a *civitas* of individual citizens with "institutional aspects" (Hammer 2014: 30).

To make salient antique constitutionalism's two aspects and their dynamic and reciprocal interrelation is not to treat antique writers as advocates of democracy.

Especially in the Athenian context of the fifth and fourth century BCE, democracy was, on the contrary, the subject of harsh critique. Writing against the backdrop of the long and tumultuous Peloponnesian War (431–404 BCE), with democratic Athens veering to oligarchy and even tyranny (411, 404 BCE), Thucydides, for example, indexes Athens's military policies to its leaders and to an emancipation of Athenian private ambitions and interests (2.65.7). He describes Athenians' overreaching, *pleonexia*, as driven by their imperial or, in Pericles' word, "tyrannical" desire, guiding and guided by their leaders, to possess more, including other people(s) and cities (1.122, 124, 2.63, 3.37, 6.85) (Balot 2001; Wohl 2002).

On the fifth-century stage, Aristophanes' *Knights* (611–680), performed in 424, as well as Euripides' *Orestes* (870–945), performed in 408, offer lampoons of the despotisms of their contemporary Athenian democracy (Munn 2000: 118–119, 374 n. 31; Morgan 2003). With Athens' democratic institutions and policies reflecting the desires, opinions, and judgments of the Athenian people, the relationship between constitution as the city's governing body, on the one hand, and constitution as the city's way of life, on the other, was especially close. Figured as a relation of identity in *Knights*, Aristophanes names the leader of "the people," "The People" (*dêmos*, *Dêmos*), and depicts both characters as sharing the same orientation to ambition and private interest (630–680; 788–1276).

Making the democratic regime a mirror of late fifth-century Athenian democracy in *Republic* 8, Socrates describes its decline into tyranny (557a–562a). In *Laws* 3, the Athenian, for his part, makes Athenian democracy (693d) the mirror of Persia's despotism (701b–e). Aristotle, similarly, presents as tantamount to tyranny regimes in which the multitude holds "supreme power" "not as individuals, but collectively," as a "many in one" (*Politics* 1292a4–12; also 1298a32, 1312b6). Drawing a correspondence between democratic decrees and "the edicts of the tyrant" and claiming that both "override the laws" (1292a20–25), Aristotle maintains that "where the laws have no authority, there is no constitution" (1292a32–33). From the vantage point of Athens's fifth- and fourth-century "intellectual critics" of popular rule (Ober 2001), the late-fifth- and fourth-century Athenian *dêmos* was analogous to the tyrant appearing across the tragedies, who ruled in his own interests, treated the law as the product of his art and the city as his private possession.[8]

If tyranny was the gold standard of unconstitutionality across the classical period, the hallmark of constitutionalism, by contrast, was whether a city's citizens had a "share" or "partnership" in the constitution (Schofield 1996; Rhodes 2009: 60–61).[9] What having a share signified varied, for, as Aristotle explains, citizens participate relative to their constitutions (*Politics* 4.14–16). Sometimes citizens participated by holding offices, deliberating, and judging, sometimes by way of mechanisms that held deliberators and judges to account, such as scrutiny, *dokimasia*, and final accounting, *euthunai* (Euben 1997: 94–99). At the very least, as is apparent across the texts of antiquity—from Aeschylus' *Oresteia* and Sophocles' *Antigone*, to Xenophon's *Constitution of the Lacedaimonians* (8.5), to the writings of Plato and Aristotle—sharing in the constitution depended on citizens acquiescing willingly to their city's laws. We might call this the necessary or minimum condition of constitutionalism. As the Athenian puts it in Plato's *Laws*, where citizens do not voluntarily accept a city's laws or participate freely in the constitution, there is no constitution deserving of the name (690c, 832b–c, 712e–713a). Without citizens sharing in the constitution, by willingly acquiescing to their city's laws, there can be no *koinonia*, *civitas*, commonality nor *res populi*. It is in this sense that, as P. J. Rhodes has said of the Greek world, "the city was its citizens" (Rhodes 2009: 61) (Figure 2.1).

FIGURE 2.1. Democracy Crowning Dēmos (the Athenian People). This relief on the anti-tyranny law of 377/6 B.C. depicts Democracy crowning Dēmos (the Athenian People). Source: AGORA American School of Classical Studies at Athens: Agora Excavations *Agora Image: 2009.05.0084:* Photographer: Craig Mauzy. 2 August 2008.

Taking sharing in the constitution as a necessary condition of constitutionalism makes sense of the antique opposition to tyranny, a regime which offers few, if any, opportunities for holding the governing body to account and in which laws are obeyed not freely or willingly but due to the imposition or threat of force. It helps to explain another common feature of antique thought, the preference, from Thucydides' *History* (8.97.2), to Plato's *Laws* (681d–e, 693d–e), to Aristotle's *Politics* (1279a37–b6, 1294a30-b13), Polybius' *Histories* (6.10–11, 6.18), and Cicero's *De Re Publica* (1.45, 1.69), for mixed constitutions. Either through the mechanism of checks and balances preferred by Polybius, or through the blending or fusion preferred by the earlier Greeks, mixed constitutions seek to ensure that both elites and masses participate (Hahm 2009: 178–198; Lintott 2009: 269–285; Lane 2014: 260–274). Taking sharing in the constitution to be a necessary condition of constitutionalism also helps to explain antique critiques of extreme democracy: in the absence of the rule of law, there will be no constitution to share in. The imperative of the rule of law to antique constitutionalism may be traced to Solon, the sixth-century Athenian lawgiver and poet, who defined *eunomia*, government according to good laws, *eu-nomoi*, as that which "makes rough things smooth, stops excess, weakens hubris, and withers the growing blooms of madness. It straightens crooked judgments, makes arrogant deeds turn gentle, puts a stop to divisive factions, and brings to an end the misery of angry quarrels." To Solon, *eunomia* is "the source among human beings for all that is orderly and wise" (Gagarin and Woodruff 1995: 26).[10]

The rule of law may be imperative to constitutionalism. Depending on *its* source, however, it can also mean trouble. From the tragic stage to the texts of philosophy, the dual and reciprocal aspects of constitutionalism suggest that constitution is a norm that chronologically and qualitatively precedes legislation. Aristotle is especially clear on this point. Cautioning that "laws are not to be confounded with the principles of the constitution" (*Politics* 1289a16–17), he insists that "laws are, and ought to be, framed with a view to the constitution, and not the constitution to the laws" (*Politics* 1289a14–15, 1282b10–11). In the depiction of Solon presenting his laws to the Athenians, as in the accounts of mythical lawgivers across antiquity, including Lycurgus of Sparta and Minos of Crete, the rule of law is represented, by contrast, as originating not in the constitution but in what Danielle Allen has called a "specific named" lawgiver (2005: 390–392). (Figure 2.2.)

The stakes of these alternatives—constitution first, then laws, or lawgiver first, then constitution—are nowhere better exemplified than in Plato's *politeia* dialogs, specifically, the *Republic* and *Laws*.[11] We have seen that these dialogs are committed to the dual and reciprocal aspects of constitution and thus to constitution as a norm that precedes legislation. In their respective representations of the "best" city of

FIGURE 2.2. Portrait statue of Solon along the balustrade. Carol Highsmith. 19 July 2012. Library of Congress Thomas Jefferson Building, Washington DC. https://commons.wikimedia.org/wiki/File:Loc-solon-highsmith.jpg. Source: Library of Congress/Carol M. Highsmith/LC-DIG-highsm-02101.

the *kallipolis* and the "second-best" city of Magnesia, however, the *Republic* and *Laws* position the source and authority of law neither in the governing bodies of these cities nor in their way of life, but instead in their founder-lawgivers: Socrates, Glaucon and Adeimantus, in the case of the *Republic*'s *kallipolis*; the Athenian, the Spartan Megillus, and the Cretan Cleinias, in the case of the *Laws*' Magnesia. In these idealized "cities in speech" (*Republic* 369a, *Laws* 702d–e), as in the approaches to constitutionalism explored so far, "the *politeia* and its *nomoi* [laws] cannot be separated." But in these cities, as Melissa Lane has recently shown, "[i]t is the [laws] which define and constitute the identity of the [constitution]" rather than the other way around (2013a: 112).[12]

The remainder of this chapter explores the effect of this reversal on constitutionalism. I argue that the *Republic* and *Laws* present the constitutions of the *kallipolis* and Magnesia, framed with a view to the laws of their founder-lawgivers, as *failing* to meet even the minimum necessary condition of constitutionalism noted above, that is, the condition of citizens sharing in the constitution by willingly acquiescing to their city's laws. That failure, I maintain, reinforces the dialogs' overall commitment to constitution as an irreducible and reciprocal interrelation between governing body and citizen way of life. Taking that failure and reinforcement into account highlights Plato's proximity to Aristotle and to the poets on the topic of constitution. It also orients to a new appreciation of the education to and for political constitution offered by Plato's *politeia* writings. Scholars often take the *kallipolis* and Magnesia to be Plato's guarantee of constitutional virtue. In what follows, I make a case for reading these cities instead as Plato's representations of the ethical and political costs of seeking such a guarantee.

THE ART OF EXTRA-CONSTITUTIONAL RULE

Melissa Lane explains the following "causal sequence" in Plato's *politeia* dialogs: first, the founding of the city by founder-lawgivers "articulated in terms of the framing of laws"; then the upbringing and education of the city's rulers; then the laws of the city, produced by the rulers in keeping with the "significant" laws first established by the founder-lawgivers; the rulers' laws then "inculcate the values which support them through education in a virtuous circle" (2013a: 111–112, 110). Lane points out that the founder-lawgivers of the best and second-best cities in Plato's *politeia* dialogs are "in a sense extra-constitutional." So, too, are their governing bodies, for the establishment of the philosopher-kings as rulers of the *kallipolis* and of the legislator/rulers of Magnesia (770a, 835b) is not itself legislated (Lane 2013a: 113). In light of this, it may be more accurate to say that the governing bodies of these cities are extra-constitutional and that their founder-lawgivers are *extra*-extra-constitutional. It is from these respective positions outside the constitution that the founder-lawgivers determine, and the rulers legislate and enforce, the laws that govern the institutions and way of life that together constitute the *politeiai* of the cities.

In *Republic* 6, Socrates calls the founder-lawgiver a "constitution-painter" (501c). The Athenian introduces legislation as an art, *technē*, in *Laws* 4 (709b–710b) and the lawgiver as a painter of constitutions in *Laws* 6 (769a–e), referring in *Laws* 7 to himself, along with Megillus and Cleinias, his co-founder-lawgivers, as "rivals of the poets," "artists and performers of the most beautiful drama," who construct a constitution, *politeia*, "as the imitation of the most beautiful and best way of life," which "the true law alone" can bring to perfection (817b).¹³ Thus understood by reference to "true" laws posited by extra-extra-constitutional founder-lawgivers that "define and constitute the identity" of the *politeia*, constitution becomes the work of an art, a *technē*. Cleinias refers to "constructing a city in speech, just as if we were founding it from the very beginning" (702d). The Athenian speaks of "molding a city and citizens from wax" (746a–b). The art of constitution, so understood, is a *technē* in Aristotle's sense, which is to say that it designs its product according to a blueprint, a form, *eidos*, originating in the soul or mind of the artist, and lying outside the product as its cause, principle, or rule, *archē* (*Metaphysics* 1032b23, *Nicomachean Ethics* 1140a10).

There is a clear and apparent advantage to approaching constitutionalism by reference to an (extra)-extra-constitutional art of rule. When constitutions are thus established, their virtuous circularity appears to be guaranteed. Socrates puts it this way in *Republic* 4: "*once it gets off to a good start*, our constitution will be a virtuous circle" (424a-b, my emphasis). In order to "get off to a good start" constitution-painters must, as Socrates says in *Republic* 6, wipe the slate clean, "refusing, right from the start, to have anything to do with any individual or city, or draft any laws, until they were either given a clean slate or had cleaned it for themselves" (501a). In the *Republic*, wiping the slate clean for the constitution of the *kallipolis* calls for banishing everyone over the age of ten (541a). In the *Laws*, "molding [the] city and citizens [of Magnesia] from wax," "from the very beginning," calls for pre-emptive purges (735b–737a).

The extra-extra-constitutional art of rule thus takes its bearings not from these cities' existing governing bodies or from the "way of life" (*Politics* 1295a40), "habits" (*History* 2.36.4), or "characters of the citizens" (*Republic* 544e), but rather, as noted, from the *eidē* of their extra-extra-constitutional artists. Aristotle makes this very point about the *kallipolis* when he remarks that while those who are not rulers are in the majority, "about them nothing has been determined" (*Politics* 1264a14–15). Calling the philosopher-kings of the *kallipolis* "a mere occupying garrison" (1264a26–27), Aristotle asks "upon what principle" (1264a19–20) the "real citizens" (1264a27–28, i.e., the majority) in the *kallipolis* would submit to the rule of their rulers? Aristotle might have asked the same question of the *Laws'* Magnesia. For that city, as comes to light at the end of *Laws* 3, is a Cretan colony, which Cleinias, with nine of his fellow citizens, has been mandated to constitute (702b–d). Although culturally Spartan and Cretan (707e–708d), its laws are borrowed and adapted from primarily Athenian law (Morrow 1960; Schofield 2006: 76; Annas 2010).

It is to be noted that the "slates" of both cities must not only be cleaned at the start. They must be kept clean as well. To this end, the laws of *kallipolis* mandate extensive eugenics programs (459d–461e), while those of Magnesia mandate more purges (740e, 929c–d) and manifold punishments and penalties (774a–e, 784d, 854d–855c, 864e, 866b, 914b–d, 917d), including a broad application of the death penalty for all and sundry infractions (854e, 856c, 860b, 915c, 933d–e, 937c, 938c). Thus oriented to force, and established and ruled by laws created by extra-extra-constitutional founder-lawgiver-artists, Magnesia and the *kallipolis* appear, not unlike the regimes depicted across the tragic stage, as tyrannies under the color of law. The *Laws'* Athenian suggests as much when, ventriloquizing the voice of a lawgiver, he recommends pairing a "young tyrant" with a lawgiver in order to set up the quickest and most effective constitution (709e–712a). As Mario Vegetti has remarked, constitution appears, under such conditions, as "a system of centralized power that guarantees the sequential achievement of the chain of means, in short the dictatorship of one who knows the model that is to be created and is able to derive from it the rational planning of the whole of society" (2013: 8).¹⁴

There is an important difference between the depictions of tyranny across the antique texts and Plato's depictions of the *kallipolis* and Magnesia, of course, and that is that the founder-lawgiver-artists of Plato's cities in speech legislate not in their own private interests but in the name of the good, with a view to establishing, by way of their "true" laws, as noted, virtuous constitutions. Or so Plato has them say. And readers often believe them, taking them to speak on Plato's behalf.[15] Plato's *politeia* dialogs give no grounds, however, for assuming that their characters, including the Athenian and Socrates, speak for Plato. As Stephen Halliwell has maintained, there is "no reliable hermeneutic for tracing a monologic authorial stance (about anything) within Platonic dialogue" (2009: 19). In any case, Socrates says in the *Theaetetus* that "the arguments never come from me; they always come from the person I am talking to" (161b). Perhaps, then, we ought not to take what Plato has the founder-lawgiver-artists say about their art of rule as the dialogs' final word on constitutionalism. Indeed, if what Socrates says in the *Theaetetus* is true for the *Republic* and the *Laws*—that is, if, like the arguments of the *Theaetetus*' Socrates, those of the *Republic*'s Socrates and of the *Laws*' Athenian come from *their* interlocutors—then what appears in Plato's *politeia* dialogs as the view of the founder-lawgiver-artists and is taken by some readers to be the position of Plato will actually be the view of Glaucon and Adeimantus (Socrates' interlocutors in the *Republic*) and Cleinias and Megillus (the Athenian's interlocutors in the *Laws*), all of whose views the dialogs present as in need of revision.

On this way of reading Plato's *politeia* dialogs, expanded below, it follows that when Plato depicts Socrates and/or the Athenian claiming to legislate in the name of the good, they may be better read as legislating in the name of what appears good to their interlocutors. That is itself complicated, however, for what appears good to Glaucon and Adeimantus in the *Republic* and to Cleinias and Megillus in the *Laws* seems to change over the course of the dialogs. At the start of the dialogs what appears good to these characters are the ethics and politics with which they are familiar: in the case of Cleinias and Megillus, the Doric institutions and practices they grew up with, oriented, as already noted, to success at war and military courage (626a–c); what is familiar to Glaucon and Adeimantus is the tyrannical justice associated in *Republic* 1 with Socrates' interlocutor, Thrasymachus, whose hold on the brothers' imagination is made plain in *Republic* 2 (358e–362c, 362e–367a).

When the Athenian makes the case that the Spartan and Cretan constitutions are only apparently good, the Dorians of the *Laws* are portrayed as being receptive to a different constitutional arrangement (632d–633a). The brothers of the *Republic* positively demand an alternative to Thrasymachean justice (358b–d, 367b–e). Enter Magnesia and, by way of the analogy between soul and city, the *kallipolis*, which cities the Athenian and Socrates present as alternatives to what initially appeared good to the interlocutors, but whose differences turn out to be largely apparent. The Athenian, to be sure, challenges the Doric laws for their orientation to war. Yet the legislation he proposes for Magnesia conspicuously orients to military courage and war as well (753b, 755c, 756a, 796e, 809c, 813e, 814c, 829a–b, 942c–d). Socrates challenges Thrasymachus' account of justice as the advantage of the rulers (338c) and a creature of law (339b), to be sure. Yet the justice of the *kallipolis* requires that all parts of the city submit to the rule of the rulers (428a–434d) and is itself a creature of (the founder-lawgiver-artists') law. Despite repeated invitations from Socrates and the Athenian to think twice about the laws, institutions, and practices they put forward for the *kallipolis* and Magnesia, respectively, Glaucon expresses satisfaction with the justice Socrates proposes for the *kallipolis*, and Cleinias willingly, even eagerly, acquiesces to the Athenian's legislation for Magnesia.[16] And why not? What is on offer mirrors what appeared good to the interlocutors in the first instance, namely, the ethics and politics with which they are familiar.[17]

What is to be made of these careful and elaborate appearances? What is to be made of them in their own right and also in light of the counter commitment running through Plato's *politeia* dialogs, discussed earlier, to positioning rule within the constitution by reference to a city's governing body and way of life? It could be that Plato presents the arts of extra-constitutional rule as a guarantee of constitutional virtue. Or it could be that Plato offers the *Republic*'s "garrisoned" *kallipolis* and the *Laws*' colonial Magnesia and their extra- and extra-extra-constitutional rulers alongside the account of constitution as an irreducible and reciprocal interrelation between governing body and the way of life of citizens to prompt his readers to ask the very question that Aristotle asks, namely, "upon what principle" *would* the "real citizens" of the cities in speech submit to the rule of their rulers? What if Plato, in other words, represents the arts of extra- and extra-extra-constitutional rule in the ways he does, not to guarantee constitutional virtue but to bring to appearance the risks, dangers, and costs not only of tyranny, oligarchy, and extreme democracy but also of seeking a guarantee against such unconstitutional regimes? What if, in short, the clear and apparent advantage of approaching constitutionalism by reference to *apoleis archai* positioned above and outside a political association turns out to be itself only apparent?

On this way of reading the *Republic* and *Laws*, Plato makes the *kallipolis* and Magnesia resemble tyrannies to illustrate the dangers for ethics and politics of seeking a constitutional guarantee. Read in this way, these dialogs, like the tragedies of Aeschylus and Sophocles, challenge the arts of extra-constitutional rule they stage by making manifest the conditions under which extra-constitutional arts of rule produce, using Aristotle's phrase, "the very reverse of constitution." So read, Plato depicts the founder-lawgiver-artists of the idealized cities' (non)constitutions as "rivals" of the tragic poets (*Laws* 817b) in order to position himself in his artistry as the poets' ally in the project of bringing to light the costs of displacing by a lawgiver the irreducibly dual and reciprocal relation of constitution.

Approaching Plato's *politeia* dialogs in this way requires not only thinking twice about identifying Plato with the *Laws*' Athenian and/or the *Republic*'s Socrates, but also about taking the interlocutors in these dialogs as "stand-ins for the reader" (Menn 2006: 43; Cotton 2014). Instead, like and unlike the spectators at a play (Monoson 2000: 206–226), readers stand outside Plato's texts, taking their critical distance from what appears while at the same time sharing in *their* constitution. So read, Plato's dialogs offer an education in place of a guarantee, an education that, by staging the dangers of the arts of extra-constitutional rule, orients to an art of constitution which, as itself a mode of activity in Aristotle's terms, has within it its own end (*Nicomachean Ethics* 1040b4-6). Bringing the making characteristic of *poiesis* together with the doing characteristic of *entelecheia*, this art orients to constitutional virtue by way of ethical and political *self*-constitution.

It is impossible in this chapter to make a full case for rereading Plato's *politeia* dialogs in this way.[18] In what follows, I offer the contours of such a reading, beginning with what I called earlier the necessary or minimum condition of sharing in a constitution, that is, the willing acquiescence on the part of citizens to their city's laws, in the absence of which, as Malcolm Schofield has put it, citizens, as in tyrannies, are "simply the slaves of their rulers" (2006: 80). Aristotle expresses his concern about whether the *kallipolis* meets this minimum condition when he claims, as noted, that "nothing is determined" about the "real citizens" of the *kallipolis*. That is not quite true, however. In *Republic* 4, for example, Socrates takes up the question of the *kallipolis*' "ordinary majority" and concludes that they willingly obey the rulers and their laws when they are moderate (431c–d). The *Laws*' Athenian, as we have seen, makes the willing obedience of citizens (684c) central to constitution when he insists that where citizens do not voluntarily accept a city's laws or participate freely in the constitution, there is no constitution deserving of the name (690c, 832b–c, 712e–713a).

If citizens willingly obey the laws of the *kallipolis* and Magnesia, as Socrates and the Athenian appear to claim, then these political associations *will* be constitutions properly so called, both by the dialogs' own lights as well as by the lights of the accounts of constitution offered by Aristotle and the poets. If, however, despite what the Athenian and Socrates *say* about citizens willingly obeying, Plato presents citizens' willing obedience as only apparent, then the *kallipolis* and Magnesia will fail the minimum condition of constitutionalism and so will count as no constitutions at all.

WILLING ACQUIESCENCE IN THE *LAWS*?

The innovative "double-method" (719c–d) of legislation, a centerpiece of the *Laws*, prefaces the laws the Athenian proposes for Magnesia with preludes (720a). The goal of these preludes, which explain the laws' purpose and intent (721e), is to persuade those subject to the laws to obey them (721e) rather than relying on force alone (721e–723b). In the Athenian's famous analogy (720a–e), just as free doctors do not prescribe medicine without the consent of their patients, so too is the double method—preludes first then laws—meant to safeguard the freedom of Magnesia's citizens and their willing consent to the laws by leavening the "despotic prescription" of "unblended law" with persuasion (722e–723a). The Athenian's disanalogy here is to slave doctors; in contrast to free doctors they issue their prescriptions "like a headstrong tyrant," quickly and effectively, and then rush off (720c, 723a).

The double method may be introduced to safeguard the willing obedience of the citizens of the new colony but it is depicted as doing no such thing. Instead, insofar as the laws are enforced whether the citizens are persuaded or not, the "legislation remains at its core a threat" (Schofield 2006: 85; Hitz 2009: 367–381). Maintaining that "Plato could hardly have been unaware" of this, Malcolm Schofield claims that whereas the legislation and preludes stand as threats to Magnesia's actual citizens, they can be "*justified* (to us, the critics, complicit in the design of the system)" "as encapsulating the voluntary outcomes that *would* be achieved" following deliberation with a "rational person of more expert understanding." Schofield continues: "Preludes simply embody the *outcomes* of such deliberations, and as such are regarded as satisfying the citizens' entitlement to persuasion. It can be more precisely formulated as the stipulation that citizens are entitled to the opportunity to be persuaded—and the claim that they will consent if they are reasonable" (2006: 85–86). The preludes are justified, in other words, insofar as they persuade "us" that they would be persuasive to those who are able to deliberate properly.

Who is Schofield's "us" ("the critics, complicit in the design of the system"), to whom he claims the proposed legislation *is* justified? "[C]omplicit in the design of the system" are, presumably, the founder-lawgiver-artists, namely, the Athenian, Spartan, and Cretan. Insofar as the Dorians acquiesce to the preludes and laws the Athenian proposes, none of them seem to be "critics" of the legislation. It is, rather, *readers* of the *Laws*, like Schofield himself, who are critical of the claim that the preludes persuade. Readers may be conscripted into complicity in the system's design (i.e., if Cleinias and Megillus are treated as stand-ins for the *Laws*' readers). But what if readers refuse to identify with Cleinias and Megillus? What if the dialog gives readers good reasons to find the preludes no more persuasive and justified than do Magnesia's citizens? What if the dialog thereby prompts its readers to withhold *our* complicity in the design of the system?

In my view, the dialog prompts its readers in precisely these ways by having the Athenian undermine the double method discursively, formally, and substantively even as he puts it forward. Just after introducing the method toward the end of *Laws* 4 (719c–d, 721e), for example, the Athenian indicates that he will turn next to the laws of the new colony. Instead of offering legislation, however, *Laws* 5 opens with its own prelude (726e–734e). For the duration of the prelude, indeed, for the entire length of *Laws* 5, only the Athenian speaks. His interlocutors, Cleinias and Megillus, are completely silent. There is no dialog at all. At discursive odds with the mode of engagement of free doctors with their patients to which the preludes have just been analogized, the Athenian's prelude is delivered not dialogically but "monologically" (Nightingale 1993: 285), which is to say, in the manner of a slave doctor.[19]

Almost midway through *Laws* 5, the Athenian declares that the prelude is over (734e), but rather than turning next to law, as he says he will (734e), he offers what turns out to be another prelude (735b). When he later indicates that he *has been* enacting laws (744d), it is difficult to tell what is law and what is a prelude (738b, 739a, 744c). In *Laws* 6, moreover, he offers a law first (772d–e), followed by a prelude (773a–774a), rather than the other way around, as per the method. In *Laws* 7, he announces a series of laws with no preludes at all (800e–801e). In all of these instances, the Athenian erases the very distinction between preludes and laws that is supposed to inform the double method. He may be seen to anticipate this erasure when he introduces the double method in *Laws* 4 with the claim that he has, so far, offered only preludes (722d), whereas his speeches in *Laws* 3–4 include what are presented as laws (689c–690d, 705e, 721b–e).

Things appear to change over the course of *Laws* 7, 8, 10–12 where the Athenian clearly signals and sets apart his actual laws (824b–c, 842e, 844d, 845e, 907d–e, 909d–e, 910b–c, 919d–920b, 921a–d, 928a, 943a, 944c). Yet the ground rules of the double method are consistently contravened in these parts of the dialog too. In *Laws* 8, there are laws that go on for pages (842e–844d), while in *Laws* 7 and 10, the preludes and laws are intermediated by prayers (823d, 887c–d). The difference between preludes and laws is undermined substantively, when, for example, the Athenian includes penalties for disobedience in the preludes in *Laws* 9 (854c–d, 862d–863a, 870d–871a). Relying on the very thing they were supposed to exclude so as to be distinguishable from laws, these preludes are full of force. If, then, the Athenian introduces the double method to secure the willing obedience of Magnesia's citizens, Plato has him present the double method in ways that underscore that obedience will be guaranteed, willing or not.

If the *Laws* thus invites skepticism about the willing obedience of Magnesia's citizens, it does so in other ways as well, most obviously, perhaps, by the Athenian's insistence that the citizens and rulers of the new colony will be bound to their laws as slaves (762e, 715d, 772b–d). Scholars have noted that to be bound to laws as slaves may not be the same as being bound as slaves to people (Annas 2010: 71–91). Indeed, the Athenian refers to his fellow Athenians as having "lived as the *willing* slaves of their existing laws" (698b emphasis added) during the period of Persia's assault on Greece.[20] He seems to be suggesting that, in relation to law, there can be slavery and freedom at the same time. Socrates' engagement with the laws of Athens in the *Crito* sheds some light on this paradoxical idea. There, Socrates says that Athenian laws "do not rudely impose their commands, but give citizens the alternative of obeying or persuading the laws that the laws are wrong" (51e–52a). The laws of Athens preserve the willing obedience of citizens because and insofar as the laws can be persuaded otherwise.

The same cannot be said about the laws governing the new colony, however. For although, as noted, Magnesia's laws are borrowed and adapted primarily from Athenian law, the law establishing how the new citizens are to relate to their laws is from Sparta (634d–e), and it prohibits negotiating with the law or, indeed, any questioning of the laws in public at all. With this "law against dissent" (Fraistat 2015) more literally enslaving the citizens and rulers of the new colony to their laws, and with those laws themselves relying, as we just saw, not on persuasion but on force, the laws the Athenian prescribes for the new colony are shot through with force. It thus appears that the citizens of Magnesia obey their laws not freely and voluntarily, but through coercion and under the threat of punishment.[21]

Megillus and especially Cleinias wonder about hardly any of this. On the contrary, they willingly acquiesce to the policing and surveillance that are the hallmarks of the Athenian's legislation (783e–784d, 794a–b, 856b–c, 929e–930a), to its shaming, threatening, and punishing (784d), to its painful and restraining education (808d–e), and, as noted earlier, to its emphasis on military courage and war (753b, 755c, 756a, 796e, 809c, 813e, 814c, 829a–b, 942c–d). This should not be a surprise, for, as also noted earlier, the legislation the Athenian proposes, in all of these ways, mirrors their native constitutions. That they are persuaded by the laws the Athenian proposes is proof positive that they have *not* been persuaded that constitutions oriented to war and to military courage are defective, however. Moreover, that they are persuaded by the laws proposed by the Athenian indicates that his early ministering to the specificities of their constitutions and to their concerns as his interlocutors, as would a free doctor, has been ineffective. Perhaps for this reason, from the delivery of his monologic speech in *Laws* 5, to his increasingly punitive and dogmatic legislative prescriptions in *Laws* 9–11, which he issues with impatience (890d–e) before rushing off to the next one (857b–c, 886e–887a), the Athenian, during the second half of the *Laws*, seems to change tactics, treating Cleinias and Megillus as would a slave doctor.

Just before introducing his double method, the Athenian says to Cleinias and Megillus that "everything they now say should be imagined as said in the presence of the future citizens of the colony." One scholar suggests that "such a move or device is required by the logic of the legislative project ... Legislation has to take place in public" (Zuckert 2009: 84). That is true. If, however, the Athenian is from here on out legislating for the new colony as if in public in the presence of the future citizens, then the "law against dissent" applies, which means that, like the citizens of the new colony, Cleinias and Megillus are not permitted to persuade the Athenian otherwise; thus they are effectively enslaved to *his* law. That is to say that in relation to Cleinias and Megillus (the Athenian's co-founder-lawgivers-artists), as in relation to the citizens of the new colony, the *Laws* presents the distinction between willing obedience and force as a distinction without a difference.[22] Under such conditions, the rule of law operates not as a safeguard of constitutionalism by preserving freedom and voluntary acquiescence; instead it undermines constitution by underwriting coercive obedience and force.

WILLING ACQUIESCENCE IN THE *REPUBLIC*?

The way Plato has Socrates present the willing acquiescence of the *kallipolis*' ordinary majority suggests something similar. As noted, Socrates describes the willing obedience of *kallipolis*' citizens as a function of their moderation. He says that they are moderate when their desires are "controlled by the desires and wisdom of the discerning minority" (431c–d). Plato has Socrates use not *sôphrosynê* but *kosmiotês* to describe the "moderation" of the ordinary majority's desires. That should give pause. Socrates has just introduced *kosmiotês* as "a mastery of pleasures and desires and that a person is described as being in some way or other master of himself." He goes on, "But isn't the phrase 'master of himself' an absurdity? The master of himself must surely also be the slave to himself, and the slave to himself must be master of himself. It's the same person being talked about all the time" (430e–431a). Speaking of an individual soul as simultaneously master and slave may be absurd but it may not be as absurd to speak of a city in that way (*Laws* 627a–c). Thus, as Socrates describes it in *Republic* 4, *kosmiotês* is the mastery of the desires of the many by those of the few to whom, if we complete Socrates' analogy from soul to city, the many are enslaved. Under such conditions, that is, when citizens are "moderated" by being ordered exclusively from without, their obedience is determined not by their own will but by the will of their rulers.[23]

Aristotle is right, then, to wonder upon what principle citizens of the *kallipolis* would submit to their rulers: by imposing laws that the ordinary majority neither participate in constituting nor to which they willingly acquiesce, the philosopher-kings do indeed function as a "mere occupying garrison" (*Politics* 1264a20–28). Recalling that the laws regulating the *kallipolis* are not actually produced by the philosopher-kings but instead by the extra-extra-constitutional founder-lawgiver-artists, we might also re-pose Aristotle's question, and ask: do the *philosopher-kings* willingly acquiesce? To this question, too, the *Republic* appears to answer "no." On the contrary, as Roslyn Weiss has demonstrated, Plato depicts the philosopher-kings themselves as altogether compelled: compelled to ascend to the Good, compelled in their courses of study, compelled to order their own souls, compelled to rule the city, and compelled to do so in accordance with the laws of the founder-lawgiver-artists (2012: 70, 81–83, 103–112, 118–119, 74–77, with references to the *Republic*). In the language of *Republic* 10's account of *mimêsis* (596e–598c), we might say that the rule of law in the *kallipolis* (and Magnesia too) is at a third remove from the citizens who are compelled to live under it and at a second remove from the rulers who are compelled to submit to, recreate, and enforce it. With its rulers and citizens thus depicted as being obedient because they are compelled or ordered, but not *willing*, the *kallipolis*, like Magnesia, appears to fail the minimum test of constitutionalism.

A VIRTUOUS CIRCLE?

Against this backdrop, let me return to Socrates' claim in *Republic* 4, anticipating the account of the *kallipolis* in *Republic* 5, that: "once it gets off to a good start, our constitution will be a virtuous circle." Socrates goes on: "If you can keep a good system of upbringing and education, they produce naturally good natures. These, in their turn, if they receive a good education, develop into even better natures than their predecessors. Better in general, and better in particular for reproduction. The same is true in the animal kingdom" (424a–b), for "like always produces like, doesn't it?" (425c). If in this passage Socrates appears to be underwriting the art of extra-extra-constitutional rule as that which, by getting the constitution off to a good start, guarantees its virtue, that appearance is deceptive. For, during the course of his account of the *kallipolis*, Socrates gives Adeimantus and Glaucon reason after reason to greet this claim to a constitutional guarantee with skepticism.

Socrates says that the "system of upbringing and education" the *kallipolis* keeps and the "natures" that system produces are "good." Are they?[24] That Plato has Socrates compare that upbringing and education to processes in the "animal kingdom" might give pause, especially when Glaucon distinguishes the education of animals from human education just pages later (430b) on the ground that the former, unlike the latter, is a kind of mindless conditioning (Mara 1997: 123; Berger 2015: 158–159). The conditioning of *kallipolis*' humans as animals comes up again in *Republic* 5 when Socrates presents the city's eugenic programs by reference to the techniques Glaucon uses to breed his pedigree cocks and hunting dogs (459a). That Socrates slyly slides from referring to the philosopher–rulers as "guardians of the herd" (451c) to calling them "our herd" (459e) implies, too, that the education and upbringing mandated for the *kallipolis* produces its humans, rulers and ruled alike, as animals (466d).

If we leave to one side these doubts about how good the upbringing of the *kallipolis* is and turn to Socrates' claim that in respect of that virtuous constitution "like will always produce like," further questions arise, not least because Socrates, in his account of the *kallipolis*, offers example after example of the opposite The "noble lie" of *Republic* 3 which founds the *kallipolis* describes those born with gold in their blood as sometimes giving birth to silver- or iron-blooded children, and vice versa (415a–c). In *Republic* 5, Socrates announces that children born to philosopher–rulers are sometimes "defective" (460c). Given the brothers' own pointed remarks about the importance of reproduction to the constitution of a city (449d–450a, 450c), it might be expected that they would query Socrates' inconsistencies. But they do not. Nor do they wonder about how the *city* will reproduce itself: with only rulers permitted to breed (459d), non-defective ruler children going to war with no way to guarantee their safety (467d), and all other children in the city aborted or killed (461a–c), the *kallipolis* appears doomed from its inception. Most obviously, perhaps, if the *kallipolis* is meant to exemplify the "virtuous circle of the constitution" and if "like always produces like," why do Glaucon and Adeimantus make nothing of the fact that, in *Republic* 8–9, the perfect city devolves into tyranny? Not a "virtuous circle" at all, much less a guarantee, the *kallipolis* appears instead to be, in Aristotle's phrase, "the very reverse of a constitution."

THE ART OF CONSTITUTIONAL RULE

Treating the *Laws*' Athenian as akin to Lycurgus and Minos, scholars sometimes take the *Laws* to show "how a philosopher could have influenced the laws of a city," and thus to indicate "something about what should be tried in the future" (Zuckert 2009: 57). In my view, Plato stages Magnesia's arts of extra-extra constitutional rule and also those of the *kallipolis* not to advocate for constitutions of this kind but instead to invite a critical distance from them. Treating constitutions created *ex nihilo*, in accordance with extra-constitutional laws, like "a pudding to be made by a receipt" (McIlwain 1940: 4),[25] Plato's *politeia* dialogs, like Aristotle's ethical and political writings and the plays of the poets, orient to an art of rule not as a private and/or extra-constitutional practice, replete with coercion and compulsion, but as something shared, an irreducibly reciprocal relationship between individuated citizens and collective institutions.

Aristotle maintains that "the best laws, though sanctioned by every citizen of the state, will be of no avail unless the young are trained by habit and education in the spirit of the constitution" (*Politics* 1310a 15–18). Plato's *politeia* dialogs suggest the same. In the *Laws*, for example, Plato has the Athenian claim that he is not legislating but educating. As part of their education, the citizens of Magnesia, the Athenian insists, will study their laws, along with the lawgiver's writings, and also a record of the conversation of the *Laws* itself (811c–e): "the written transcript of [the Athenian's] conversation with the two old Dorians [is to] become the basic text or, we might say, the constitution of the regime" (Zuckert 2009: 140). This means that the education the Athenian proposes will teach the founder-lawgiver-artists' laws, while concurrently exposing the coercive and compulsive nature of those laws and the constitution they frame. Seen this way, Plato's Athenian may, in the end, be less like Lycurgus than like Solon. According to Plutarch, Lycurgus "did not commit his laws to writing" for he wanted them to be "implanted" in the hearts of Sparta's youth (1998: 21).[26] Solon, by contrast, left his laws in writing for the Athenians to implement. When asked if he had left the Athenians the best possible laws, Solon replied, "The best they would accept" (1998: 58–59). Perhaps, then, Solon left his laws in writing to leave the Athenians to accept, which is to say, to read and interpret his laws, make them their own, and, in so doing, to share in their constitution (Figure 2.3).

Plato and Aristotle and the poets, by way of their writing, bring to appearance not only the ethical and political perils of constitutions made by the force of extra-extra-constitutional laws but also, and like Solon, the power and possibilities of political *self-*

FIGURE 2.3. Athenian decree. Detail of a marble stele inscribed with a decree of the Athenian *boulē*, c. 440–425 BCE. Source: Wikimedia/Future Perfect at Sunrise/Public Domain.

making, the art of political self-constitution. In this way they may be seen to anticipate what Hanna Pitkin has said more recently and in a different context:

> The constitution we have depends upon the constitution we make and do and are. Except insofar as we *do*, what we think we *have* is powerless and will soon disappear. Except insofar as in doing we respect who we *are*—both our actuality and the genuine potential within us—our doing will be a disaster. Neglect any one of these and you will get the idea of ... constitution very wrong. (1987: 169)[27]

CHAPTER THREE

Codes

BARRY WIMPFHEIMER

"Culture" and "law" are both slippery terms that evade simple definition. The dialog of culture and law that has transpired across academic disciplines since the 1990s has produced, through incremental accretion, a method of putting law and culture in conversation that takes advantage of the terms' slipperiness to combine the two in a single unbounded discourse.[1] This deconstruction goes beyond studying culture in law (using law as a static field in which culture manifests as literature, art or society) or law in culture (using culture as a static field in which law is an institution, a set of practices or an intellectual space). By considering both law and culture as discursive terms that open up ways of organizing human interactions and ways of thinking, scholars are able to think of both as dynamic (always changing) modes of organizing or describing social interaction. This allows for the realization that culture is always already law and law is always already culture because both are perpetually becoming themselves alongside each other.[2]

One of the places in which the adjacent discourses of culture and law vie for control is in the consideration of texts, specifically legal ones. The legal discourse encounters a legal text and approaches the text with a set of assumptions about its meaning and a set of practices that allow texts to contribute to the production of that meaning.[3] While cultural discourse has a vaguer set of assumptions and practices and may even cede interpretive authority of a specific text to the legal discourse, people within the cultural discourse can empower themselves to employ reading practices that allow the putative legal text to speak to social practices, moral assumptions, ethnic diversity, and political relationships.[4]

The legal code is the quintessential legal text. A set of formally arranged precepts, the code lends itself to intense consideration within a legal discourse. Even when a code is ancient, removed from the reader by a millennium or more, its genre invites legally trained eyes to read the normative content like a lawyer, distilling specific outcomes into general concepts or principles, comparing cases with analogous ones to discover nuances in the implicit legal reasoning. These lawyerly reading practices and their results are only a small part of a cultural study of law. There is an implicit challenge to reading law codes as culture. This challenge—of understanding the cultural impact of ancient law code—has not just been felt in the present. Earlier readers, including ancient ones, sometimes felt the need to make ancient law codes more culturally meaningful, and met that need by producing narratives on the margins of the law codes or, more rarely, in the codes themselves. These narrativizing behaviors produced narrativizations: stories designed to provide historical, cultural, or moral context for the law codes. As a scholar tasked with producing a cultural reading of ancient law codes, I think it important to see the narrativizing elements of this task as taking place with a tradition of such narrativizations.

The ancient editor who framed a Mesopotamian law code with its origin myth, the late antique rabbi who produces a morality play in order to understand a set of biblical law code verses and the contemporary scholar fusing law and culture in the study of ancient law codes are all engaged in attempts to produce narrativizations of the law codes.

Legal codes possess an implicit barebones narrative setting established by the voice of the legist speaking with authority to an audience. This implicit narrative scene of political and social authority is often intensified through more elaborate narrativizations that provide greater context for this basic scene of legal transmission. In the modern case, the script of legislative procedure (how a bill becomes a law) plays an important role in a heightened narrativization: representative legislators produce legislation through motions and votes of parliaments and thus reflect the will of greater society. This narrative heightens the implicit political and social authority of statute collections and law codes. Historical origin stories also contribute to the narrativization: in the modern American context, the utilization of the "founding fathers" within legal conversations produces a myth of origin that implies an entire backdrop of revolution and creation that is part and parcel of the US legal story and that lends a majoritarian ethos to otherwise authoritarian legal documents.

This chapter focuses on ancient legal codes—formal lists of normative precepts. It will introduce the legal codes of four different ancient cultures, and draw attention to accretions of narrativization within the reception of these corpora. After providing an initial overview of the four ancient cultures and their legal codes, the chapter will explore in detail the production of one such elaborate narrativization of an ancient legal code— an example in which the narrativizing replots the law code's own text to produce it as a more fully developed story. The example demonstrates the ironic fact that while the interpreted legal code contains features that encourage this narrativization, the specific narrativization also undermines some of the cultural work inherent to the original code. This paradigm will concretize the claim that the foisting of heightened narrativizations upon ancient legal codes risks occluding some of the cultural meaning of these texts.

ANCIENT LEGAL CODES: AN OVERVIEW

Four different "cultures" produced the law codes extant from antiquity. The Mesopotamian, Israelite/Jewish, Greek, and Roman cultures are not only different ancient cultures, they have also spawned separate academic subfields that only occasionally overlap.[5] Despite the advantages of thinking of them as a group, they are rarely considered in this fashion.

The term Mesopotamia translates literally as "between rivers." The earliest Western civilizations were located between the Tigris and Euphrates rivers that originate in Turkey and flow through Turkey, Syria, and Iraq. The materials identified as part of ancient Mesopotamian legal culture include materials from beyond the geographic boundaries produced by the Tigris and Euphrates (Westbrook 2003a: 1). Seven separate cuneiform legal codes ranging from 2400 BCE–500 BCE have been unearthed by archaeologists of the ancient Near East over the last two centuries.[6] Though these are extant in different regional languages (Sumerian, Akkadian, and Hittite), most of them are in Akkadian (even outside the region of Akkadian dominance) and several commonalities within the group testify to their participation within a common tradition (Westbrook 2003a: 4). These documents are so stylistically similar that they are somewhat interchangeable despite the millennium and a half that separates the earliest and latest exemplars.

To term the second culture "Jewish" requires a retrojective nomenclature; the term Jewish cannot be responsibly used before the sixth century BCE and some would deem it appropriate to use only in the first century CE. At the same time, to call this culture "Israelite" on the basis of its earliest exemplars severs the valuable linkages between these earliest examples and later Jewish codes.[7] The Israelite/Jewish culture has preserved several legal collections ranging in composition from approximately eighth century BCE–600 CE. The earliest legal codes within this tradition are the ones preserved as embedded codes within the prose historiographies of Exodus, Leviticus, Numbers, and Deuteronomy. These are referred to as the *Covenant Code, Deuteronomic Code* and *Priestly Code*; sections of the *Priestly Code* are sometimes separated out as the *Holiness Code*. Controversy rages about the respective ages of these codes, but one can date the *Deuteronomic Code* to the seventh century BCE and the *Priestly and Holiness Codes* to about a century later (Westbrook 2003a: 9; Westbrook 2015: 47). In the late second temple period, around the turn of the first century CE, the elite scholastic population of Judea splintered into different religious sects who disagreed over matters of law and theology. Sectarian legal codes from the first century CE have been unearthed and examined in the last half century as some of the Dead Sea Scrolls.[8] (Figure 3.1) Two

FIGURE 3.1. Portions of the temple scroll, labeled 11Q19, one of the longest Dead Sea Scrolls. Second century BCE. https://commons.wikimedia.org/wiki/File:Temple_Scroll.png. Source: The Israel Museum's Dead Sea Scrolls Digital Project.

rabbinic legal codes, Mishnah and Tosefta, date to the second and third centuries CE. Mishnah is a voluminous code with over four thousand individual legal precepts and a threefold subject organization into orders, tractates, and chapters. It covers all aspects of life from the sacred (temple rites) to the profane (tort law). Tosefta adheres to Mishnah's structure and functions as both a commentary and a supplement. Though not codes, the two Talmuds (Palestinian and Babylonian) record oral statements that originated as codes and preserve the ideal of precepts as the default mode of expressing law for several centuries after the oral publication of Mishnah and Tosefta.[9] (Figure 3.2)

While classical Greece (the fifth and fourth centuries BCE) is unrivalled for its ancient artistic, scholarly, and literary production, the Greeks did not produce (or leave behind) a significant corpus of legal codes (Gagarin 2005b). The law of homicide, a single section, is all that has survived from Drako's law code (seventh century BCE) (the code responsible for the adjective "draconian"). A single law inscribed on a stone at Dreros in Crete in the seventh century survives as well. The seventh–sixth century Athenian Solon is reputed to have reformed Drako's laws through the promulgation of his own law code, but only fragments of Solon's code survive to the present. The rich legal inscriptions found in Gortyn on Crete, and dating from the seventh to the fourth centuries BCE, do much of the heavy lifting on behalf of Greek codes with the caveat that these elaborate inscriptions emerge from a relatively obscure civilization about which only little is known (Willets 1967; Davies 2005) (Figure 3.3).

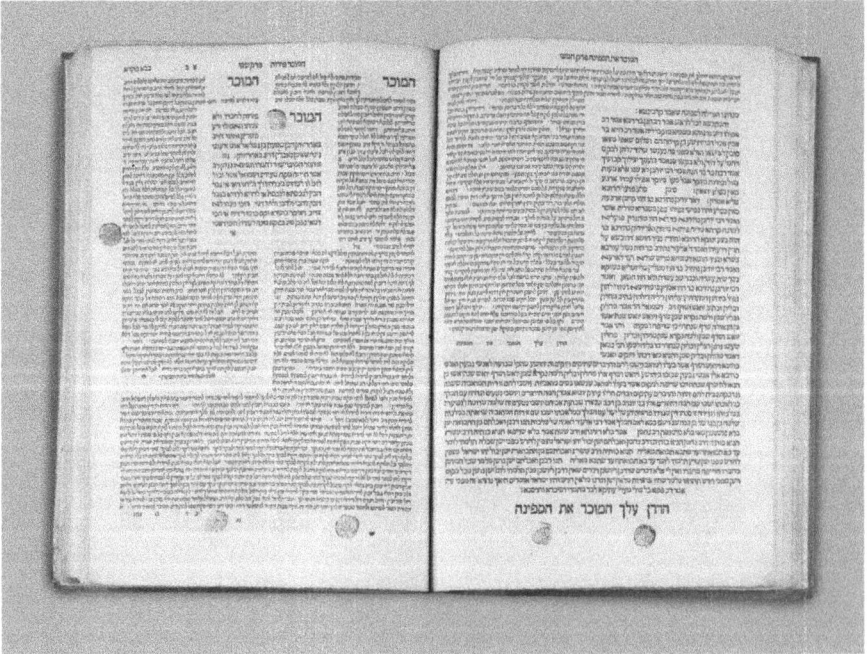

FIGURE 3.2. The first complete printed edition of the Babylonian Talmud. Source: Courtesy Sotheby's New York.

FIGURE 3.3. Law Code of Gortyn (fragment describing inheritance law), fifth century BCE. Louvre Museum. Source: Wikimedia/Jastrow/Public Domain.

Among the ancient legal cultures, Roman law has spawned the largest modern field of study. Roman law is largely responsible for the dominant image of law-as-code that emerges from antiquity. There are three important data points for Roman legal codes. The earliest code, the Twelve Tables (fifth-century BCE), survives not as complete text but as citations found in later, particularly legal, writing (Westbrook 2015). One of the sources that preserves material from the Twelve Tables is Gaius' *Institutes* from the second-century CE, a work that sets the organizational tone for subsequent Roman law (Gordon and Robinson eds. 1988). The *Institutes* is one of several works that served as the basis for Justinian's sixth-century CE *Corpus Juris Civilis*, a set of works that includes the *Digest*, the *Code*, the *Novels*, and *Institutes*. Like either of the Talmuds, the Digest is an important source of legal theories and opinions that emerged from thinking with codes in the centuries leading up to the work's production (Figure 3.4).

Raymond Westbrook propounded the view that the relatively unified corpus of Mesopotamian and biblical law codes not only encouraged a strong narrative of unity within their cultures of composition but also served as the grounding for early legal codes in Greece and Rome (Westbrook 2014). Fighting against the resistance of scholars who wish to keep their fields (biblical law and Roman law) exceptional, unique, and original,

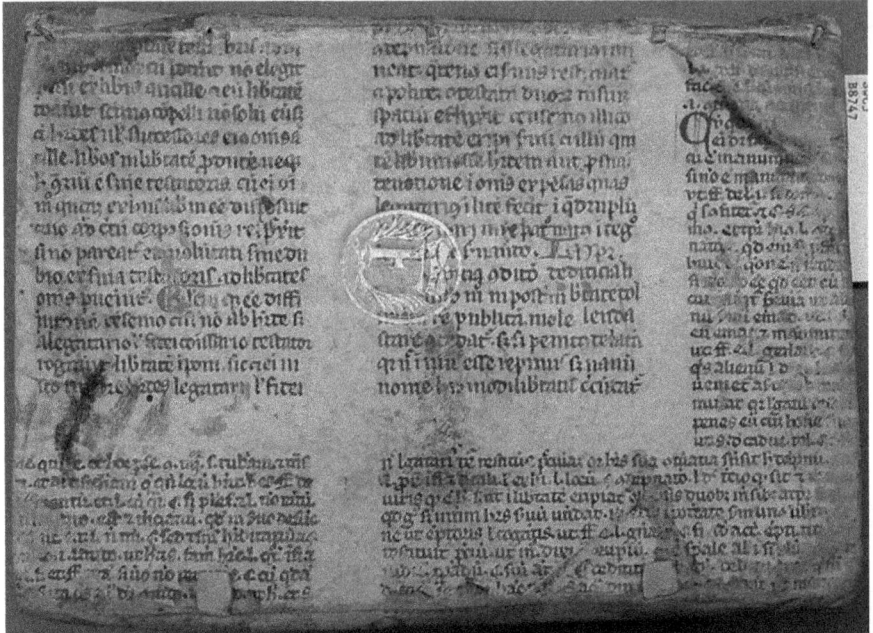

FIGURE 3.4. Justinian's Digest. Portion of an early parchment ms. leaf from a glossed copy of the Codex Justinianus. Source: Provenance Online Project (POP) from the Kislak Center for Special Collections, Rare Books, and Manuscripts at the University of Pennsylvania/ Flickr/CC BY 2.0.

Westbrook notes the generic, organizational, ideational and statutory similarities across the legal codes in these different cultures and argues that a scholastic movement of long duration both produced and consumed these legal codes as educational training.[10] Westbrook's thesis provides the groundwork for the remainder of this chapter: a consideration of the poetics of ancient law codes followed by an instantiation of these poetics within a specific example of interpretive narrativizing from the Jewish legal tradition.

MODERN RESONANCE OF "LAW" AND "CODE"

A scholar encounters an ancient text containing a series of statements connecting scenarios with outcomes. The outcomes are corporeal punishments or financial penalties. Without much effort, the scholar concludes that the ancient text is a law code. In naming it a law code, though, the scholar unintentionally introduces through the two words "law" and "code" a set of assumptions about the history, nature, and function of the ancient materials.

In contemporary usage, the word "law" is identified with the state, enforcement, and politics. Though it invokes a theoretical discipline as well, law is linked to practice. Law stands as an opportunity for recourse in (democratic contexts) a world of individual autonomy and right. Despite its engagement with worldly realities, though, modern law is also a rich theoretical lens through which to examine society. One of the core interventions of the cultural study of modern law is identification of the insufficiencies of this theoretical lens for capturing legal ideas, realities, or the various ways in which law is experienced by legal subjects. The ancient text cannot be presumed to exist within the framework of a modern state, its politics and its mechanisms of enforcement. One can presume (though this is also not unproblematic) that individuals depicted in scenarios do not have autonomy or rights in the modern sense of those terms.

The word "code" does profound if unacknowledged work within modern law. The "code" bespeaks comprehensiveness; in its most ideal sense, a code is capable of speaking dispositively to all of the human interactions in which law is necessary.[11] While some would distinguish between common law and statutory systems with respect to the code, this distinction does not greatly figure in the conceptual work that the term code enacts as the default image of law. Law is often conceptualized as a series of rules that work together to create a system. If law is the object of the individual fantasy for legal recourse, the code is the text in which one expects to find redress. The ideal code is law-as-an-object—a perfect articulation of life as it should be that is presumed to exist on its own, independent of manipulation or interpretation. In this sense, the code is imputed objectivity, standing above the fray of human entanglements that necessitate law's intervention. Empirically, of course, no legal codes are comprehensive—no set of rules could ever anticipate all of the potential complications of lived life. Codes are also not entirely hermetic objects since they are produced by subject authors, are interpreted (and applied where law is a practice) by subjects and affect (where law is enacted) different subjects (Balkin 1994).

When considering ancient law codes, it is worth an attempt to shed the modern resonance of these terms. It might be worthwhile to consider labeling them descriptively as lists of statements that connect actions with consequences. There is a strong scholarly argument to be made that none of the Mesopotamian, Israelite/Jewish, Greek and Roman "law codes" (excluding Justinian's corpus from this list) were ever practically implemented as lived law (Finkelstein 1966; Bottéro 1992; Westbrook 2003a). This fact alone fundamentally alters one's understanding of the corpus and its work within society. Rather than a set of precedents that both depict actual cases and stand as models to be implemented in new judgments, these sets of legal statements were theoretical, scholastic, and unenforced. They were often produced within a specifically cultic or sacerdotal setting and some of them, unsurprisingly, apply the same generic forms to cultic and sacerdotal actions and objects.[12] The problem of historical context—most acute with respect to the so-called Gortyn Code because nothing is known about the adjacent culture—is profound with respect to all of these ancient legal codes (Davies 2005).

All of the legal codes mentioned above are thinly narrativized, implicitly, by dint of their genre: in all cases the text speaks authoritatively to the reader with a list of scenarios and consequences. In some cases, additional narrativization has been transmitted alongside the legal code in the documents within which we find these codes. The Mesopotamian codes, for example, generally incorporate a prolog and epilogue. These parenthetical frames attempt to concretely embody the voice of the code and to provide a historical context (i.e., reform of corruption) that further positions and justifies the code's precepts. The biblical codes are embedded in narratives of such epic scope that one is hard pressed to read these codes *without* assuming that the voice of the law is God's through Moses and that the historical context is something other than the Israelite sojourn through the desert after emerging from slavery in Egypt.

In other cases of ancient legal codes, additional narratives are suggested just outside the immediate vicinity of the document, in nearly contemporaneous traditional understandings of context and purpose. The opening chapter of Mishnah Tractate *Avot* (Ethics of the Fathers) uses a chain of transmission to connect Moses' receiving of the Torah on Sinai with the Mishnah's own laws; the implication is that the authoritative voice that stands behind Mishnaic precepts is the voice of God filtered through traditional transmission.[13] Sherira Gaon, an important tenth-century rabbi, propounded the widely held idea that the author of the Mishnah only collated earlier oral traditions into a formal authorized code because of an intellectual devolution that threatened the continuity of the tradition (Levin 1921). Similarly, the interpretive history of the Twelve Tables understands that these rules were produced as a specific response to class warfare and the need to curtail corrupt class-based abuses (Westbrook 2014). These last two traditions are narrativizations that in some sense undermine the authority of the code by conditioning the existence of these respective codes on unfortunate societal circumstances.

The above are macro-narratives that work to describe the entirety of the corpus of the respective legal codes from the outside, painting a picture of historical context. There are smaller narrativizations, though, that are produced through internal examinations of the texts of the respective codes themselves.[14] Lawyerly attention to the particular details of cases and their underlying reasoning can generate both underlying principles of jurisprudence and baseline operative cultural assumptions. These might work off a deep structural reading of a passage of the Gortyn Code to argue for specific ways in which the code reflects social assumptions and moral categories. Alternatively, and commonly, scholars can compare two separate ancient codes (either codes that derive from the same culture or those that emerge from different ones) to produce relative evaluations of the moral and ethical character of a specific code or the proximity of a code either to cultural mythology or to historical events (Greenberg 1960; Finkelstein 1981). Both the deep structural approach and the comparative approach are ways of making the basic materials of a law code have a more profound meaning.

In light of the problematic potential bias of the terms "law" and "code" and in recognition of the narrativizing that inheres in attempting to make ancient law codes meaningful, the remainder of this chapter will proceed with caution. The chapter will first attempt to more fully characterize the technical poetics of the ancient law codes while resisting the urge to narrativize. It will then explore an example in which an ancient reader produces an unusual, even outrageous, narrativization. An exploration of this narrativization will create a moment in which the law code can speak back to the narrativization attempt and resist it.

THE POETICS OF ANCIENT LAW CODES

Ancient legal codes are collections of precepts. A precept is a statement of fact employed within a legal register. Precepts routinely prohibit or mandate, but they can also establish the outcome of an action or set of actions within a specific register of legal cause and effect. The poetics of a precept are relatively uncomplicated. Scholars long ago attended to a fundamental difference within ancient code writing between casuistic presentations which articulate a legal fact through the presentation of a scenario and its outcome, and apodictic articulations which assert legal facts in straightforward syntactic sentences (Mackenzie 1964; Alt 1966).

Consider the biblical example of homicide. The Decalogue at Exodus 20:13 states "You shall not murder," an apodictic formulation. The *Covenant Code*, though, expresses the idea casuistically at Exodus 21:12–13: "He who fatally strikes a man shall be put to death." The apodictic assertion is an imperative asserted to a second-person subject. Casuistic articulations are third-person descriptions. This third-person feature combines with the protasis–apodosis format to introduce a progressive aspect into the scenario: while "you shall not murder" is an admonition before the fact, "he who fatally strikes … shall" produces a series of moments in time—the moment of the crime and the moment of the punishment. This change in temporality gives the casuistic formulation a higher degree of narrativity.[15] Since the ancient legal codes are primarily narrated casuistically, there is a basic micro-narrative inherent to most precepts.[16] Individual casuistic laws are like tiny stories.

Even while casuistic articulations have a higher degree of narrativity, they might best be considered scripts rather than full-blown narratives.[17] Casuistic sentences in the ancient codes generally describe events within a relatively confined temporal plane (two points in time) and with minimal attention to characterization, drama, affect, and even plot.

Like poems, codes are written in an extremely formal register (Wimpfheimer 2011: 13–21). Like poems, they are more susceptible to a hermeneutic lens that privileges authorial intent as the site of textual meaning.[18] Even so, the work of the reader is crucial in determining the ultimate meaning of a precept. Focusing on a single precept can change the meaning of both the individual precept and of the code as a whole. A contrast in one direction (rather than another) pushes the meaning of the set in that direction. Rabbinic law codes, for example, routinely contain precepts that address specific categories of legal subject such as man. But the term "man" can be a generic inclusive term for human being or it can contrast with human beings not legally considered in the same category (women, children, foreigners, etc.).

The individual precept speaks descriptively with a voice from nowhere. The set of precepts is similarly direct and makes no additional effort to identify its speaker. If the precepts are understood as transcripts of once-oral events, the failure to identify the speaker is understandable since the original speaker would have been obvious to the oral audience. But as a written genre it is striking that codes do not identify their speakers. This informs a basic feature of the poetics of the genre: there is no need for the authority of an author—the precept and its larger code speak authoritatively.

Form criticism is a commonly employed technique of textual criticism in which scholars employ genre as a tool for sifting texts into literarily consistent groupings. One of the most basic form-critical moves is the separating of biblical legal codes from adjacent narratives. From a form-critical perspective, it is easy to separate these evidently Mesopotamian codes from their surrounding narrativizing frames. The debate within the scholarship tends to become polarized, forcing one to choose whether to read the code absent the frame or integrated within it. The same is true for the biblical narratives—one can choose to read the codes separate from the Israelite narrative or integrated within it. A better alternative to this dichotomous choice is attending to the gaps between the implicit limited narrative scenes of the codes themselves and the explicit comments about the historical and legal context one finds within the framing prologue, epilogue and (in Hammurabi's case) sculpture.

The Code of Hammurabi is the best-preserved ancient Near Eastern Code. The famous diorite stele preserves three additions to the set of statutes: a prologue, an epilogue, and a carved image (Figure 3.5). The prologue and epilogue frame the rules as associated with Hammurabi, they connect Hammurabi with reforming tendencies, and they associate him with ancient Near Eastern mythic deities. The stele is topped by a sculpted image of Hammurabi's standing before the sun-god Shamash. Shamash is handing a stick and ring to Hammurabi. Without entering into the morass of complications regarding this material, note that the prologue, epilogue, and image are all engaged in an attempt to narrativize the contained laws.[19]

The image of the standing Hammurabi before the seated Shamash makes a strong visual argument for divine imprimatur for the royal personage and, by extension, the laws etched underneath. It almost doesn't matter which divine figure is seated in the throne (the prologue makes Hammurabi Shamash-like though his authority is from Marduk) (Grimme 1907). The voice from nowhere becomes the voice of the king authorized by god. The self-authorizing format of the precept and code has been married to the clear power structure of gods and monarch which connect to known mythologies.

To some extent (and to the surprise of form critics), it is sometimes the case that the frame narrative of a law code usurps primary position from the code itself. The first historical reference to a Western code refers to the laws of Urukagina around 2350 BCE. None of the specific precepts of this code survives; all that is recorded in cultural memory is the narrativization that asserts that King Urukagina produced a code as part of a reform of corruption (King 1910). The code itself is not extant, but the memory of its existence is transmitted along with the ethical impetus that motivated it. The Urukagina reforms protected ordinary people from abuses of power by the politically powerful. Hammurabi's prologue and epilogue draw upon this tradition and frame Hammurabi as a modern day Urukagina, employing these laws to ennoble the downtrodden.

FIGURE 3.5. Detail of Hammurabi's Stele, showing the cuneiform writing style in legible form. Source: Flickr/Gabriele Barni/CC BY 2.0.

The biblical texts avoid some of the artificiality of the prologue/epilogue format by overwhelming the law codes in their new environment.[20] The sheer size of the epic biblical narrative that frames the codes subsumes the codes under the larger narrative frames. Unlike the window-dressing of the epilogue and prologue, the biblical materials fully envelop the law codes and ensure that the voice of nowhere becomes understood as the voice of God through Moses.[21] The eruption of the first person voice as God within some casuistic formulations works as a specific cementing of the unification of the divine narrativization with the content of the laws themselves.[22]

The poetics of ancient legal codes necessitate a movement from the simple register of the precept to the more complicated and subtle set of precepts and finally to narrativizations that place sections of a code or the entire code within a hermeneutic frame. Attending to these poetics, I turn now to an example from the corpus of rabbinic literature—the corpus of texts produced by rabbis who lived between the first and the eighth centuries CE. This example provides an opportunity to evaluate the gap between a law code and its narrativization; the gap is present in this case despite the fact that the narrativization is produced out of the materials of the code itself. The hermeneutic relationship between the code and its interpretive narrativization will allow the code, in this case, to resist the narrativization and make an argument for its own cultural meaning.

MIDRASHIC NARRATIVIZATION OF BIBLICAL LAW

Ancient readers, not unlike modern scholars, employed analogy, juxtaposition and contrast (among other tools) to detect patterns in the codes they received from their historical predecessors. The rabbis who were active between the first and eighth centuries were incredibly precise and careful readers of the biblical text who occasionally licensed themselves to employ midrashic modes of interpretation that resemble post-modern freeplay (Stern 1996; Yadin-Israel 2004; Yadin-Israel 2014). The example to which I now turn is one in which the rabbis transform adjacent precepts into temporal moments and turn a set of three laws into a three-act play. While one can debate whether authorial intent is either a desideratum or something one can ever confidently attain, it is extremely unlikely that these precepts were designed to be read as an extended narrative.[23] The violence of this interpretative move makes this an excellent opportunity to evaluate the features of the biblical legal text and of rabbinic legal interpretive culture that encourage this interpretation.

The legal cases that comprise the *Deuteronomic Code* range across a wide panoply of topics that are arranged either haphazardly or through some form of free association (Tigay 1996). Three adjacent biblical laws—about the status of the conquered woman, about primogeniture and about a rebellious child—become the basis for a rabbinic narrativization that produces a recognizable story.

Deuteronomy 21 details what should happen if an Israelite warrior is smitten by a woman residing in a conquered city:

> When you take the field against your enemies, and the Lord your God delivers them into your power and you take some of them captive, and you see among the captives a beautiful woman and you desire her and would take her to wife, you shall bring her into your house, and she shall trim her hair, pair her nails, and discard her captive's garb. She shall spend a month's time in your house lamenting her father and mother; after that you may come to her and possess her, and she shall be your wife. Then,

should you no longer want her, you must release her outright. You must not sell her for money; since you had your will of her, you must not enslave her. (*Deut*. JPS 1985)

This elaborately narrated casuistic presentation licenses the practice of military sexual conquest, but domesticates it to the cultural norms of marital sexuality. The captive is humanized by the consideration with which she is to be married rather than raped. The text legislates the woman's beautification as a piece of her absorption and empathizes with the captive's need to process the transition from one culture and patrimony to another. The passage reflects little naiveté. Understanding that physical attraction drives the warrior's desire, it anticipates a possibility that the warrior will wish to discard the woman after he has had his way with her.[24] The Hebrew text for "you no longer want her" has a clear sexual meaning. The text asserts control of the meaning of the sex act; the warrior who rapes his conquest must treat the object of his lust as a free Israelite woman rather than as chattel that can be manipulated for financial good.

The subsequent section of the *Deuteronomic Code* describes a scenario in which a man's older son (of two) is the child of his despised wife and his younger son the child of his beloved wife.[25] While the patriarch might wish to dispose of his estate in the direction of the more beloved family, he is bound by primogeniture to bequeath a double portion to the older son.

This primogeniture section is immediately followed by the case of the "rebellious son." A boy who rebels against authority is seized by his parents and brought to a town tribunal at which the parents testify. The elders convict the boy and the boy is stoned by the people of the town to eradicate evil from society. Three seemingly separate laws—the conquered woman, primogeniture and the rebellious son—are proximate but have seemingly little connection with one another.

Some of the clearest articulations of rabbinic interpretations of the Bible from Late Antiquity (second–sixth centuries CE) are found in the writings of Rashi, an eleventh century commentator to the Bible. Distilling a narrativization that is present but less fully developed in several texts from the earlier rabbinic period, Rashi writes:

> The *Torah* only addresses itself to evil desire: if the *Holy One Blessed be He* did not permit [the desired woman], [the warrior] would marry her in prohibition. But when he marries her, he will eventually hate her, as it says afterward "If a man has two wives ..." and he will eventually father with her a rebellious son. That is why these passages are juxtaposed. [26]

Rashi personifies the law code's speaker as "The Torah," a Hebrew term for Pentateuch and asserts that the verses do not describe a social ideal, but a pragmatic response to baser human urges which will ultimately have disastrous consequences, leading to a despised wife and a son who is executed as he comes of age.

Rashi distances the lawgiver from the moral choice at the center of the warrior's relationship with the conquered woman. The law (Torah is the text personified as a subject) is not invested in this conquest, but responds to expected real-world lusts by regulating them.[27] This part of the interpretation is not a stretch; a historically responsible text critic who presumes a goal of authorial intent might understand the text to be working to contain the warrior's lust. Rashi moves beyond this reactive component of the warrior's case; taking advantage of this sense in which the biblical lawgiver is antagonistic to the warrior's sexual conquest, the midrashic reading puts the scenario of the desired woman in temporal sequence with the adjacent passages to tell a story: "A man who meets his wife at war will come to despise her and have a family split between beloved and despised children; the result of having despised children will be a rebellious son, whom society will have no choice but to execute." This narrativization not only has the benefit of disavowing biblical moral responsibility for sexual conquest, but it also helps justify the strikingly unethical execution of a rebellious adolescent.[28] Fault for the boy's death lies not with the tribunal or the people who actually stone him, but with the warrior who could not control his lust, and introduced the conquered woman into Israel as his despised wife and the rebellious child's mother.

There are, in my view, at least eight pressure points within the framework of legal interpretation that are essential to the interpretation of a legal text within a larger cultural discourse. These eight sites are relevant and present aspects of the cultural study of law in modernity as well, but they are amplified within the ancient setting that precedes the modern state and made more acute by the distance inherent to the reading of ancient codes. The eight pressure points include some that are literary (poetics, literary dynamics, hermeneutics and narrativity) and others that are connected with the force of law in the world (power, authority, society, and scope).

Consider these eight features, which I will delineate more specifically, with respect to Rashi's narrativization. The distinction between apodictic and casuistic formulations is a matter of concern to textual poetics. It is specifically the progressive temporality of the casuistic formulation that makes it possible to read the law of the conquered bride as reactive to existing social practices rather than as advocating such practices. An apodictic phrasing of the statute of the conquered woman (e.g., "a woman acquired in battle must be treated as a wife") would communicate a greater degree of a priori intention. In contrast, the higher degree of narrativity within casuistic formulations ("e.g ... When you take the field ... and you see a beautiful woman") open up the possibility that the place of law in the scenario is entirely in the apodosis—in the outcome of the scenario rather than the *ab initio* articulation of the scenario itself. Where an apodictic articulation necessarily justifies the sexual conquest, the casuistic formulation leaves a reader uncertain about the law's interests and intervention. The poetics of the casuistic statute introduce a degree of ambiguity that is more fully opened up by the midrashic narrativization.

As for literary dynamics, biblical scholars consider the individual precepts of Deuteronomy to be only loosely associated with one another, with verbal echoes or larger organizational patterns justifying an almost random ordering (Tigay 1996). Even so, biblical scholars concede a loose biological ordering to this triptych of cases that begins with a sexual encounter, continues with a domestic polygamous squabble and finishes with the execution of a rebellious son.[29] While the legislator may not have intended the full midrashic narrative, there is something implicit in the biblical text that contributes to the temporal dynamics of the sequence. Perhaps more consequentially, the midrashic story allows the biblical text to maintain its progressive aspect of multiple points in time. But where casuistic formulations provide legal consequences for legal scenarios (legal cause and effect) that is presumably guaranteed by legal procedures, the midrashic story makes the punishment of the desirous warrior a natural and automatic consequence of his action.

The midrashic interpretation is charged by a fundamental question of hermeneutics that has bearing on the questions of power and authority. Rashi echoes midrashic readers in presuming a divine author of the *Deuteronomic Code qua* Hebrew Torah.[30] This despite Deuteronomy's own claim to be voiced by Moses. Identifying the author, though, only begs the question of hermeneutic context. If Moses or God is speaking, does their speech communicate a pure ideal of how people should act in the world or does it reflect an encounter with preexisting cultural practice, with uncontrollable human sexuality or with a set of customary norms which the speaker is powerless to undo? Ancient legal codes are produced in a form that often asserts legal realities without rationales or justifications. As such, they can be read as communicating within a preexisting set of communal structures in which the assertion of legal facts is just an extension of royal, priestly, military, or divine authority and that authority might or might not reflect cultural realities.

The midrashic story draws additional attention to Foucauldian aspects of power that are present in legal codes. Rather than simply embodying extant social structures, legal codes are implicated in the process of producing such power structures. This is true both at the level of the biblical text, in which the *Deuteronomic Code* produces power dynamics through its formulations, and in the rabbinic interpretation. When the rabbis narrativize Deuteronomy's cases as part of an effort to ethically remake the received canons in their legal tradition, they assert their own control over the text and their interpretations become themselves vehicles for new assertions of cultural power.[31] By imputing divine authorship and then framing that authorship as reactive and somewhat impotent, the rabbis claim for themselves the ability to eliminate the laws of the conquered woman and the rebellious son as precedent. Hermeneutics becomes a vehicle for an assertion of power that grants cultural authority (Halbertal 1997). This claim to power can work either with or against communal and institutional authority structures.

Consider the possibility that the *Deuteronomic Code* reflects priestly aspiration rather than reflecting lived practices. The production of a code that aspires to control the unruly rape authorized by the military and its authorizing force, the king, is itself a claim to power that is entwined in competing authority structures. The rabbinic interpretation that writes the code as a story and considers the law reactive to, and not supportive of, military rape, is a true heir to the priestly writers. But the path from religious pragmatism (priestly writers) to religious pragmatism (rabbinic reader) travels through an assumption that the text speaks from God (or at least Moses) and represents the ideal rather than pragmatic circumstance. When the rabbis wrest control of the meaning of the text from the imputed divine legist, they are actually, in this example, restoring the text to a social context quite similar to the one in which it was produced.

The midrashic story constructs biblical law as operant within a framework of preexisting cultural practices or norms. The desirous warrior is ontologically prior to the law that governs his actions. This reality suggests a specific relationship between the legal code and the culture that produced it and which it reflects. Because of their formal simplicity and straightforwardness, legal codes (particularly ancient ones for lack of other information) are often accepted as direct reports of cultural realities. The question of scope is an examination of the relationship between a given law code and its broader culture. Does it reflect cultural reality *in toto*? Could it instead reflect the cultural reality of a specific sub-culture associated with its production? Might it entirely be an idealistic fantasy produced by a narrow sub-culture? The midrashic narrativization provides an example of ancient legal theorizing that is capable of narrowing the scope of a set of laws so that it is not considered representative of or addressed to the wider culture. The law is addressed specifically to the warrior class who are unable to curb their appetites and must be accommodated in some fashion. It does not reflect an ideal, but a poor accommodation with disastrous results.

One of the colonialist techniques of modern anthropology was the presumption that ancient law reflects a primitive stage in human and legal development. When applied to ancient legal codes, this allowed modern scholars to assume primitive notions of justice, morality, and vengeance. The midrashic interpretation shares this assumption by considering the very idea of the law of the conquered woman a primitive response to base tendencies: "Torah only addresses itself to evil desire." Implicit in this statement is the judgment that the Bible is addressed to a primitive, not a civilized rabbi. The rabbinic story undermines the notion that Torah ideology is reflected in the licensing of sexual conquest. Disgusted by this idea, the rabbis presume that it speaks to base tendencies. Close examination of the biblical text demonstrates that the *Deuteronomic Code* is itself more ambivalent.[32] The biblical text, it needs to be emphasized, encourages the woman's beautification and produces a ritual of mourning so that she can be productively absorbed into Israel; it is not fair to read the passage as entirely antagonistic to the practice. One can resist the rabbinic narrativization much as one can resist the evolutionary anthropological model in general. "Primitive" legal redress can even, occasionally, be characterized as superior to seemingly evolved possibilities. Consider the present case of the conquered woman. Wars have been a constant fact of human life from the ancient period to our own day. "Raping and pillaging" is an all too familiar description of what victors do to the victims, their homes and their civilizations. The *Deuteronomic Code*'s legislation of the conquered woman legislates to treat the woman with dignity and insists upon her humanity within a culture in which she might easily have been treated like chattel or worse; certainly victims of war crimes in our present day are often treated worse. By flattening the legislation into a primitive statement that is obliterated by rabbinic ethical thinking, the rabbis suppress the biblical text's insistence upon the dignity of the victim as expressed through beautification of the body, the recognition of traumatic loss, and the insistence upon her elevation to a full position as an Israelite woman.

Having considered poetics, dynamics, hermeneutics, power, authority, scope and anthropology, let us turn to narrativity itself. While sections of the legal code can be read as narrative, the legal code would not be confused for a coherent short story much less a novel or epic. This fact makes the code susceptible to narrativization. Narrativizations can take the form of narrativizing individual statutes; this is particularly easy to do with casuistic hypotheticals (Bartor 2010). The rabbinic narrativization of the three cases expands the narrative time of the original hypothetical to include scenes from later in the relationship between the warrior and his beloved. In expanding to different scenes, the story also pans backward to place a broader cast of characters into the narrative. While the biblical casuistic precepts contain but a few characters, the case of the rebellious son introduces, in addition to the child and his parents, town elders and the larger community of Israel. By expanding the desirous warrior into the case of the rebellious adolescent, the rabbinic interpretation makes the broader community a relevant set of characters in the narrative. So while the law speaks to the warrior as one legal subject, it also speaks to the rest of society, as another. In connecting the case of the violently acquired bride with the rebellious adolescent, the midrash connects two precepts that police the borders of the community and ensure conformity. While the original telling of the bride's story in the Bible encourages a reader to sympathize with her experience, the connection of her story with that of the adolescent son marks her as someone whom the larger society should view with suspicion. By combining the precepts, the midrashic story shifts the casuistic law which seems to address the warrior class to the framework of a cautionary tale addressed to society at large.

The rabbinic narrativization produces a story that makes it easier to tease out some of the ways in which legal rules interact with literary, social, and political aspects of cultural discourse. The simplicity of the law code as a textual genre sometimes masks its implicit narrative of authoritarian pronouncement. It also elides the role that the reader plays in producing the meaning of the text. Introducing the interpretive story and its manipulation of the original law code makes this aspect of the reading of law codes extremely visible while creating the opportunity to reflect, more carefully, on some of the hidden cultural aspects of the original text. Both the original text and the interpretation have something to say about sexual desire, gender relationships, power dynamics, and the relationship between legal strictures and the cultural practices they strive to regulate. The interpretive narrativization, whose only intervention in the original law code is turning sequence into consequence, stands in judgment over the ethics of the original text. But judgment, with its implied evolutionary sense of betterment is not unproblematic. The biblical text is able to resist this claim to improvement. And in that resistance there exists the possibility for ancient legal codes to function not as primitive, archaic, or displaced, but as alternative.

Ancient law codes are lists of rules that were preserved in documents that have survived from four different ancient societies. Some of these documents have been preserved continuously while others have been lost for centuries or millennia before being unearthed. The blatant genre requirements of these codes make them seem to operate within a narrow legal world and to encourage a minimal set of lawyerly reading practices. But these codes are not just legal documents. They are arguably the most important archive of ancient society and culture. Historians turn to these documents to unearth important clues to ancient civilizations. The reading practices of a cultural study of law allow scholars the opportunity to extract these texts from the narrow confines of formal legal analysis and allow them to speak to larger matters of culture. There are dangers associated with such reading practices, though, for they allow contemporary interests and mores to color the meaning of these ancient texts. And as one tries to make these materials more meaningful, one risks transforming them into grander and more sophisticated narratives. Some caution is advisable.

CHAPTER FOUR

Agreements

ROBERTO FIORI

Whether or not we accept the theory of the "social contract," the importance of agreements in society cannot be underestimated. Every day we are reminded that to live in society means we either agree or disagree with other people. Given their social importance, and considering that law is a way to regulate society, one could think that no legal system could fail to reserve a central place for agreements, so that from the perspective of a legal history of agreement it would suffice to describe the various forms of contracts, treaties, and settlements over the course of time. However, every legal system is also the product of culture. No legal institution can be taken for granted, but ought to be weighed according to the ideas and values of each civilization.

MODERN SUBJECTIVISM AND THE WILL

In one of the most influential writings for the development of the modern vision of law, the *System of Modern Roman Law* (*System des heutigen römischen Rechts*) by Friedrich Carl von Savigny, the "legal relationship" (*Rechtsverhältniss*) is represented as the relationship between two people that is determined by a rule of law which grants to the individual will a sphere that it can rule without interference from any other will, and whose object-matters are the willer's own person and the outer world (von Savigny 1840: 331, 333). The whole of private law is thus seen as the reproduction, on a global scale, of the structure of the *Rechtsgeschäft*—a concept created by German Natural law that can be rendered as "legal act"—whose simplest scheme is the declaration of the will of a subject about an object.

It is clear that if the primary structure of the "legal relationship" is based on will, agreements become the most important driving force of the system: not just because of their relevance in modern economy, but especially because of their ideological value. For this ideology, agreements are indeed both the expression of the individual's liberty to decide upon his own goods or acts, and the medium through which the individual can dispose of a reified world. If considered from a certain perspective, this is today the ideology of the whole Western legal culture. However, even if this representation of law is so common to us that we may perceive it as "natural" and therefore almost unavoidable, we must remember that it is the historical result of a number of factors (Fiori 2011a).

One of the most important of these factors is the Christian idea of religion. Christianity has inherited from the religion of the Jews the doctrine of a covenant between Man and God. However, in Jewish religion, it was a covenant between God and the whole elect people, who was chosen by Yahweh and who chose him as their sole god among the many deities worshipped in the Near East—probably reproducing the formulas of obedience of the international treaties of the time (Liverani 2003: 180, 378). On the contrary, in

Christian religion, which is not an "ethnic" but a universal religion, this covenant has become a personal relationship between the individual believer and God, aimed at the salvation of the soul. This has led to the conviction that alongside human tribunals there exists also an internal forum, based on the conscience of each believer. It has favored the rise of an individualistic dimension to ethics, which lies at the root of Kant's distinction between a "moral" and a "legal" sphere of duties:[1] the first being founded on an individual perception of universal values, and the second on the coexistence between individual choices and the respect for the liberty of the others, in accordance with a universal law.

In Christian religion, a breach of this covenant brings about personal sin. This idea is strictly linked to the salvation of the individual soul and was unknown to ancient ethnic religions, which considered a religious offense to be a danger to the whole community.[2] To avoid the risk of sin, canon law has assigned great importance to the fulfilling of promises: a good Christian should never lie. Therefore—unlike in Roman law, as we will see—in canon law every promise is binding (Calasso 1967: 267) and the initial contractual will, just like the believer's individual choice to worship the sole God, encompasses the whole regulation of the relationship.

Another important feature of Christian religion is the distance created between Man and Nature. In many traditional cultures, plants, animals, human beings and gods are all part of a natural order; respect for legal and religious rules is often aimed at the preservation of this order. Christianity has changed this holistic vision of the world into an individualistic one: God is the creator of the world and Man, the only creature made in God's image, has received the world into his possession: just as the Christian God is a legislator to Man, the latter is a legislator to the natural world. Nature is no longer an active part of reality, in some way sacred, but the reified object of the will of Man.

These ideas are, of course, part of the entire European culture, but during the Middle Ages and the Renaissance they had a strong influence on law only within the limited field of canon law. The medieval jurists of the civil law, although naturally influenced by the Christian vision of the world, developed their doctrines with a strict adherence to the Roman sources, so that the general categories changed—particularly under the influence of Aristotelian philosophy[3]—but not the actual rules of law, preserved in Justinian's *Corpus iuris*. It was only during the seventeenth century, with the advent of the doctrines of Natural law, that the rules of canon law were introduced into the institutions of civil law through the medium of the Spanish Late Scholastics. Also in civil law, mere promises became binding (Diesselhorst 1959; Calasso 1967; Wieacker 1973; Gordley 1991) and the will was seen as the expression of one's liberty within his own property (Grossi 1973).

It was at this point that such ideas were dramatically emphasized in a subjectivistic and individualistic perspective (Fiori 2003a: 200–212). On the one hand, one of the most distinctive traits of Natural law was the assertion of the existence of natural rights, belonging to the individual not as part of a system, but inherent to Man (Tierney 1997). On the other hand, modern philosophy reduced the only certainty of knowledge to the perception of the Self (*cogito ergo sum*): whereas in ancient and medieval cultures subjectivism was considered as a limit to the knowledge of reality, during the seventeenth century the "subject" became instead the starting point for every contact with the world. Moreover, this vision was aided by the development of new grammatical theories caused by the speculation on modern languages, particularly French. At the center of the new grammar was the scheme "subject-verb-object": a pattern that, because of the believed parallelism between logic and grammar, was considered a primary model of reasoning. This was also adopted by the jurists in describing what came to be called the *Rechtsgeschäft*.

At the end of this process, justice and law no longer expressed the collective ethics of the community. "Ethics" was conceived as the sum and the harmonization of the individual conscience, and "law" as obedience to the orders of authority. The doors were opened to a positivistic conception of law, distinguished by ethics essentially because of the presence of a sanction. The ambition of the modern state to achieve complete control of the legal system, the free market ideology and the fragmentation of modern society have done the rest: rules are no longer binding because they convey the feelings and the beliefs of a community, but because they are established by a political authority; each citizen has, so to speak, a "personal" relationship with the law; within his sphere of autonomy he is the ruler and his will is the law. The interaction between legal subjects is thus completely based on agreements.

LAW AND SOCIETY IN ROME

In antiquity, and particularly in Roman law—which, considering its importance for the development of the Western legal tradition, we can assume as our primary reference—we find a completely different framework.

First of all, the ancients could never have pictured the "legal relationship" in terms of a structure "subject-action-object," nor looked at the law in a subjectivistic perspective. In classical antiquity the notion of subject has another value, and the idea of object is completely lacking. Latin *subiectum* is a calque of Greek *hypokeímenon*, a term that in Aristotelian philosophy had a twofold meaning. It was, ontologically, the material substratum that remains the same during the transformation of the substance (Aristotle, *Physics* 190b20; *Metaphysics* 1024a9 and 985b10); but in a logical-predicative sense it was what the discourse is about (Aristotle, *Categories* 1a20; 1b10–11; *On interpretation* 16a1–17a7)—a semantic value that is still the primary meaning of the word in English, but which has become secondary in other European languages. Accordingly, Greek and Latin grammatical theories used the idea of "subject," as opposed to the "predicate," in the sense that today is rather given to the "object," and there was no hierarchy among the parts of the phrase: the functions of words were defined by the declensions and their relationship to the verb, on equal footing (Lepschy 1992). It was, however, not just a matter of terms. As we have said, ancient and medieval philosophies believed in the possibility of a true knowledge of the world, while individual perception was often seen as a hindrance to knowledge, rather than as a firm starting point (Gill 2006: 36, 391).

What is more, the Roman idea of law was not positivistic. The root of the *ius* were the *mores*, the ancestral customs of the community. Even if at the end of the Republic, because of the influence of Greek historiography, it was imagined that many *mores* had been created by royal statutes, these customs had, in fact, been followed from time immemorial. The legal rules on which social life was founded were perceived as essential for the survival of the community, and since gods and men were in a way parts of the same society (Scheid 2001), the infringement of these rules was considered not only as a legal wrong but also as a religious offense: the best way to describe it is perhaps to use the adjective "cosmic" (Sabbatucci 1981). It is probably because of this vision that the Romans only rarely voted *leges publicae* about private law—and when they did, the laws were often related to social issues such as debt, citizenship, or marriage[4]—whereas the statute was the usual source for constitutional and criminal law, i.e., for those parts of law which were more tied to the political choices of the *res publica* (Serrao 1973: 794–850; 1974: 5–130). Even during the Empire, the *constitutiones principis* related to private law never altered the principles developed and refined by the jurisprudence (Gualandi 1963; Coriat 2014). In those rare instances when it happened, the jurists did their best to limit the interference of the *lex* and to restore, through their *interpretatio*, the "natural" logic of the system.[5]

Like many ancient peoples, and particularly in the archaic period, the Romans believed in the existence of a cosmic order that had to be preserved, lest its violation might cause a breach of the *pax deorum* and put at risk the survival of the community (Fiori 1996). It was a hierarchical order: each part of the universe had a position that ought not to be altered, therefore everyone should behave according to his or her role. One of the most important Roman virtues—and certainly the one that the Romans considered a distinctive feature of their culture, especially when compared to the Greek—was *gravitas*, the capacity of something or someone to be "heavy," i.e., to stay put at their place, according to hierarchy (*maiestas*) (Dumézil 1969: 125–152). The *honestas* was not simply "honesty," but the virtue to conduct oneself according to one's role (*honor*) (Jacotot 2013), and the reliability (*fides*) of each member of society was calculated on his social position (Fiori 2008: 465–481): according to an archaic rule of the civil procedure, if there were no witnesses, the defendant could be acquitted only if his social standing and ethical standards were equal or superior to that of the plaintiff, otherwise he had to be found guilty. In this respect, Roman society was divided not only between patricians and plebeians, but also between *boni* and *mali*, the first term indicating the rich and respectable, the second the lower orders. This division lasted—even developed in different forms, because of the general changes of Roman society—until the end of the Republic, when the *nobiles* were called *optimi* and their political supporters *optimates* (Fiori 2013: 169–249). There was not a universal idea of "just": just was what was appropriate to one's social condition.

These ideas had probably survived from Indo-European conceptions of law and society. According to an influential theory, India, Rome, and early Ireland have preserved the oldest legal and religious traditions of the Indo-European peoples, because the interpretation of law and religion was assigned to colleges of priests (Vendryes 1918: 265–285). Indeed, notwithstanding the obvious differences among these historical cultures, we find in each of them a similar system of values. When we read that in Roman law it was considered "more appropriate to the status" (*honestius*) for a patron to take his freedwoman as a concubine rather than as a wife, even if, in general, marriage was considered more "honest" than concubinate (see below), we are reminded of a passage of the *Bhagavadgītā* where it is said that it is better to perform imperfectly one's own duty than to perform well the duty of another (*Bhagavadgītā* 3.35) as each member of society has their own rules of conduct, according to stages—originally, modes (Olivelle 1993: 73)—of life and class.[6] There is also a striking resemblance between the assertion by Ovid—in a passage which is the rendering in verse of a priestly doctrine—that before the establishment of Jupiter's order, based on *maiestas*, the universe lived in equality (*Fasti* 5. 11–52),[7] and the statement of one of the most important tracts of early Irish law, the *Senchas Mór*, where it is stated that before the lawbook was drawn up, the world was in (a chaotic) equality, whereas after its completion everyone received his rank (*Corpus iuris Hibernici*, 348.10–11). It is a quite different culture from ours: but we must remember that still at the end of the eighteenth century, the Prussian civil code provided different tribunals and different compensation for injuries, depending on the status of the victim (Koselleck 1981). Although theoretically part of Christian doctrine, the ideal of *egalité* among all men is actually very recent, and was only accepted in ancient societies to a certain extent.

All this has to be borne in mind when dealing with Roman law generally (Garnsey 1970). To the Romans, law is more a science than a set of rules: it is the technique (*ars*) that the priests—and, after them, the lay jurists—follow to understand what is appropriate, according to the natural order; this is, of course, portrayed by them as a universal projection of their society. The *ius* is therefore mostly based on tradition: the "law of the citizens (of Rome)" (*ius civile*) includes not only the peculiar provisions of the "national" law of the Romans (*ius Quiritium*), based on customs (*mores*) and statutes (*leges*), but also the law known to other peoples (*ius gentium*) and accepted in Rome because it is perceived as being compliant with the natural order. It is what the anthropologists call a traditional culture: gods, men, and nature are all part of the same system; the world is ordered by the same rules of the community, therefore the survival of the community is bound to the respect of these rules, which are discovered by the jurists through their *ars*. This vision of the world is hierarchical, objective, and holistic, not egalitarian, subjective, and individualistic; consequently, the law is seen as a set of rules that descend primarily from rationality, rather than from the commands of authority.

In such a context, the role of the will is less essential, in comparison with what we experience today. What is important is the preservation of the order, which is the necessary condition for the survival of the community: changes are allowed, but they should comply with this general scope. This does not mean, of course, that will and agreements had no part in the development of the law and in the legal life of the Romans. It means, however, that their role must be studied not abstractly but historically, taking into account the development of Roman culture and society.[8]

AGREEMENTS IN ARCHAIC ROMAN LAW (EIGHTH–FOURTH CENTURIES BCE)

In the studies of Roman law the importance of archaic law is often undervalued.[9] This attitude can in some ways be understood. The available sources are quite scant when compared to those which refer to the classical period, and those that have come to us followed paths that appear quite heterodox to the student of law: not only the books of historians, but also—and sometimes especially—antiquarian studies, and even works of poetry. However, when we find that the ideology of the late Republic and of the Principate can still be fruitfully compared to other Indo-European cultures, we understand that traditions were in Roman culture so binding that the study of the archaic period is essential to a real understanding of Roman law.

It is probably the first phase of the regal period—often called the Latin monarchy—that had the strongest influence on the formation of the traditional Roman vision of the world.

During this period, the Roman economy was based on agriculture and livestock. The land was divided into small parcels which were the private property of families, or in large areas in the collective ownership of the *gens*. The head of the family (*pater familias*) held absolute power over both the things and the subordinate persons of the family, and exerted large autonomy in private matters: neither the king nor the *gens* could interfere with his powers. He was the only one in the family to be *sui iuris*, that is, he was not subject to any other member of the group.

This autonomy was, however, not conceived as an individualistic issue. The respect of the father's *potestas* was the respect for the traditional order, and when two fathers entered into an agreement what was significant were the binding effects of the agreement, rather than the agreement itself. The community was not considered to be the sum of its members, the result of a "social contract" of free individuals; on the contrary, its members were, at different levels, parts of a group that in some way preexisted , because only the group as a whole had a relationship with the gods: without a group, the individual was nothing.

The preeminent importance of the social effects of the agreement is shown by the fact that during this period the parties could either agree to enter into a customary institution of social relevance, or cover their agreement using ritual forms that granted the social significance of the transaction.

An example of the first case was clientship. It was a vertical relationship between a *gentilis*, who took the name of *patronus*, and a subordinate, called *cliens*. The client agreed to work and to fight in wars for his patron, increasing his wealth and power; the *gentilis* granted to the client access to the *gens'* lands and protected him within the group with his higher *fides*. Another example was the *sodalitas*, which was also an association, but at a more aristocratic level: the *sodales* were all *gentiles* and formed a war-band and a political lobby (Figure 4.1). Since both these institutions descended from the Indo-

FIGURE 4.1. Reliefs on a sarcophagus depicting farmers gathering legumes and milking sheep from Villa Casali Necropolis, Rome, detail. Source: DEA / A. DAGLI ORTI/De Agostini/Getty Images.

European past, they were structured according to ancient customs. The duties of *clientes* and *sodales* were defined from time immemorial, and the agreements (*pacta*) that could be adopted among comrades were probably aimed at specific accomplishments, e.g., cattle-raiding or actions in war, but they did not define the general duties of the members of the association.[10]

In other cases the agreement should take the form of a ritual act. The simplest was the *sponsio*, in the beginning probably an oath, later a formal promise to give or do something. The second was called *mancipatio*, and consisted of the weighing of copper or bronze to be given in exchange for power over a valuable thing (*res mancipi*) or a person. The formality of this act should not be explained by a love for ritual, but was rather due to the lack of written records and with the oral forms of transmission of memory: the solemnity ensured the presence of witnesses who could provide future proof. However, although formal, neither the *sponsio* nor the *mancipatio* were rigid. The first, being merely a promise, could contain whatever one wished: it expressed the duty that the promising party assumed on the basis of the agreement. The second might serve several purposes thanks to the various utterances (*nuncupationes*) that could be pronounced during the ceremony: it could be used to sell, to hire animals or persons, to provide sureties for a debt through the subjection of the debtor to the creditor, to acquire power over one's wife and—no later than the XII Tables—to adopt children and to bestow an inheritance on a third party who would later pass it to the heirs of the deceased.

It is thus apparent that, contrary to what it is often affirmed, in archaic law there was a large number of possible transactions. Thus we should not be surprised to find the same terminology, but not yet with the same technical meaning, that will be later found in the classical sources—*emere* (to buy), *vendere* (to sell), *locare* (to let), *conducere* (to hire), etc. Indeed, what is typical of archaic law is not the absence of transactions, but the fact that, unlike classical law, their economic content and the related agreement of the parties remained in the background. Rather, what was in plain view was the performance of the ritual, because it created a socially relevant bond between the parties: the relationship had a legal value only when it was recognizable by the community.

A very instructive example of all this is marriage (Fiori 2011b). In Roman law, the basis of marriage was seen in the agreement (*consensus facit nuptias*). However it was, so to speak, a "qualified" agreement. There were several stable unions: between slaves, the *contubernium*; between free persons, marriage or concubinate. Also in concubinate the will to live together was important, because it distinguished the concubines from the occasional lovers but it did not imply, as in marriage, the sharing of the same social position between husband and wife. To have marriage, there was therefore the need of the specific will to be married (*affectio maritalis*). This peculiarity of marriage was expressed, at a social level, by many markers. The wedding was a ritual ceremony, during which auspices were assumed, sacrifices and banquets were performed, and the wife was publicly brought to the house of the husband. After the ceremony itself, the most important social markers were taking part in rites and dress (Figure 4.2).

There was, first of all, a difference between married women and concubines. The former shared the same *dignitas* as the husband, while the latter was a partner of lesser social condition. Therefore, according to a law attributed to Numa Pompilius, only married women could make sacrifices to Iuno, the wife of Jupiter; her altar could not even be touched by a concubine.[11] Only married women could wear ribbons (*vittae*) in their hair and the *stola*, which was a light colored cloth (as opposed to the gaudy dresses of the prostitutes).

FIGURE 4.2. Roman marble sarcophagus with relief depicting nuptial rite. Source: DEA / A. DAGLI ORTI/De Agostini/Getty Images.

There were, however, distinctions also among married women, based on *dignitas*. It took centuries to extend to all married women the privileges originally reserved to the patricians and that were denied even to the patrician women who had married a plebeian. In 296 BCE, the patrician *matronae* prevented the patrician wife of a plebeian from sacrificing to the altar of the goddess *Pudicitia* (Figure 4.3), so she created the cult of the *Pudicitia Plebeia*, which was originally reserved for the noble plebeian families (Livy 10.23.3–10): even among "honest" women, in fact, a different ethic was required, based on social hierarchy (Langlands 2006: 365). The *stola* was originally reserved for the patrician women; later it was permitted to plebeian women if they were not descended from slaves (*ingenuae*). Only during the third century BCE were freedwomen permitted to wear it, providing that they were married to other freedmen or were concubines of their patrons. The same social markers were reserved for children: in the beginning, only patrician boys could wear the *toga praetexta*, distinguished by its broad purple border; only over time were the *ingenui* allowed to wear it, while the descendants of slaves had to wait until the third century BCE.

In a community where social bonds were so strong, agreements were important for settling disputes. Any controversy was an issue for the whole community. Since the parties had to swear their claims, the one who was found guilty lost his reliability (*fides*) and, if he did not comply with the sentence, was reduced to slavery[12]—or, according

FIGURE 4.3. The goddess Pudicitia (Vatican, Musei Vaticani, first century CE). Source: B&Y Photography / Alamy Stock Photo.

to some theories, lost every right within the community, being declared *sacer* i.e. an outlaw without any property or family connections (Fiori 1996). This could also have consequences for his friends and relatives, because all the social relations of the parties were involved in the trial. The litigants not only brought witnesses—who could be publicly dishonored if they refused to give testimony, and would be flung from the Tarpeian Rock if they lied—but also *laudatores*. These were relatives or friends who pleaded, on their *fides*, that the party they were supporting in the trial was trustworthy—a role that was quite important, if we keep in mind the ancient rule we recalled before, that a *bonus vir*, a "man of good standing," should be preferred by the judge to a *malus* even when there were no witnesses (Fiori 2013). Sometimes sureties were required; here it was the guarantor who risked being enslaved instead of the party. A civil trial was a very dangerous procedure for the parties and their supporters. It is highly probable that it was a quite rare event, and that the social groups involved tried desperately to avoid it. We know for certain that the Romans granted the possibility of a settlement (*pacisci*) at different stages: between the parties, before or during the trial,[13] or within thirty days after the judgment; with the help of a third person, because after the thirty days the debt was publicly declared in the Comitium, so that the debtor could find someone who would take the debt upon himself to satisfy the creditor.[14]

This system was more or less reproduced in international relationships as well. As long as the Romans had contact with the peoples of Italy, they found a common tradition of international customs and religious cults, and could therefore develop a system of rules quite similar to those that we have seen in private law.[15] In the background are the agreements, but most in evidence is the *fides*. A promise (*sponsio*) made by the commander of the army had to be ratified by both the *populus* and the senate, otherwise it created obligations only for the general: the real treaty (*foedus*) was stipulated with the consent of the people and the senate by the representative of Rome who swore to respect the clauses of the treaty. The oath was, once again, the main device used to create obligations: just as a private perjury would have polluted the *pax deorum*, so that the community could avoid the wrath of the gods only by expelling the criminal, an international *sponsio* not ratified led to the general being handed over to the enemy, and the breach of a *foedus* would cause a war that—being "unjust" for the people at fault—could not count on the favor of the gods and was therefore hopeless (De Martino 1973; Cursi 2014).

AGREEMENTS IN CLASSICAL ROMAN LAW (THIRD CENTURY BCE–THIRD CENTURY CE)

The period of the so-called Etruscan monarchy (seventh to sixth centuries BCE) must have been a quite exceptional moment in Roman history. For the first time, Rome was included in the trades of the Mediterranean, and this obviously led to relevant changes in society. As already mentioned, in a time before the Etruscan kings, the community was composed of the *gentiles* and their *clientes*, devoted to the cultivation of the gentilician lands. The growing importance of Rome as a center of trade brought to the city a number of people from abroad, especially Etruscans and Greeks who, not being interested in agriculture, did not need to have access to the gentilician lands and thus did not become clients of the *gentiles*. This new social class, which would eventually take the name of *plebs*, found its place in the Roman constitution with the reforms of the Etruscan kings, who adopted the Greek model of the city-state and created an assembly of all citizens based on census, in imitation of the Solonian timocratic system.

In private law, however, there were very few changes. There were probably two separate worlds coexisting. On the one hand, the patricians and their clients kept on using the old *ius Quiritium*, as their economy had not drastically changed. On the other hand, the plebeians involved in international trade followed the law merchant in the Mediterranean markets. The *ius Quiritium* was protected by a procedure, organized by the city-state and governed by a magistrate, known as 'actions of the law' (*legis actiones*). On the contrary, the law merchant was probably protected only through private arbitrations: it may be significant that the Latin word *arbiter* seems to be borrowed from the Punic language, indicating a professional who acted in the markets as broker, witness, advisor, and arbitrator (Martino 1986).

Things really only changed between the end of the fourth and the first half of the second century BCE, with the growing importance of Rome both within Italy and the Mediterranean at large.[16] By this point, the Roman economy was no longer centered on agriculture: trade was also vital (Figure 4.4). It was both an economic and a social change. The struggles of the fifth and fourth centuries had led to the formation of a new aristocracy, the *nobilitas*, composed not only of the patriciate, but also of the most eminent plebeian families; below this class was the equestrian order, a bourgeoisie devoted to commerce and the production of goods, while at the bottom were the lower classes. The population had greatly increased and society had become so complex, that the social role of formal acts had become worthless. There was no longer need to use solemnity as a tool to help memory, because of the diffusion of writing in everyday life. This induced

FIGURE 4.4. Roman merchant ship. Source: Flickr / Carole Raddato / CC BY-SA 2.0.

the Republic to take care of informal transactions in international commerce and grant them, for the first time, judicial remedies.

The medium though which this new protection was granted was not the statutory law (*lex*), but the power (*imperium*) of the praetor, the magistrate who was in charge of the jurisdiction. He created a new civil procedure termed "formulary" because it was no longer based on the spoken word, but instead on written documents (*formulae*).

It is quite interesting, for our purposes, to notice how the structure of this new procedure was based on the agreement between the parties (Fiori 2003b: 67, 121). In the old *legis actiones*, the judge was a private citizen whom the magistrate asked "to show the *ius*" (*iudicare*): he had no command over the parties, so that the binding force of his verdict was based completely on the *ius Quiritium* that the judge had "shown." In other words, the verdict was binding not because of some "power" of the judge, but because the sentence revealed the law, which was itself binding. The new formulary procedure was instead created by the praetor to protect transactions or economic positions which were considered foreign to the *ius*: therefore, in the absence of a "law" to be executed and of a power of the judge, the verdict would be completely ineffective. The solution was found by asking the parties to exchange promises, written in the *formula*, that they would carry out the sentence. The binding force of the verdict was therefore in the agreement between the parties to accept the sentence of the judge: if the judge established that the defendant was wrong, the latter should pay to the plaintiff a sum of money equal to the value of the claim; if he was found to be right, the claimant should consider him free from his promise. Because of the structure of this procedure, the judgment took into account the controversy, but was properly directed to ascertain whether or not the promised sum of money was due: this is the reason for the strange rule in the formulary procedure, that the judge could never order the specific performance, but only condemn the defendant to a monetary redress. It was a development of the archaic idea of self-condemnation that is typical of the oath: the *pater* could not take orders from the public magistrates as to his personal affairs if it was not provided by the law. Thus, he was asked to voluntarily take upon himself the duty to redress the other party if the judgment went against him. When it became apparent that this new procedure, less formal than the *legis actiones*, could also be profitably used for the claims of *ius civile*, the *legis actiones* were doomed and at the beginning of the Principate they were abrogated. At this stage, the whole judicial protection of Roman law was ultimately founded on the agreement between the parties to the case.

Thanks to this new procedure, the praetor could now provide judicial remedies not only to the *ius Quiritium*, but also to institutions perceived by the Romans as existent in the law of every people (*ius gentium*) and to a number of economic needs completely foreign to the *ius*. When these needs found protection in the tribunal of the praetor, they started to be perceived in some way as legal institutions, and were collectively called "praetorian law" (*ius praetorium*) because their protection was based on the praetor's power.

At this moment, private transactions could also be relevant if they were not covered by a formal act, and the purpose of the act—loan, sale, hire, etc.—came into focus. The way the Roman jurists describe this system is, however, still tied to how the obligation arises. Gaius, a Roman jurist of the second century CE, writes that four kinds of obligations may arise from a contract: some are contracted by conduct, others verbally, by the very fact of writing down the obligation, or by consent (*re, verbis, litteris, consensu*) (Gaius, *Institutes* 3.89). In a loan (*mutuum, commodatum*) or a *depositum*, the obligation arises only when the thing to be loaned or given in custody is handed over; in a *stipulatio*, similar to the *sponsio*, but open to foreigners, the obligation arises through formal utterances; in the *nomina transscripticia*, only when the debt is written down in the *pater familias*' account book; in sale, hire, partnership, and mandate, it is enough that the parties agree to the obligation.

It is important to note that Gaius does not speak of "contracts," but of "contracted obligations." Even if the importance of the agreement is more apparent than before, the idea of the social bond, the duty to perform, is still more relevant: while in modern law the contract "is" the agreement and the obligations are only its effect, in Roman law the contract "is" the obligation and the agreement is its—albeit necessary— precondition (Fiori 2012: 40–75). The contract, as already stated, is not seen as the expression of the liberty of the parties to dispose of their wealth, but as the justification for the creation of a duty upon a *pater familias*. In the new Roman society, this has become quite normal, but in the concept of contract we probably still find the remnants of the ancient feeling that only the *pater familias* himself could limit his autonomy (Figure 4.5). When even in the formulary procedure any sentence was carried out against the whole of the defendant's property, which was sold to satisfy the creditor, and a declaration of *infamia* was issued against the insolvent debtor (Kaser and Hackl 1996: 383-407), we understand that the social importance of undertaking a duty was far greater than the simple economic relevance of the debt.

The centrality of obligation is further demonstrated by the doctrine of the *conventio* as outlined by the jurist Ulpian in the third century CE (Ulpianus 4, *On the edict*, Digest 2.14.7 pr. 2 and 4). He writes that simple agreements (*pacta*) do not give rise to any obligation, therefore they do not receive protection in the formulary procedure but can

FIGURE 4.5. Stipulation of a contract or will (Italy, Rome, Museo della Civiltà Romana, first century CE). Source: DEA / A. DAGLI ORTI / Getty Images.

only be referred to by the defendant in his defense. To create an obligation and to be therefore protected by an action, the agreement must match a specific type (*nomen*) of contract—the ones that Gaius described in the passage cited above. However, even if this does not happen, the agreement gives rise to an obligation, and therefore to an action, if because of it one of the parties has suffered a loss (*causa*): in this case, the contract is "atypical" but nonetheless is a "contract." It is quite clear, from this doctrine, that the praetor did not protect, with actions, the agreements in themselves, but only the obligations that might arise from them: the *res publica* chose to give the strongest remedy only to those pacts which were socially or economically relevant.

That the classical conception of contract is a novelty still full of archaic features can be seen also in the transformation of the idea of *fides*. As has been said, in archaic law *fides* was the reliability of each member of society, calculated on his social position: the *boni*, the rich and respectable people, had *fides* to the highest degree. This idea of reliability was, of course, based on personal acquaintance. However, in the society of imperialistic Rome and in its international trade, the parties were often strangers both to each other and to the judge: it was impossible to know who was the more reliable and to ascertain the duties of the contracting parties according to their actual status. The Roman jurists thus substituted for the concrete and personal archaic *fides* an abstract and impersonal new *fides*, which was modelled on the reliability of a *bonus vir* and was therefore called *bona fides*. When the parties agreed to adopt a certain contractual scheme, they were automatically bound to all the inherent duties, even if not expressly enumerated: "good faith" was the principle by which it was possible to take account of the implied terms of the contract, and to judge as if the parties were both *boni*. This may seem a "democratic" solution. In some ways it is: but if we think about it, it is the aristocratic ethics that is still dominant, being pervasive also in the more modern fields of law, such as commerce. It is an ambiguous representation, that we can decipher when we read one of the most important treatises on Roman ethics of this time, Cicero's *de officiis*. All those who follow the traditional ethics of the ruling class, are *boni cives*; those who follow the conservative parties are *optimates*, but only those who are truly part of the ruling class are socially *boni* and *optimi* (Fiori 2011a; Fiori 2014a). It is, as we can see, a long-term history in the sense set out by Fernand Braudel: even in the world economy of imperialistic Rome, the core values outlined by the priests based on Indo-European concepts are still operating centuries later.

There were, however, also important innovations. During the second century BCE, Hellenistic philosophy influenced the Roman higher classes. This process was already advanced by the last century of the Republic, when it was common for the young *nobiles* to travel to Athens or to other Greek cities to study. As for the science of law, it is probably an exaggeration to talk about a "Hellenistic period" of Roman jurisprudence (Schulz 1953), since the latter already had a strong intellectual tradition, and the influence of Greek philosophy was generally confined to the adoption of some new methods for the distribution of the subject matter, such as the use of definitions. However, in some cases, Greek philosophical doctrines affected also the substantive law. Indeed, we must consider that at that time philosophy was not a science among others, but was "the" science: it comprised not only logic, ethics, metaphysics, but also what we call today "hard sciences" such as mathematics, physics, and astronomy. If a jurist was asked to give a legal solution that involved knowledge of one of these subjects, he had to look to philosophy. One example will suffice. For some lawyers, if someone asked a goldsmith to make him a ring, the contract might have a different nature depending on whether or not a transfer of ownership occurred: if the gold was provided by the goldsmith, the property passed to the client, and the contract was a sale; if, instead, the gold was supplied by the client, there was no transfer of ownership, and the contract was a hire. However, in a building contract, even if the materials were given by the builder, the contract was a hire if the house was built on land belonging to the client: in fact, according to Stoic philosophy, the latter had given that part of the *res* which did not change notwithstanding its transformation (*substantia*).[17]

The influence of Greek culture was also felt in international law. As previously mentioned, among the peoples of Italy there were enough common customs and cults that, until the third century BCE, Rome could use a set of rules quite congruent with its legal and religious traditions. However, when Roman hegemony expanded over the Mediterranean, it had to adapt to Greek diplomatic models. Rome maintained the legal forms of the international treaties (De Martino 1973: 13), but the content of the agreements changed: until the third century BCE the relationships were based on an "alliance" (*societas*) that had a military meaning; after that date the treaties speak of "friendship" (*amicitia*), a notion of good relations in peacetime that was borrowed from the Greek *philia*, although it relied on a traditional Roman concept (Cursi 2013: 195).

Marriage, however, was still strongly dependent on ancient Roman customs. To find a solution to the ethical and social disorder of the late Republic, at the beginning of the Principate, Augustus issued some laws directed towards retrieving the importance of *dignitas* in marriage.[18] It was therefore stated that the freeborn could not marry actresses, prostitutes, women found guilty in public trials, and that the senators could not marry even freedwomen. In these cases, as before, the only honorable union was concubinate: even in the advanced society of the Empire, agreements seem to be more a social than a private affair.

AGREEMENTS IN LATE ROMAN LAW (FOURTH TO FIFTH CENTURIES CE)

From the second half of the third century CE, the Empire underwent a significant transformation.[19] The Principate had been, at least formally, a continuation of the Republican constitution, even if the centralization of power had gradually brought in the adoption of bureaucratic methods of government. This also affected the role of the jurist, who became part of the imperial chancery. When the emperor declared himself "Lord and God" (*dominus et deus*), the Empire took the form of a Dominate. The monarch was portrayed as the only source of law, and jurisprudence lost its critical force: it is "the bureaucratic period," a time of codifications and statutes, not of commentaries and responses (Schulz 1953).

All this was in line with the general conditions of the economy and society of the time: the crisis of the slave system brought about an increase of free laborers, who suffered in many cases a social and legal diminution and were bound, along with their descendants, to their professions. It was a static system, with strong social gaps, which led to the final dissolution of the political structures of the Republic and the Principate.

A role was also played by Christianity, whose universalistic ideals dissolved the close correspondence between religion and the organization of the city that was typical of Roman religion (Scheid 2013). The idea that all men are equal before God interfered with the Roman conception of marriage, and the prohibitions of the Augustan legislation were still followed in the fourth and fifth centuries to prevent the marriage of a senator with women of very low status or of reproachable behavior (*Codex Theodosianus* 4.6.3 in 336 CE), but in the sixth century even these limitations were refused by Justinian's laws (*Novellae* 117.6 in 542 CE). However, the classic Roman idea that the will of husband and wife to be married should be continuous, and that when it was over they could divorce at any time, was substituted for the Christian principle that marriage was indissoluble, and that the initial agreement was forever binding.

This is also the time of the so-called "vulgar law," i.e., a simplified approach to the classical categories (Levy 1956). As for contract law, the fourfold distribution of contracts formulated by Gaius was no longer understood, and the moment of the arising of the obligation was identified in all contracts with the agreement, while the conduct, the words and the writings were all reduced to formal requirements. This attention to the inner dimension of the will is probably due to philosophical and Christian influences, and has the effect of stressing the importance of the scope of the contract, identified with its *causa* (Kaser 1975: 366).

Justinianic reverence towards antiquity will revive some classical ideas, but an irreversible process has been triggered: Antiquity is at its end, and with it the ancient system of values.

CHAPTER 5

Arguments

DAVID MIRHADY

SPEECH WRITING

In his play *Clouds,* the comic writer Aristophanes suggests that if his comic hero Strepsiades (who is a dunce) trained with Socrates as a speechwriter he could earn popularity, as well as considerable sums of money (*Clouds* 466–468). His is only the first of a number of texts that suggest skepticism and even hostility about the perceived corruption of speechwriting (or "logography"), the activity that exemplifies Greek legal argumentation.[1] The essayist and rhetorician Isocrates seems embarrassed to admit that he ever had any connection with the courts (Isocrates 15.36–8) despite the six forensic speeches (16–21) that are attributed to him on good authority. Aeschines criticizes Demosthenes simply by referring to him as "a certain speechwriter" (1.94; cf. 2.180) and by mentioning that he teaches techniques of speech that include deception (1.117, 170). He also levels a charge against Demosthenes in his capacity as private logographer that has vexed every commentator on Demosthenes ever since, namely, that Demosthenes wrote a speech for the banker Pasion, presumably our Demosthenes 36, and then revealed its contents to Pasion's opponent Apollodorus (Aesch. 2.165; cf. Plutarch, *Dem.* 15.1–2), for whom he wrote our Demosthenes 45. Speeches 36 and 45, if they are actually both by Demosthenes, do show a remarkable flexibility on the part of a single individual to invent powerful arguments that both praise and vilify the same individuals (Figure 5.1).

Universally recognized as the greatest of Athenian speechwriters, Demosthenes himself appears to have been sensitive to criticism of his involvement in others' private disputes. At the end of the speech *Against Zenothemis* (32.32), the speaker, Demon, admits that Demosthenes, his relative, helped him with his arguments, and he quotes

FIGURE 5.1. Bronze juror's identification ticket (*pinakion*), inscribed with name, patronymic, and deme, fourth century BCE. This identification ticket carries the juror's name: Demophanes; the first letters of his father's name: Phil.... ; and his deme: Kephisia. Source: American School of Classical Studies at Athens: Agora Excavations.

what Demosthenes said to him when asked for help: he denied ever having come forward to plead any private cases since he entered political life. In another speech, however, these scruples do not prevent Demosthenes from using Lacritus' activity as a teacher of law court pleading against him (35.41). The rhetorician Anaximenes also includes advice about how to deal with this issue in his handbook (*Rhetoric to Alexander* 36.37–42). There is no doubt, however, that from the time of his debut on the forensic stage, Demosthenes distinguished himself as its master. His own legal campaign to recover the inheritance left to him by his father, which is documented by no fewer than five surviving speeches (27–31), is a *tour de force*. It served not only to win his dispute, even if he did not recover his entire legacy (Plutarch, *Demosthenes* 6.1–2), but also helped to advertise his skills to a broad range of clients who kept him employed writing speeches for them for much of the rest of his life.

DOCUMENTARY EVIDENCE AND ATHENIAN DEMOCRACY

What made Demosthenes' argumentation so effective was not simply his abilities with language and narrative (although these are estimable and were as highly admired in antiquity as they are today) (Jaeger 1938; Pearson 1976: 39–74), but his mastery of the technical aspects of law. In particular, his success was due to his employment of the various forms of documentary evidence that were available to the Athenian logographer: documents such as laws, witness testimony, contracts, and challenges. These documents, and the arguments that surround them in the speeches from the Athenian courts, are important windows into the culture of democratic Athens. The laws themselves testify to the Athenians' devotion to the law, echoing important claims in the historians Herodotus and Thucydides, in Greek tragedy, and elsewhere (Herodotus 7.104.4; Thucydides 2.37; Euripides, *Suppliants* 306–313, 434–437). Witness testimony was offered by any free adult male who was present at the incident in question and so knew the truth, without regard to his economic status or citizenship. Contracts provide glimpses of commercial life, and challenges to torture slaves, which occur frequently in the speeches although none is ever accepted and carried through, illustrate the lives of slaves and how their status was defined by their vulnerability to violence. Challenges to settle disputes based on oath-swearing often refer to facts known by a woman, who could not appear in court to give witness testimony, and who otherwise would rarely make an appearance in any kind of public venue aside from religious festivals.

As Demosthenes himself points out in his first speech, he is competing against opponents who are not only adept at speaking—by which he is presumably referring to their abilities with language and narrative—but who are proficient in preparing their cases (27.2). They understand their position vis-à-vis the law, the need to collect witnesses, and the strategies to be employed in documenting maneuvers employed at preliminary hearings. In the democratic courts of fourth-century BCE Athens, as much as character invective, emotional pleas, probability arguments, and cogent narrative played their roles, it was the successful preparation and employment of documentary evidence that was the key to success. Demosthenes says in defense of himself in the political sphere: "the man who prepares what he is going to say is the true democrat" (Plutarch, *Demosthenes* 8).[2] Aristophanes puts an exclamation point on it: his comic litigant Strepsiades says that if he was going to lose a case because he had no witnesses, he would hang himself (*Clouds* 776–780).

There is some irony in Aristotle's description of such documentary evidence as "artless proofs" (*atechnoi pisteis*).³ The term reveals that for him they were forms of argumentation that lay outside the rhetorical craft or *technê* of the orator. They were formulated by someone other than the speechwriter and delivered intermittently by the court secretary during breaks in the oral delivery of the litigant's speech (Mirhady 1991a: 5–28). Aristotle's characterization of the documents as "artless" stems both from the fifth-century sophists, who privileged arguments based on probability over more formal means of proof and dispute resolution,⁴ such as oath swearing, and from a fairly widespread distrust among elite circles regarding statements committed to writing. From the end of the fifth century BCE, when the ideology of Athenian democracy saw a pronounced shift away from the unchecked popular sovereignty of the democratic Assembly to one limited by the sovereign authority of law (Ostwald 1989 170, 303–320; Harris 1994: 130–152), especially written law (Andocides 1.87), the written word took on ever-increasing importance within the Athenian judicial framework.⁵ The Athenians learned their lessons partly from illegal decisions that were rashly taken by the democratic Assembly when it conducted trials against Athenian generals and executed several of them for minor mistakes. That bit of illegality led in 404 BCE to a bitter defeat against Sparta in the long Peloponnesian War. Power was then seized by the "Thirty Tyrants," who themselves arbitrarily executed many of their democratic opponents. Fidelity to the law became a watchword when the democracy was re-established shortly afterwards.

First and foremost there was the text of the laws themselves, which each juror was sworn to uphold as part of his oath as a judge (Mirhady 2007). As Carey writes, "the juror's oath, and the strenuous efforts of Athenian litigants to prove that the law supports their stance on the subject at issue, indicate that the jurors did feel bound by the law and that for the most part they consciously sought to make their decisions conform to the law" (1996: 34 fn 8).⁶ Simultaneously with the shift to the sovereignty of law, the advent of public arbitration forced a further commitment to the written word (Harrell 1936). Almost all private disputes had to be heard first before a democratically selected (i.e., by lottery) public arbitrator ([Aristotle], *Constitution of the Athenians* 53.4–5). Unlike the private arbitrator, who was often empowered by the parties in dispute to impose a resolution on them, the public arbitrator's decision could be appealed. What gave his role special force, however, was that only the evidence that had been produced before him, committed to writing and deposited in his evidence jar (Figure 5.2), could subsequently be brought before a democratic court (*Constitution of the Athenians* 53.2; cf. Demosthenes 54.27). All evidence thus had to be committed to writing and disclosed both to the arbitrator and to the opponents. This process of committing evidence emanates from sometime in the 370s BCE, when it appears that witnesses were no longer required to give testimony in court (Bonner 1905). While their presence was still required, they did not speak: their pre-recorded testimony was simply read aloud to the court by the court secretary. Demosthenes describes the situation:

> having given his testimony with the other witnesses (at the arbitration), he made no denial of the fact, when, standing by the plaintiff's side in the popular court, he heard his testimony read. (29.18)⁷

From this passage, it is apparent that the witness in court does not even have to affirm what is read. If he wanted to deny it, he would have had to do so under oath.

Among the canon of Attic (i.e., Athenian) orators' writings that survive, Demosthenes' are the first to have been composed only after the final great shift to written evidence

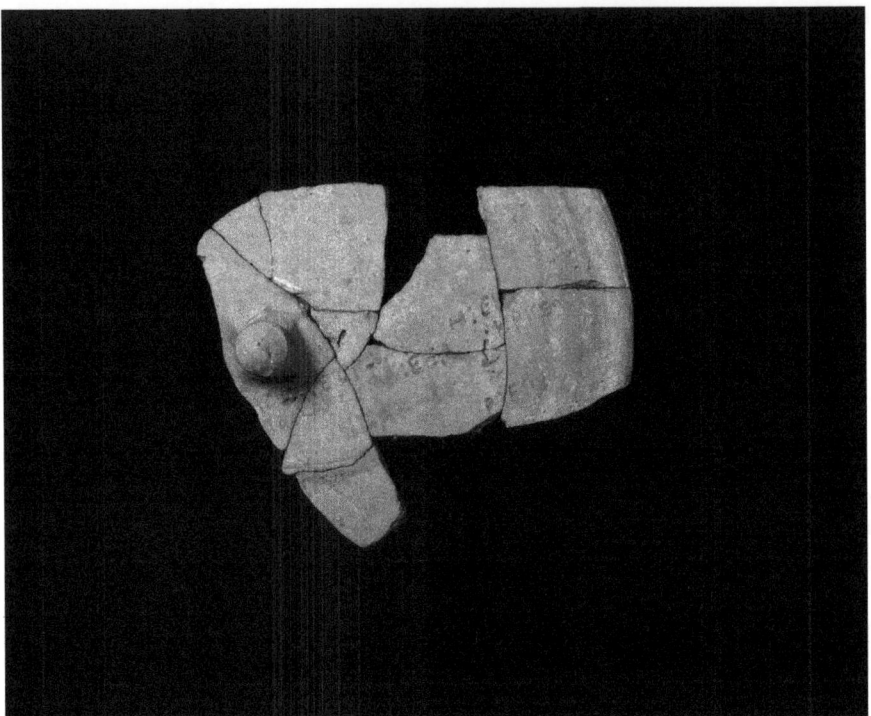

FIGURE 5.2. Fragment of the inscribed lid of a cooking pot with dipinto, fourth century BCE, which seems to list documents that were stored in the pot until needed for a trial. The text reads: "Of the written copies, the following four are inside: *diamartyria* (testimony) from the *anakrisis* (preliminary hearing), law on the abuse of heiresses, challenge of testimony, oaths of litigants; Antenor put the lid on." Names of litigants and, possibly, other relevant persons follow. Source: American School of Classical Studies at Athens: Agora Excavations.

is complete. The earlier orators, Antiphon, Andocides, Lysias, Isocrates, and Isaeus, all employed *atechnoi pisteis* to some extent, but Demosthenes is the first to be able to exploit the full ramifications of the shift.[8] With a convert's zeal, Demosthenes' devotion to the use of these documents also far outstrips that of his later contemporaries, Aeschines, Lycurgus, Hyperides, and Dinarchus.[9] The earlier speechwriters all relied on witnesses who stood before the court and said something—we do not know what exactly—which confirmed the truth of something the litigant claimed. Perhaps they said as little as "what he said is true." Demosthenes, however, had a fixed, written document read aloud, whose precise meaning and consequences everyone present could assess and whose content both parties to the dispute were aware of in advance. He emphasizes this point in *Against Stephanus* (45.44–5):

> bear in mind that the reason why the law requires people to give evidence in written form is that it may not be open to them to strike out any part of what has been written, or to add anything to it ... Who will ever be convicted of giving false testimony, if he is to depose to what he pleases, and be accountable only for what he pleases? No, the law does not thus make a distinction in these matters, and you must not listen to such

a thing either. The straightforward and honest course is this: What stands written? To what have you deposed? Show that this is true. For you have written in your plea in answer to the complaint these words, "I have given true testimony in testifying to what is contained in the deposition"—not "to this or that in the deposition."

The rhetorical handbooks of Aristotle and Anaximenes lay out systematic advice about how to argue both for and against each item of documentary evidence,[10] but these are somewhat compromised by a freedom of thought that stems from their development in a classroom. Their advice is not necessarily practical, since much of it would be unpalatable in an Athenian court. Arguments that Aristotle recommends against written laws, for instance, are not found in the Attic orators at all.[11] However, when Aristotle gives a conceptual framework both for when argumentation is needed against statute law and for when it is needed in favor of statute law, his recommendations do suggest lines of argumentation that are reflected in the law court speeches, namely, "that justice is something true and beneficial."[12] Although Aristotle's point is that speakers might argue against the law on this basis, in fact they seem to recruit these lines to argue in conformity to the laws.

The source for the argumentation that truth and justice coincide may be an oath that prosecuting litigants had to swear after winning a conviction in homicide cases: "the winner must cut up the cuttings, and swear to the vote—and this is traditional for us still even now—that those judges who voted for him voted what is true and just" (Aeschines 2.87).[13] Sometimes such argumentation seems to reflect what is supposed to be correct evidentiary procedure (rather than oratory) (Antiphon 6.18, 6.24, 6.26, 6.32; Demosthenes 18.271, 31.3; Dinarchus 1.1, 11; cf. Dem. 23.147). Indeed, the juxtaposition of "truth" and "justice" seems in general to reflect questions of fact and law: "What need was there for pretexts, speeches, special pleas? Justice is plain, the truth easy, and the proof brief" (Lycurgus 1.33).[14]

THE ARGUMENT THAT JUSTICE IS TRUE AND BENEFICIAL

Aeschines and Demosthenes trace the argument that laws are just and beneficial back to the lawgiver Solon: "you enact the laws in all cases with regard to what is just, not for the sake of unjust profit or favour or enmity, but looking solely to what is just and beneficial" (cf. Demosthenes 20.94, 22.11). Sometimes, however, it is recognized that laws have to be *interpreted* in a way that is "beneficial": "it is the function both of a good citizen and of a just judge to interpret the laws in such a way that for the rest of time he will benefit the city" (Lysias 14.4).[15] The speaker makes explicit the idea that the verdict be just, and that it be beneficial for the judges themselves (Hyperides 2.13). Of course, the judges are, in a sense, agents for the city. The just and beneficial verdict may also provide a harsh lesson for wrongdoers (cf. Aeschines 1.196, 3.8; Demosthenes 48.58; Isocrates 18.35).

Just as speakers argue that justice and what is beneficial should be a concern to the judges, they also argue that they themselves are similarly motivated: "I have now helped as much as has been my part of the prosecution, disregarding everything other than justice and what is beneficial to you" (Dinarchus 1.114).[16] One speaker even seems willing to bend the law against himself if it serves the common interest: "if I am acquitted of the charges, by justice, law, and what is beneficial, do not abandon me to the savagery of the prosecutors. But if by dying I contribute at all, as these men say, to the common safety, I am ready to die" (Demades 1.4). Of course the opposite motivations are attributed to the opponent (Demosthenes 18.82, 18.277, 19.132, 57.5).

So much for argumentation about the laws themselves.

OTHER FORMS OF EVIDENCE

For the other documents, the speechwriters likely took as their starting point the simple list of documents placed in the evidence jar after the arbitration or the *anakrisis*, the preliminary hearing before the magistrate. This list consisted of the written charge (*enklêma*), witness testimony (*martyria*) and challenges (*proklêseis*) to settle the dispute based either on the torture of a slave or an oath being sworn (*Constitution of the Athenians* 53.2). In Aristotle's canonical treatment of these documents in *Rhetoric* 1.15, the written charge gives way to a discussion of laws. The discussion of witness testimony expands into a discussion of both witness testimony and contracts (since a contract's credibility depends in any case on its being supported by witness testimony and its persuasive function rests on its being somewhat like a private law between the contracting parties). Challenges give way to discussions of torture and oath, the dispute-ending procedures about which challenges are typically made. The practical reality of such argumentation differs markedly in many respects from the prescriptions of the handbooks. The handbooks suggest, for instance, a clear break between narration of the events at issue and the proof for that narration. In the speeches, narrative and proof are closely integrated. In the earlier logographers, especially Lysias and Isaeus, narrative and proof appear to be largely directed by the narrative strategies of the writers, documentary evidence appearing in a largely ancillary role. In Demosthenes this independence disappears: the documentary evidence itself provides the roadmap to the narrative. Likewise, Aristotle gives pride of place to his "artistic proofs" (*entechnoi pisteis*), arguments based on circumstantial evidence (*tekmêria*) and probabilities (*eikota*), from the character of the speaker, and from the emotional response of the listeners.

In his private speeches, Demosthenes reverses this order. Indeed, Aristotle himself admits that documentary evidence is found in law court speeches in particular (*Rhetoric* 1.15.1). As Demosthenes says to the judges at the end of his second speech *Against Aphobus*, "you have heard sufficient proofs from witnesses, from evidence, and from probabilities" (Dem. 28.23; cf. 30.25). Written witness testimony is his proof par excellence. In the public trials (cf. Dem. 18–26), however, the facts of the cases give way to political considerations (Figure 5.3).

DEMOSTHENES' ARGUMENTS

In the following pages, I want to retrace some of Demosthenes' argumentation in the speeches that he wrote concerning his own inheritance. His strategies vary according to the situation, but his devotion to the use of documentary evidence is clear throughout. From the beginning of his first speech *Against Aphobus* (27), Demosthenes has his opponent over a barrel. He attacks every material aspect of his case and backs up each line of argument, first with admissions (*homologiai*) wrested from Aphobus (Demosthenes 27.10, 24, 34, 39, 42–43), and then with witness testimony that confutes each point in what is left of Aphobus' defense (27.8, 17, 22, 25–26, 28, 33, 41, 46). Aphobus is one of three guardians to whom Demosthenes' father entrusted his estate until Demosthenes came of age. According to Demosthenes, they have stolen almost everything, so he has

FIGURE 5.3. A Klepsydra (waterclock) used to time speeches in the Athenian courts. Original in front with replica above showing the flow of water out of the top pot into the lower one. Source: American School of Classical Studies at Athens: Agora Excavations.

initiated litigation against each of them. Demosthenes clearly had to anticipate the need for such witness testimony long before his encounter at the popular court, and he laid the foundations for his case early. The witnesses he provides, despite what has been written by Sally Humphreys (1985) and Stephen Todd (1991 and 1993: 19–39; 96–97), are not necessarily partisan.[17] Many were admittedly friends and relatives of Demosthenes, but his opponents were also supposed to belong to this circle. Most of Demosthenes' witnesses cannot even be identified from the text of the speech, though of course they would have been identified in the text of the testimony itself, which we do not have. Like so much else in democratic Athens the identity and status of the witness, besides his being a free male, and likely a citizen, was irrelevant (Mirhady 2002). A witness was similar to the judges who were to decide the case; he was simply a free man, though one who had some relevant, specific knowledge. Some of the judges are already familiar with the broad outlines of the case, so Demosthenes can claim them as friendly for his side, implicitly calling on them as his witnesses (57; cf. 29.49). Where Demosthenes is not in a position to produce witnesses, such as on the point of his maternal grandfather's indebtedness, he makes clear that this is due to a trick by his opponents, which left him with no time to locate a knowledgeable witness. Only then does he resort to other forms of evidence (*tekmêria*: 28.2).

In his construction of the events of his case, Demosthenes must teach (*didaskein*: 27.3) the judges not only about the events themselves, but what sorts of evidence about those events are most significant (*megistos*), precisely accurate (*akribos*), and clear (*saphos, phaneros*). He thus constructs several hierarchies of evidence, which vary somewhat according to the circumstances of the case and the sorts of evidence available. In his first speeches against Aphobus, his opponents themselves are at the top of his list. They are his "greatest" (*megistoi*) witnesses as they once registered Demosthenes' estate in the highest tax bracket (27.7; cf. 28.4), even if they were compelled to do so because the size of the estate made it impossible to hide (27.8). Demosthenes' description of his opponents as "witnesses" involves, of course, an obvious conceit; the opponents do not appear as witnesses (*martyres*) in the technical sense at all. No statement from them will be read aloud in court stating that they had entered him in the highest tax bracket. Nevertheless they did do so, and nobody denies it. Beyond the significance (namely, probative value) of the evidence, the second hierarchy involves accuracy or extent of detail (*akribeia*), as the judges must gain "accurate" knowledge (27.1, 7, 9). Thus, after the important but blunt evidence of the tax bracket, Demosthenes goes on to detail his father's precise property holdings (27.9–17). A third hierarchy involves the clarity of the presentation (27.1, 47–48), which results from the accumulation of points that are demonstrated in support of Demosthenes' claims.

ARGUMENTS BASED ON WITNESS TESTIMONY

Most of the witnesses whose testimony Demosthenes has read aloud are anonymous.[18] Someone, we do not know who, needs to say, for instance, that Aphobus was in charge of a factory that should have generated revenue of thirty *minae* per year (27.18). It seems likely that in all these cases, which involve partial admissions on the part of Aphobus, the witnesses were part of a preliminary hearing, perhaps a public arbitration, who were there for the express purpose of witnessing what exactly each party said under questioning: "take and read for them these testimonies of those before whom they answered" (27.41).

Admissions (*homologiai*) are particularly powerful because of the Athenian principle that those things upon which there is an admission are binding (*kyria*; cf. Demosthenes 56.2 and Isocrates 18.24). The first witnesses that Demosthenes identifies, in speech 27, are the two guardians he has not yet charged, Demophon and Therippides, and his uncle (by marriage) Demochares, though he claims there are many other (unnamed) witnesses (27.14, 18). Aphobus admitted to Demochares certain facts of the case, to which Demochares now gives witness (27.15). Demosthenes places repeated emphasis on the fact that Aphobus gave written acknowledgement to the other guardians that he had received a dowry, though he does not produce this document (27.14, 16). He is also able to make use of the accounts that were submitted in writing by his guardians (27.19) and of answers that they gave, in the form of transcribed testimony, at preliminary hearings (27.42). The fact that his opponents disagree among themselves in the recorded documents adds particular weight to Demosthenes' position (27.43; cf. 28.3). He ridicules the immateriality of the points supported by Aphobus' witnesses (25–26) and Aphobus' inability to provide witnesses on the material points (27.21, 49, 51, 54, 28.1): "demand that he provide witnesses on each point" (27.51). Aphobus' witnesses' testimony about the baseness of Moeriades' character is a red herring; they ought to be saying where

Demosthenes' slaves are. Aphobus also ought to have witnesses for goods delivered (27.21). It is important to recognize that Demosthenes does not impugn Aphobus' witnesses directly; he simply argues that their testimony is immaterial.

Too much has been made of the possible corruptibility of witnesses in Athens (Cohen 1995: 107); the references to it are relatively rare. Where they occur, as in *Against Onetor 1* and *Against Conon*, the false witnesses are described as having been in league with the opponent throughout; they are co-conspirators against the speaker. Demosthenes argues that while Aphobus has made various statements, he has given no demonstration, no *epideixis*, of them, the *epideixis* to consist of witness testimony (27.51). Demosthenes makes no demand here for witnesses of a particular status or impartiality; he simply demands witnesses.

ARGUMENTS BASED ON WILLS

While arguing his case, Demosthenes is, of course, like all litigants, constructing a rhetorical epistemology, a system, supported by arguments, whereby some sources of knowledge are deemed more credible than others for persuasive reasons. In the epistemology that Demosthenes constructs, it is interesting to note his argument that more accurate or exact (*akribesteron*) knowledge could actually be gained, not just from witnesses' testimony, but from the text of his father's will, which has gone missing:

> You would, however, have had more exact knowledge of the matter, if they had been willing to give up to me the will which my father left; for it contained (so my mother tells me) a statement of all the property that my father left, along with instructions regarding the funds from which these men were to take what had been given them, and regarding the letting of the property. (27.40)

Aristotle, strangely, makes no provision for wills in his scheme of *atechnoi pisteis*; it is likely that he saw them as a form of contract, which, in turn, he considered a sort of particular law (*Rhetoric* 1.15.21). Demosthenes employs arguments about laws twice in *Against Aphobus 1*. The first time he simply refers to a law that expresses the commonly known Athenian principle that dowry monies in arrears are owed 18 percent interest (27.17). The second time he actually has several laws read aloud (27.58). The interpretation of them has been vexed, but Demosthenes argues, based on inference from them, that his guardians were required to lease out his estate at a rate that would have realized about 12 percent per annum. The result would be an enormous sum.

ARGUMENTS BASED ON CHALLENGES

On close examination, Demosthenes' employment of these laws appears unclear and hardly to his credit. Such a precipitous increase in the value of the estate seems wishful thinking. But the judges do not have the benefit of close examination. Within the overall context of his arguments it is important for Demosthenes that he simply appear faithful to the letter of the law, to be using the law on his side. In response to questioning by both Demosthenes and the public arbitrator, Aphobus appears to have issued Demosthenes a challenge, saying that he was willing to show that Demosthenes' estate was worth ten talents and that if it was not, Aphobus would make up the difference (27.50–2). Aphobus then placed some testimony concerning his challenge into the evidence jar. Demosthenes clearly did not accept the challenge, since it was predicated on a claim by Aphobus—that such ten talents represented all the items that belonged to the estate—that he had not yet demonstrated.

In this speech, moreover, Demosthenes is not interested in arguing on the basis of challenges. They are typically used when a dispute hangs on information that is known by a slave, who could be tortured, or a woman, who might swear an oath. Demosthenes parries the thrust of Aphobus' challenge first by saying that Aphobus should simply demonstrate his claim to the arbitrator, and then by claiming that the challenge was immaterial (27.52), a desperate act by his opponent when he was backed into a corner both by Demosthenes and by the impartial public arbitrator, who had asked a series of tough questions (27.50). But Demosthenes refers to no challenges of his own, since in this case he does not need them. The challenge belongs to the realm of extra-judicial settlement, to which private arbitration also belongs. It is an informal, oral realm of dispute resolution, governed by the traditional rules of aristocratic culture that had existed in Athens for hundreds of years.[19] In the first sentence of his speech, Demosthenes makes clear that Aphobus' actions have precluded a settlement within that realm (27.1). The private arbitrators that might have intervened would have been intimates (*oikeioi*) of both sides and thus have had clear knowledge upon which to decide between them. Since the democratic judges have no direct, accurate knowledge, Demosthenes must construct an epistemology that is based not on intimate familiarity, but on the rules of the democratic court. In the subsequent speeches, of course, he will have to make recourse to arguments based on challenges, indeed, challenges which he made even before the first speech and which he might have used in it but did not.

EX TEMPORE ARGUMENTS?

Against Aphobus 2 (Demosthenes 28) continues the same dispute and was delivered in response to Aphobus' first speech in defense of himself before the popular court. It therefore raises questions about the extent to which the text that we have actually reflects the arguments that Demosthenes must, to some extent, have had to extemporize. One result of this would be, of course, that he could not rely to the same extent on prepared, written testimony. What he does use is recycled: the same testimony that is read at 27.8 is read again at 28.10, and so on. The thrust of Demosthenes' speech is directed at answering a charge by Aphobus that Demosthenes' maternal grandfather had died indebted to the state (thereby making Demosthenes also a state debtor through inheritance). Again, however, the same hierarchy of proofs come forward. Demosthenes demands witnesses (28.1): "This is the pretence he uses; but he offered no witness testimony that my grandfather died indebted to the state." He also lays even greater emphasis on the missing will, which he now refers to as "witness testimony" (*martyria*) (28.5): "having destroyed such important witness testimony, they expect to be believed by you without any rational support." Demosthenes clarifies the close relationship between the credibility of the will and witness testimony: "it was necessary, as soon as my father died, to call in many witnesses and call on them to seal the will, so that if anything became disputed it would be possible to go to this text and discover the truth of everything" (28.5). Aphobus and the other guardians did actually produce documents to support their claims, lists that had been duly sealed. These Demosthenes dismisses as incomplete, simply memoranda from which many items that should have been in the will were left out (28.6). We may wonder whether these documents might not have had vastly more credibility than Demosthenes acknowledges.

ARGUMENTS CONCERNING FALSE TESTIMONY

Against Aphobus 3 (Demosthenes 29) was delivered sometime after the first two speeches.[20] Demosthenes won his first confrontation before the popular court. Now Aphobus has countered with a suit for false testimony against one of Demosthenes' previously unidentified witnesses. He has also dispersed his property to friends in an attempt to foil Demosthenes' attempts to get hold of it, so that he will have to litigate against Onetor, one such friend. In this suit, however, he is again faced with "teaching" (*didaskein*) the judges, so that they may learn "with greater accuracy" (*akribesteron*: 29.4), and many of the circumstances regarding evidence remain the same. This time, however, the suit concerns false testimony, so Demosthenes must face this issue head on. Aphobus claims that Demosthenes' witness, Phanus, lied when he testified that Aphobus admitted that Milyas, whom he had wanted to torture as a slave, was actually a freedman. Aphobus' brother Aesius had joined in this testimony with Phanus, but now recants (29.15). Demosthenes' arguments about his own motives for using Aesius' testimony and Aesius' current recantation reveal several things about witness testimony in general:

> He now denies it, because he has allied himself in the suit with Aphobus; but at that time he gave this testimony along with the other witnesses, for he had no desire to perjure himself, or to suffer the penalty which would straightway follow. Surely now, if I had been getting up false testimony, I would not have put this man in my list of witnesses, seeing that he was more intimate with Aphobus than with anyone else in the world, and knowing that he was going to plead for him in the suit, and that he was my adversary. It is not likely that one would call as witness to a false statement one who is an opponent, and a brother of his adversary. (Dem. 29.15)

Aesius was clearly a partisan of Aphobus, yet Demosthenes enlisted his testimony to Aphobus' admission that Milyas was a freedman. For Aesius to have refused to give testimony would have required his swearing an oath in which he would have had to claim that he did not know whether Aphobus had made this admission. His perjury would have been manifest—it was the sort of thing he was bound to know—and would likely have entailed legal penalties (see 49.20).[21] The arbitrator is likely to have played a role in compelling such testimony (cf. 29.20).

Demosthenes' discussion of the motives for false testimony (29.22–4), which, he claims, are absent for his own witnesses in this case, reveals some striking similarities with the accounts in the rhetorical handbooks of Aristotle and Anaximenes (Mirhady 1991a: 14–15). He says that his discussion is based on probabilities (*eikota*). Indeed, it is the sort of discussion one would find in handbooks about how to deal with this topic, since they also deal with probabilities. He lists three motives: bribery, friendship, and enmity, and these same three are mentioned as a group by Anaximenes (*Rhetoric to Alexander* 15.5). He also describes his witnesses as "respectable people" (29.24), which corresponds with Aristotle's "reputable" people (*Rhetoric* 1.15.19). Demosthenes also resorts to a challenge to torture a slave in this speech, which is somewhat necessitated by there being witnesses on both sides whose testimony conflicts:

> I knew, men of the jury, that I should find the whole contest centering about the witness testimony written in the document, and that it would be regarding the truth or falsehood of this that you would cast your votes, and I therefore determined that the first step for me to take was to offer Aphobus a challenge. What, then, did I do? I offered to surrender to him for examination by torture a slave who knew how to read

and write, and who had been present when Aphobus made the admission in question, and who wrote down the statement of the witness. This man had been ordered by me not to use any fraud or trickery, nor to write down some and suppress others of the statements made by the plaintiff regarding the matters at issue, but simply to write the absolute truth, and what Aphobus actually said. (Dem. 29.11)[22]

ARGUMENTS BASED ON TORTURE

The challenge was made in the marketplace, where there were many bystanders, some of whom have provided testimony. It was directed not only at Aphobus, but also at his brother Aesius (29.12, 17). Demosthenes has resorted to the challenge not only because of the conflicting testimony of witnesses, but also because the case concerns testimony that dealt with a previous challenge of Aphobus to torture a slave. Aphobus is thus caught equivocating about torture (*basanos*), which was universally approved as the surest form of proof in the ideology of the Athenian courts (29.14): "For he surely cannot claim this, that for some matters, which he himself wants, torture is clear, and for others it is not clear." Aphobus apparently counter-challenged with a different set of questions for the slave (29.13; cf. 50). Demosthenes dismisses this challenge as quickly as possible, emphasizing that the question he would have had put to the slave went to the central issue of the dispute, while Aphobus' fallacious demand concerns "other things." As he says later in the speech, "after passing over those who were admittedly slaves, he demanded to torture a free man, whom it would have been impious for me to surrender; he was not seeking to bring the matter to a test, but he wanted to make a specious argument out of the fact that his demand was refused" (29.39).

Aphobus apparently still considers Milyas a slave, despite Demosthenes' arguments that Aphobus had admitted him to be a freedman, and he has renewed his challenge to have him tortured (29.25). In response, Demosthenes has offered three female slaves for torture, who are old enough to remember that Demosthenes' father had manumitted him. Later, Demosthenes imagines that Milyas were still a slave and gives us one of our only arguments against the torture of a "slave" in Attic oratory: "let's picture Milyas being racked on the wheel, and let's examine what [Aphobus] would have hoped him to say. Would it not be that he did not know that this man had any of the money?" (29.40). The key words are "he did not know." Any challenge to torture a slave has to be premised with the claim that the slave does know. Demosthenes has provided many witnesses who testified that they did know that Aphobus had the money. Instead of charging them for false testimony, Aphobus has sought to get at this former slave, who does not know, and torture him (Figure 5.4).

FIGURE 5.4. Inscribed jurors' ballots, fourth century B.C. One ballot has a solid axle, the other a hollow axle. Source: American School of Classical Studies at Athens: Agora Excavations.

ARGUMENTS BASED ON OATHS AND TORTURE

To this Demosthenes added a further challenge, to have his own mother swear an oath regarding the manumission (29.26). This form of oath-challenge was the strongest way for the statements of a woman to come forward, since women could not appear as witnesses in court. Because women exercised few political rights in Athens, they also did not witness as many events as women in other cultures might. Indeed, Athenians must also have been loath to subject the women of their families to public scrutiny by having them swear such oaths. But in this case, the challenge was made in what was essentially a family squabble, since Aphobus was a cousin of Demosthenes (and was supposed to have married Demosthenes' mother according to the wishes of Demosthenes' deceased father). Demosthenes' mention of her is brief and to the point. He refers to the various challenges to torture slaves and to have his mother swear an oath to support his case as "just measures" (*dikaia*). They are the "greatest tests" (*megistoi elenchoi*) of what has been testified to by his witnesses (29.27). Clearly he gives them a greater role here than he had in his first speeches against Aphobus. The suit for false testimony has apparently not been preceded by a public arbitration, however, so after Aphobus introduces testimony from witnesses like Onetor and Timocrates, who give testimony regarding the monies of the guardianship, Demosthenes excuses himself for not having prepared witnesses to deal with them (29.28).

His response to his lack of preparation is fascinating. After reminding the judges that he has already won his case on these matters against Aphobus, he restates his case and says in his own voice what was in the documents that had been read aloud by the court secretary in the original case. He begins with his charge (*enklêma*) and goes on with the testimony that has become the basis for the suit for false testimony (29.31–2). About several parts of his father's legacy, however, Demosthenes does have testimony at hand, so he goes on presenting his case in the normal order, outlining the events and then backing up his narrative step by step with the reading of laws and testimony (29.33–9). But later he returns to his method of stating in his own voice the substance of what is normally the stuff of documentary evidence. At the original arbitration, when Aphobus was being insistent on his challenge to torture Milyas (cf. 29.14, 39), Demosthenes formulated a complicated counter-challenge:

> For I, in my desire to refute him in every particular, and in my attempt to make clear to you his tricks and his villainies, asked him how large the sum was regarding which he demanded to examine Milyas, as one "who had knowledge of the facts." To this he stated falsely, that it was in regard to everything. "Well then," said I, "as to this I will give up to you the one who has the copy of your challenge to me. If, after I have given oath that you acknowledged [Milyas] to be free and that you so testified against Demo, you will swear to the contrary with imprecations upon your daughter, I release to you everything for which you shall be shown by the examination of the slave to have at the first demanded Milyas; and the damages which you were condemned to pay shall be lessened by this much—that is, by the amount in regard to which you demanded Milyas, so that you may be found to have been put to no disadvantage by the witnesses." (29.51–2)

Demosthenes clearly did not formulate the challenge along lines that Aphobus would have favored, since he limited the amount at issue to what Milyas might have been tortured over instead of "everything." He also makes the stakes very high over this relatively small amount: the settlement would have entailed the two cousins swearing conflicting oaths. But Demosthenes is taking full advantage of this stock form of argumentation based on refused challenges. The refusal to settle a dispute through swearing an oath amounts to the refusal of Aphobus "to judge these things for himself" (29.53; cf. 30.2 and Arist. *Rhetoric* 1.15.30–1). Both Demosthenes and the witnesses he is defending were willing to swear oaths to the truth of their case, and thereby to settle the dispute, but Aphobus did not bite (29.54).

ARGUMENTS OVER LEGAL TECHNICALITIES

In the two speeches *Against Onetor* (Demosthenes 30 and 31), Demosthenes has apparently not had the benefit of the extensive preparation that went into the speeches *Against Aphobus*. Again, there seems to have been no public arbitration for this suit, where Demosthenes might have lined up his witnesses and forced Onetor to disclose his. Demosthenes has to rely on recycled testimony and on challenges that serve to bolster it. Under the guise of an *apotimêma*, a method by which a wife's family secures a guarantee for her dowry by laying claim to a piece of her husband's land in case of divorce (Harris 1993), Onetor has seized some of Aphobus' land that Demosthenes hoped to have as part of his award. According to Demosthenes, Onetor and Aphobus perpetrated a false divorce, which gives Onetor this opportunity. Onetor prevented Demosthenes from seizing the land, so Demosthenes has brought a suit for ejectment against him. Presumably, because of his lack of preparation, Demosthenes relies to an even greater extent on stock forms of argument (most clearly at 30.37) rather than on witness testimony. He refers to these stock forms of argument as "great and clear evidence" (*tekmêria*: 30.5). So while he still uses witness testimony (30.9), he also relies largely on conclusions drawn from Onetor's refusal of his challenges. From the outset, he recognizes that in this dispute his opponent will use witnesses who will give false testimony (30.3). One of them is Aphobus (30.38), his previous opponent, who is continuing their dispute through Onetor (30.4). The other is Timocrates, the former husband of Aphobus' wife, whose testimony Demosthenes himself uses for his own purposes (30.9). The challenges are thus needed as a second-order proof, one that backs up witness testimony when the opponents have witnesses who give conflicting evidence.

Timocrates, the former husband of Aphobus' wife, testifies that he returned his former wife's dowry in the form of instalments to Aphobus at a rate of 10 percent per annum (30.7, 9). These payments covered the interest on the money. It is unclear whether they involved any payment of the capital. Demosthenes' case is based on the assumption that none of the capital was paid to Aphobus. It should thus be Timocrates, not Aphobus, who should provide the guarantee in the form of the *apotimêma*. This, however, must be an assumption, which Demosthenes must support "from probabilities" (30.10–13), since clearly he was not in a position to provide witnesses regarding arrangements among Aphobus, Onetor, and Timocrates. The probabilities suggest that the dowry was paid by instalments only because it was known that Aphobus' property was to be under dispute; they follow from the great wealth of these men (30.10), its liquidity (11), and the harm to one's reputation that flows from not paying a dowry outright (12). Timocrates could have returned the full dowry and Onetor could have passed one on to Aphobus had they wanted to do this. Demosthenes can also argue from the actions (*pepragmena* 30.14) of his opponents, about the timing of the marriage in connection with his own litigation, which imperilled Aphobus' estate and made the payment of a dowry to him unlikely

(30.14–18). He relies on —presumably three —different anonymous witnesses, to affirm the timing of the marriage to Aphobus and its relation to the progression of Demosthenes' claims against him (30.17).

In a preliminary confrontation, Demosthenes questioned Onetor and Timocrates about the particulars of the case before anonymous witnesses (30.19, 30). He makes much of the fact that no witnesses saw Aphobus receive the instalments from Timocrates: "Is this credible to you, that with a dowry of a talent Onetor and Timocrates handed over to Aphobus so much money without witnesses? ... No one would complete such a transaction without witnesses" (30.20–1). The following passages, for all of their rhetorical charge, are critical for an appreciation of the role of witnesses in Athens. The marriage feast is described as an act of communal witnessing, in which members of one family are entrusted to those of another (Scafuro 1994). Timocrates has already testified himself that he had agreed to pass on the dowry in the form of instalments to Aphobus (9). Now Demosthenes challenges whether the instalments were ever paid, since no one witnessed them.

> As it was, they could not induce their friends, who were more honest men than they were themselves, to bear witness to the payment of the money, and they thought that, if they produced other witnesses, not related to them, you would not believe them. Again, if they said the payment had been made all at once, they knew that we should demand for examination by torture the slaves who had brought the money. These, if the payment had not been made, they would have refused to give up, and so they would have been exposed. But if they maintained that they had paid the money without witnesses in the manner alleged, they thought to escape detection. (Dem. 30.23)

Demosthenes moves in this passage from his opponents' lack of witnesses to a hypothetical challenge to torture slaves. The torture challenge becomes the second-order proof for witness testimony, even hypothetical witness testimony.

In the next passage (30.25–30), in which he wants to show that Aphobus' divorce from his wife was a sham, Demosthenes uses three kinds of evidence, which he describes as witnesses, great evidence (*megala tekmêria*) and sufficient proofs (*pisteis*) (30.25). Even after the purported divorce and Onetor's claim to the land on the basis of *apotimêma*, Aphobus continued living with his wife and working the land. Demosthenes confronted Onetor before witnesses and challenged him by offering him a slave for torture over these points. Onetor declined the challenge but admitted that Aphobus continued working the land. Demosthenes provides witnesses to the challenge, as well as to the fact that Aphobus had stripped the land, as if realizing that he would have to hand it over to Demosthenes. He uses as evidence (*tekmêria* 30.31) of there being no ill will (the likely result of a genuine divorce) between Aphobus and Onetor and that the latter had joined in the pleadings for Aphobus against Demosthenes (30.31–2). Despite this being common knowledge, Demosthenes provides witnesses. As further evidence, he notes that while Onetor's sister went straight from Timocrates to Aphobus in order not to be unmarried, even temporarily, she has not remarried after "divorcing" Aphobus (30.33). As if admitting that this inference is weak, Demosthenes also produces as a witness Pasiphon, who cared for Aphobus' wife when they were supposedly divorced and who saw Aphobus attending to her also (30.34).

Demosthenes also challenged Aphobus to allow three slave women from his house to be tortured on the same point (30.35–6). The fact that he can point to bystanders who agreed that Demosthenes' challenge to torture the slave women was just suggests strongly that such slave tortures actually took place.[23] Here Demosthenes actually has the challenge read aloud and then turns to a piece of argumentation that is clearly out of the rhetoricians' toolbox, as it copies almost word-for-word an argument in Isaeus (8.12) and Isocrates (17.54).

In his second speech *Against Onetor* (Demosthenes 31), Demosthenes deals with another sort of document, albeit one that could hardly be brought into court. These are the *horoi*, marking stones, which were set up on the disputed property to indicate that it was security (*apotimêma*) for the dowry Onetor had provided, by way of Timocrates, to Aphobus. Demosthenes provides testimony from "those who know," that Onetor had himself removed from a house on the land the *horoi* that indicated that it was security for two thousand drachmas (31.4). He then draws an inference from this removal and Onetor's inconsistency (31.8) that neither the house nor the land was actually security for anything, that the entire *apotimêma* was a fraud: "to me it seems that no greater evidence than this could be found" (5). Although he refers to the laws concerning *apotimêma* (31.8), he does not have them read.

ARGUMENTS CONCERNING VIOLENCE

An analysis of the arguments in all Demosthenes' private speeches, let alone all the other Athenian law court speeches, is beyond the possibilities of this chapter, so I shall confine myself just to one more. *Against Conon* (Demosthenes 54) has won some of the highest praise among the speeches that Demosthenes wrote for others. It is generally dated to 341 BCE and concerns a case of assault. As in Dem. 29 and 30, conflicting testimony from witnesses plays a large role, so Demosthenes must also resort to arguments regarding challenges. The speech illustrates what had become conventional arguments in the popular courts against what is portrayed as outlandish behavior by the opponent regarding his use of evidence. At the beginning of the speech the speaker, Ariston, reports that he has followed the advice of family and friends (and presumably of his logographer) by instituting a private suit for assault instead of a more serious charge. Indeed, this speech shows a remarkable interest in the law and in its purposes.

Ariston first provides unnamed witnesses for the assaults he and his servants received from sons of Conon while they were all on garrison duty two years previously (54.6). He also provides at first unnamed witnesses to the events over which he is litigating, when Conon and several others attacked Ariston and a friend, Phanostratus, in a drunken brawl.[24] A relative named Euxitheus and friend named Meidias came upon the group as they were making their way to Ariston's home. There he was cleaned up and seen by a doctor before being moved on to Meidias' house. Presumably it is now Euxitheus and Meidias who testify about Ariston's injuries, as does the doctor (54.10). A doctor (the same one?) and others also testify about the severity of Ariston's injuries and the difficulties of his convalescence (54.12).

There is a sense in which Ariston's case could now be complete: he has detailed the assault and supported his narrative with witness testimony. But he goes on to anticipate Conon, who will argue, Ariston supposes, that the events over which Ariston is litigating do not meet the threshold for a charge of assault and that Conon was really only a bystander. Ariston anticipates this line of argumentation with an *a fortiori* argument of his own, pointing out that even verbal assault is against the law, though he does not actually have that law read aloud at this point (54.17–19). Instead, he goes on to base his arguments on the laws concerning hubris and robbery (54.24), the more serious charges he chose not to bring (54.1). In so doing, he is using a tactic pioneered by Isocrates in *Against Lochites*. At the preliminary arbitration, Conon apparently spent a great deal of time insisting that Ariston's witnesses swear to their testimony (54.26), a bizarre step since the truth of testimony in non-homicide trials was supposed to be assured by the suit for false testimony alone, not by oaths. Finally, when things were getting late, Conon challenged Ariston to have some slaves tortured. Ariston argues that this was altogether the wrong time for a challenge of this kind, and has witnesses testify that it was only a delaying tactic (54.29). Finally, he deals with the conflicting testimony. He anticipates the testimony that Conon will use by actually quoting from it in his own voice (31). Conon's witnesses are his own drinking buddies (54.33); they are notorious libertines (34) and brutes (37). He mimics the talk of drunken conspiracy among Conon's gang, in which testimony was simply manufactured to suit Conon's needs (54.35). Ariston's emphasis is that his own witnesses are independent passers-by and a doctor (54.36); these are the sorts of independent, knowledgeable witnesses one ought to produce before the democratic court. Ariston condemns the attitude of Conon's witnesses towards the written document of witnesses' testimony, the *grammateion* (which he reports using the diminutive *grammateidion* to reflect his opponent's contempt for it), and their attitude about false testimony on behalf of close friends. He goes on to condemn Conon's behavior in bringing in his family and swearing outlandish oaths upon their heads to support his case. Ariston must also swear in response, but his oath is sober and conventional, which is in keeping with his entire presentation.

CONCLUSION

As just a few speeches have demonstrated, in the time of Demosthenes, evidence and arguments in Athens' law courts were grounded in rules of evidence and rhetorical conventions, i.e., on a judicial and rhetorical epistemology that was tailored to the needs of the democratic ideology within which it functioned. Gone were the days in which the Greeks gathered before a panel of aristocrats and decided their cases using oral arguments e.g., as depicted on the shield of Achilles in Homer (*Iliad* 18.497–508). Certainly there were still private arbitrators, vestiges of an aristocratic past; they were chosen by agreement of the disputing parties and were sometimes empowered to settle their disputes. Before them the rules of argumentation were less formal: slaves could appear as witnesses and sometimes women participated. But in the Athens of Demosthenes, evidence, and the arguments surrounding it, had come to rely on written documents.

Western tradition has a long history of Athenian litigiousness as "sycophancy," a sort of "meddlesomeness" (*polypragmosynê*). In fact, it is a fundamental part of the democratic process, in the modern system as in fourth-century Athens, where it was perhaps the most significant way in which the democracy could assert control of the city through the popular courts: "The laws, which for you are authoritative, have made these [members of the popular court] authoritative" (Dem. 24.118). In his survey of the ideology of Athenian democracy, M. H. Hansen includes a discussion of "Accountability" and "Publicity" (1991: 310–312), and he recognizes the role of written laws in this process. The able employment of arguments based on these written laws, testimony, contracts, wills, and challenges contributed no less to the effective running of the democracy.[25]

CHAPTER SIX

Property and Possession

PAUL J. DU PLESSIS

INTRODUCTION

How does one go about writing a "cultural history" of ownership and possession in Roman law? This is a question that I have grappled with throughout the research for this chapter. At the outset, I thought that I had a fairly clear grasp of the concept of "cultural history," but having read my way through vast swathes of contemporary literature on the topic, I have to confess that I am none the wiser (Burke 2004b; Green 2008; Burke et al. 2010; Arcangeli 2012). To that end, and so as not to produce a chapter that is both rambling and pointless, it seems prudent to start with certain basic notions. What is "cultural history" and how would one go about writing a "cultural history" of ownership and possession in Roman law? Let us start with the concept of "cultural history." Given the qualifier, it seems fair to assume that "cultural history" is not mainstream "history." After all, a general historical account of ownership and possession in Roman law can be found in countless textbooks and monographs.[1] So what then is "cultural history" in this context? For the purposes of this chapter, I have taken it to mean a historical account with specific focus on culture (in the broader sense of the term). To that end, I have relied on contemporary attempts at defining this branch of historical enquiry. Arcangeli ventures the following definition:

> What is meant today by "cultural history" is no longer the history of culture, in the ordinary sense of the term. As a field of enquiry, it is not defined by the breadth and limits of its object. It is not characterised by a unity of method either, if we consider that it is practiced in a variety of different ways. The culturalist approach aims at cutting across the traditional subdivisions of the discipline of history (political, economic, military, and so on). Its nature and scope are comparable with those of social history, against which it is constantly measured. What distinguishes it from social history as it has ordinarily been practiced is its focus on the other side of the coin: history from the viewpoint of the motives and meanings that individual and collective historical agents from the past gave to whatever they were doing, and to the contexts in which they operated. (2012: 16)

But herein lies the issue. Once it is acknowledged that the focus of this chapter is "cultural history" and, more specifically, the cultural history of two legal constructs (ownership and possession), it is a relatively short leap intellectually from "cultural history of legal concepts" to "legal culture." For, it is the final part of Arcangeli's definition: " ... history from the viewpoint of the *motives and meanings* that individual and collective historical agents from the past gave to whatever they were doing, and to the *contexts* in which they operated ... " (my emphasis) that comes closest to the idea of "legal culture." And it is here that the problems start. What exactly is "Roman legal culture" and is it possible to identify a coherent "legal culture" for such a long period of time?

Until now, the concept of "legal culture" has primarily cropped up in contemporary socio-legal literature where it has formed part of a debate concerning the various agents of legal change. With only a few exceptions, little attempt has been made to introduce the concept of "legal culture" into debates about Roman law and its growth or decline.[2] The reasons for this are mainly twofold. First, those who participate in this debate are chiefly concerned with contemporary legal systems where source material for socio-legal study (whether empirical or otherwise) is abundant. Second, the notion of "legal culture," coined by Lawrence Friedman in the 1970s, is not universally supported. It is not my intention to provide a complete summary of Friedman's notion of "legal culture" here (Nelken 2007; Nelken 2012: esp. chapters 1–3). The gist of it is this: for Friedman, "legal culture" is a collection of diverse cultural forces (if you will) that has an impact on the law (summarized in Cotterrell 2006: 83). These cultural forces precede the creation of law, but also continue to shape it once created. Friedman also distinguishes between "external legal culture" (i.e., broader societal forces) and "internal legal culture" (i.e., the culture of those involved in the creation and administration of law such as lawyers, judges and law makers) (Cotterrell 2006: 84–85). As alluded to previously, Friedman's notion of "legal culture" has come under attack in recent years. Critics of Friedman have objected to two aspects of the notion of "legal culture." First, it is too vague a concept and it is therefore difficult to distinguish between "legal culture" and "culture" more generally. In fact, some authors, such as the von Benda-Beckmanns (2010) have argued that there is no need for the notion of "legal culture" and that it would be more useful to unpack the concept into its constituent parts (von Benda-Beckmann and von Benda-Beckmann 2010). Second, it has been suggested that it remains unclear from Friedman's writings whether "legal culture" is the cause or the effect of legal change (Cotterrell 2006: 86–87). These are the main criticisms. But Cotterrell, the main critic of Friedman's notion of "legal culture," does see some value in retaining aspects of it. As he has pointed out:

> the concept of culture—and perhaps legal culture—remains useful as a way of referring to clusters of social phenomena (patterns of thought and belief, patterns of action or interaction, characteristic institutions) coexisting in certain social environments, where the exact relationship existing among elements in the cluster are not clear or are not of concern. Culture is a convenient concept with which to refer provisionally to a general environment of social practices, traditions, understandings and values in which law exists. (2006: 88)

This critique by Cotterrell will be used as the basis for this chapter. Phrased differently, this chapter will focus on "clusters of social phenomena" relating to ownership and possession in Roman law with specific reference to the origins, growth, and interaction between these two legal constructs in order to draw larger conclusions about motives, meanings and contexts. This will be used, using the terminology of Friedman, to make various claims about "legal culture" that precedes and surrounds law.

Before embarking upon this chapter, certain caveats are required. First, it would be impossible to provide a complete survey of all of the Roman law of ownership and possession from the founding of Rome to the enactment of the Justinianic project in the mid-sixth century. A comprehensive survey of this kind would not only fill a number of books, but it would also be so general and impressionistic as to be virtually useless.[3] Second, virtually any textbook on Roman law contains a detailed survey of the rules of Roman property law from the XII Tables to the Digest. These narratives are mainly internally focused only on legal rules and contain more than just a whiff of the idea of "progression" from "primitive" to "sophisticated." So, in this chapter a combination of rules of law and social phenomena will be used, rather than a narrow focus only on the rules of law. In so doing, I make no claims about historical causation as this would be a step too far. Rather, my goal is merely to set out some of the social phenomena that, in my view, require more detailed study should a comprehensive account of the cultural history of these two legal constructs ever be attempted. This would be in keeping with Cotterrell's notion of "legal ideology," a concept that he sees as more useful than a vague notion of "legal culture":

> legal ideology can be regarded not as a unity but rather as an overlay of currents of ideas, beliefs, values and attitudes embedded in, expressed through and shaped in practice ... Legal ideology is not legal doctrine but can be regarded as made up of value elements and cognitive ideas presupposed in, expressed through and shaped by the practices of developing, interpreting and applying legal doctrine within a legal system. (Cotterrell 2006: 89–90)

"LEGAL CULTURE" IN ARCHAIC ROME (THE MONARCHY AND EARLY REPUBLIC)

It seems fitting to start the discussion of ownership and possession in Roman law with the earliest credible written legal source, the XII Tables. As countless studies will attest, there are problems with the Roman narrative surrounding the creation of this law.[4] A supposed embassy by the drafting commission to Greece to consult the Laws of Solon, for example, seems unlikely and evidence for this remains scant. Also, the content (reconstructed from verbatim quotations by later authors) is open to interpretation.[5]

Any textbook on Roman law will mention that there are a number of legal rules in the XII Tables that deal with aspects of what contemporary scholars would refer to as "property law." But the rules themselves only get us so far. Rules of law can only be investigated as a reflection of society if we first understand the society that created them.[6] To uncover Cotterrell's "clusters of social phenomena" we must first establish, to the extent that our sources permit, what the XII Tables represented to the Romans of the period. As Cornell has pointed out:

> the Twelve Tables do not amount to a code in the modern sense. The Decemvirs [the ten-men commission appointed to draft the Twelve Tables] made no systematic attempt to set out the whole of the law, and the areas they did cover were not dealt with comprehensively ... Exactly why the Decemvirs chose to set out the law on some matters, but not on others, is a puzzle. But it seems most likely that their choice was determined by the need to specify the law in doubtful or disputed areas but to leave unstated rules which were settled or taken for granted. (1995: 279–280)[7]

While one may quibble about the first part of this statement (how much law does a small group of people require?), the latter part rings true. Thus, we may infer that many of the rules of property law, e.g., about boundaries, the *usus* of property (i.e., the acquisition of "ownership" of property through continuous use for a legally prescribed period of time) and the requirement of a *mancipatio* (a ritual involving the parties to the transaction, at least five adult male Roman citizens as witnesses, a set of scales and a bronze ingot) in cases of the transfer of ownership of *res mancipi* (a group of objects seemingly considered important for agricultural life) were somehow controversial. But why should these legal rules be controversial? The answer to this question is complex, but seems to relate to three larger phenomena.

The first of these is that the XII Tables was seemingly enacted after a period of conflict between the plebeians and patricians. Even if the details are questionable, it is clear that early Roman society suffered from certain social upheavals and that the Romans of later epochs believed in the "struggle of the orders" (as it came to be known) as a source of influence upon the law (Capogrossi Colognesi 1978; Capogrossi Colognesi 1981; Forsythe 2005: 216–222). From this we may deduce that property law had (or was reputed to have had) a political facet in the early history of Rome.

In second place, the notion of paternal authority (*patria potestas*), one of the cornerstones of Roman private law already visible in the XII Tables, had a profound impact on who could own and dispose of property. The head of the household was the only person with full capacity under Roman law to own property. This had a direct impact on the remaining members of his *familia*, especially with reference to the law of succession. We may therefore conclude that property during this period also had a social facet that was intimately connected to the patriarchal nature of Roman society (Capogrossi Colognesi 2014: 31–34). Patriarchy clearly had a restrictive effect on ownership and possession (especially in relation to women and minors). To this should be added the complex issue of *nexum* and the nature and causes of debt bondage. Even if the details are sketchy, there were clearly tensions between the rich and the poor regarding this issue (Cornell 1995: 280–283). This affected not only land ownership, but also free labor since enslaved debtors could not work their lands, thereby falling into more debt. Thus, property law also had an economic facet.

The final issue is that of agrarianism. It is clear that Roman society of this period was largely agrarian, that people owned small plots of land and that these were in close proximity, thus necessitating rules on dealing with common boundaries, sources of water and overhanging branches and fruits.[8] This agrarian focus formed the larger cultural environment in which the Roman law of property arose and developed and accounts for the division between *res mancipi* and *res nec mancipi*, the significance of *mancipatio* and the rules of *usus* of land. As part of this environment, it would be possible also to mention aspects of the "internal legal culture" that affected property law, such as the *legis actio sacramento in rem* (the strict ritual process that had to be performed in a court of law in relation to actions concerning property) and the fact that, before the enactment of XII Tables (and to some extent still thereafter) wider knowledge of the law and its operation in the courts remained limited to the Pontiffs (the "priests" of Roman religion, exclusively elected from the patrician class), but for the moment this is sufficient to sketch a general impression of the origins of "Roman legal culture" as it applies to ownership and possession.[9]

Thus, already in its earliest guise, the Roman law of property was about more than merely legal rules. It had political, social and economic aspects and was shaped by and existed within a larger cultural environment (Archi 1958; Manthe 2003).

"LEGAL CULTURE" IN THE MID-TO-LATE REPUBLIC

A cursory glance at any timeline of the Roman Republic in the period from the battle of Zama in 202 BCE to the collapse of the Republic in 27 BCE will reveal a period of almost continuous strife, both in Italy and abroad. This is significant for at least two reasons.

First, war requires armies and armies require soldiers. How the Roman state dealt with the recruitment and the eventual pensioning off of these war veterans (usually by granting them citizenship and land in newly established territories) (Figure 6.1) will become an important theme running through the narrative of ownership and possession, especially during the later Roman Republic. The second significant point is that war disturbs ownership (especially of land) and, in the chaos that follows, provides opportunities for those with greater resources (whether physical or otherwise) to seize and occupy land illegally. Indeed, conquest in war remains one of the main sources of land to the Romans throughout the Republic (and early Empire). It is important to stress, though, that it was not just ownership of immovable property (land) that was affected during this period. The two Sicilian slave revolts of this period also indicate that rights in movable property (slaves being arguably an important form of movable property) could, at times, become precarious when these "objects of ownership" attempted to cast the yoke of oppression aside, often with bloody consequences.

When reviewing the internally focused narratives regarding the development of ownership and possession found in most textbooks on Roman law, it quickly becomes clear that they bear little resemblance to the turbulent political and social circumstances of the period. In fact, there is a distinct impression that the law developed slowly and steadily in an oasis of calm while larger socio-political changes occurred around it. Even if it is assumed that law (as the guarantor of stability) responds to society slowly, this picture seems somewhat doubtful. Nevertheless, this narrative reveals the following. The period from the mid-to-late Republic witnesses further developments in the concepts of ownership and possession, even if the concepts, as such, were not yet fully developed (or indeed defined). But whether the identification of terms necessarily implies anything is debated. Watson phrases it as follows:

> Kaser thinks that until late in the second century B.C. ownership was not "institutionalized," that the legal control was but a mere reflection of the protection granted by the vindication [the main legal remedy of the owner], that it was not yet conceived of as a specific legal type nor contrasted with other types of legal power … Early Roman law was content with the vague phrase *meum esse* which expressed only the appropriation of the thing, not the content and limits of the power over it. But this argument does not seem to me to be wholly persuasive. First, there can be another explanation of the absence of a technical term for ownership, namely that since it is the greatest right imaginable over a thing a technical name for it is not really needed. *Meum esse* is quite sufficient. It is lesser and restricted rights which need a technical name expressive of their content. Secondly, *meum esse* does not appear at all vague … Thirdly, the claim *meum esse* was supported … by the words *ex iure quiritium* [the right of the *Quirites*—an ancient form of self-identification among the Romans]. (Watson 1968: 91–92)

This quotation neatly summarizes one of the main issues about Republican Roman law, namely the diversity of opinion regarding the origins of many of the staple concepts of the Roman law of ownership and possession during this period. At best, given the absence of any concrete information, one may speculate as to how these concepts came into being.[10] As the quotation from Watson shows, it is generally assumed that they evolved towards the end of this period.

It is important to stress, however, that these two legal constructs should not be seen in isolation from the remedies required to enforce them. Thus, alongside these, and largely as a result of the change in civil procedure used in Roman courts from *legis actiones* (a highly ritualized system) to *formulae* (a more flexible system) and the simultaneous

FIGURE 6.1. A military diploma granting its holder Roman citizenship. Source: Wikimedia/Poulpy/CC BY-SA 3.0.

growth in Praetorian innovation of the law, the remedies used to protect ownership (the *rei vindicatio*) and possession (interdicts) arose during this time (Capogrossi Colognesi 2014: 132–147). To this must be added the development of the notion of *in bonis esse* ("bonitary ownership"), a state of "legally protected possession" of an individual who, for some (innocent) reason, had not immediately acquired ownership of an object at the point of conveyance. Finally, there seems to be some development in the area of the law of servitudes (i.e., limited real rights over the property of another, such as a right of way) during this period with newer ones being created, especially in an "urban" context and existing "praedial" ones being grouped together (Capogrossi Colognesi 1969, 1976).

There are two reasons why this internally focused narrative does not seem to reflect the turbulent socio-political events of the period. First, modern knowledge of Republican Roman law remains extremely scant and consists in large parts of comments by later Roman jurists and Latin authors concerning events that happened quite some time before.[11] Secondly, contemporary scholarship remains very poorly informed about the role and significance of the earliest Roman jurists and their impact on the development of Roman law.

Identifying the "clusters of social phenomena" that make up the legal culture of the mid-to-late Republic in relation to ownership and possession is, therefore, a difficult task. As the survey of legal developments outlined above shows, possession looms large. When combined with the socio-political events of the period, it becomes clear that ownership [of land] "again" becomes (or perhaps remains?) a political issue in the mid-to-late Republic. This time, however, the politics of land ownership is not based on internal strife between rich and poor in Roman society; it now takes on an external element, especially with reference to newer territories and foreign peoples, since, for much of the early Republic, Rome was engaged in war with her neighbors on the Italian mainland in an attempt to become the dominant power, while, for much of the mid-to-late Republic, she was expanding her influence abroad through war and conquest. Evidence for this is visible in the events between the conclusion of the second Punic War in 201 BCE (when Carthage had been defeated) and the start of the Social War in 90 BCE (a war between Rome and her Italian allies in which the latter demanded greater social and legal integration into the Roman state). In just over a century, the Roman state became embroiled in the Macedonian and Jugurthine Wars, razed Carthage to the ground and suppressed two major slave revolts. The impact that these events had on the Roman legal concepts of ownership and possession must have been profound, but can only be seen in outline.

The first point to bear in mind is that Roman law at this junction was not a territorially based legal system. Access to Roman law was based on citizenship; only Roman citizens could "own" or "possess" under Roman law. Given the influx of peregrines after the conclusion of the second Punic War and the expansion of Roman territory, it seems inevitable that this system would come under pressure. Indeed, the reluctance of Roman authorities to grant their allies in Italy greater access to Roman civil law was one of the main reasons for the eventual Social War of 90 BCE.

Two pieces of evidence show the complexities of ownership and possession in Roman law during this period. The first is the episode from the mid-second century BCE described as the Gracchan land reforms (Lintott 1992). Irrespective of the problems with Appian's narrative concerning the reasons for these, it seems undeniable that certain problems had arisen regarding public land (*ager publicus*) (Capogrossi Colognesi 2014: 179–193). These lands, largely a product of Rome's successful conquests, had somehow begun to fall (illegally) into the hands of wealthy individuals. This had led to popular discontent. The legislative intervention by the Gracchi was designed to address this issue. The *lex agraria* of 111 BCE represents the culmination of a series of events that had started with the enactment of the *leges liciniae sextiae* of 367 BCE whereby Roman citizens were only entitled to hold a certain quantity of public land (Jakab 2015: 116–118).[12] The provisions of this latter law had come to be ignored, no doubt owing to the political turbulence of the period, leading to the complaints of the people that eventually triggered the Gracchan episode. The text of this law, most recently provided by Lintott, demonstrates a number of important points relating to the history of ownership and possession (1992: 41–43). Although the law is mainly concerned with public land, it demonstrates the importance of possession as a factor in determining entitlement to said land. In second place, the law provides for a system of registration of holdings of public land, which in turn suggests a system of centuriation (i.e., mapping out the extent of landholding using a grid pattern) (Figure 6.2) (evidence of which predates this law by roughly two centuries) (Jakab 2015: 116). Finally, the law also mentions "provincial land" brought under Roman control through conquest. It also suggests that, during this time, the categories of public and private land and the law that applies to them were closely connected.

The next piece of evidence is the *Tabula Contrebiensis* of 87 BCE (Richardson 1983; Birks et al. 1984). It records the outcome of a dispute over land between two communities in Spain together with the outcome of the dispute as reinforced by a Roman official. There are a number of significant points to this inscription. The first is the nature of the matter and the applicable law. As Richardson has pointed out, the parties are not Roman citizens, nor is this a matter of Roman private law:

> The case is presented in such a way that it is clear that the issues are to be decided in terms of Sosinestan law, both as to whether the Sosinestani were within their rights in selling to the Salluienses and whether, under Sosinestan custom, the Salluienses were permitted to construct their canal; but the appointment of members of an outside state (in this case the senate of Contrebia) to act as judges indicates that this is an international arbitration, of the type familiar in the Greek world, and provided for in the province of Sicily under the *lex Rupilia*. (Richardson 1983: 39)

The importance of this document should not be underestimated. For what it reveals is a willingness by the Roman authorities to apply local law, while at the same time ensuring that justice is served through oversight and endorsement by Roman officials. From a property law perspective, documents such as these demonstrate one of the main reasons why concepts such as "ownership" and "possession" are not well documented in the Republican period. Given the complexities of public vs private land and Roman law vs local law, landholding in the Roman Republic was much more pluralist than first imagined and encompassed not merely Roman land held by Roman citizens according to Roman law. The Roman state clearly also endorsed local non-Roman law under certain circumstances.

The period between the conclusion of the Social War and the end of the Republic is one of great political turbulence. The slave revolt of Spartacus had a profoundly disturbing effect on the countryside and the proscriptions ("authorized" killing and confiscation of the property of their "enemies"), first under Sulla and Marius and thereafter under the first and second Triumvirate no doubt contributed significantly to legal insecurity in relation to ownership and possession, especially of land. To illustrate the unsettled state of this period and how it impacted upon legal constructs such as ownership and possession, three aspects of Cicero's life deserve mention. First, the introduction of the

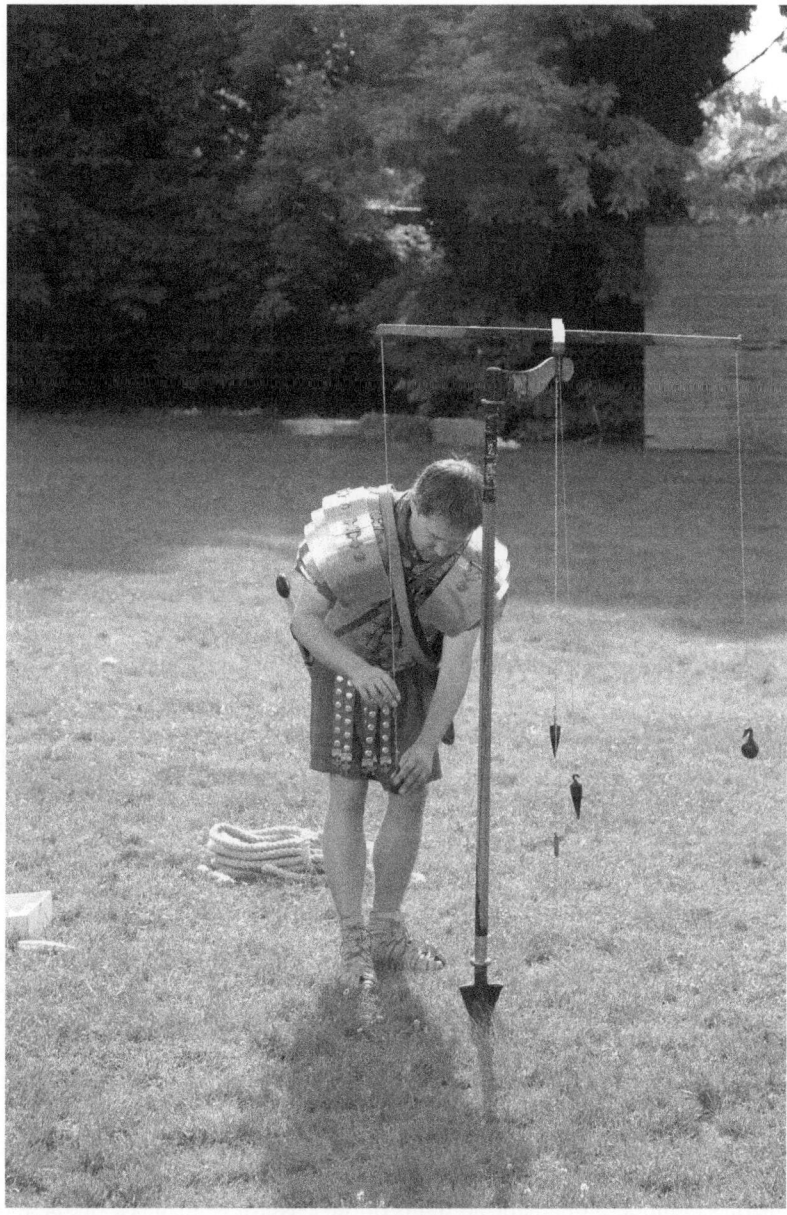

FIGURE 6.2. A *groma* [surveying equipment]. Source: Wikimedia/Matthias Kabel/CC BY-SA 3.0.

interdictum unde vi and *de vi armata*, two Praetorian legal remedies designed to deal with violent dispossession of property, at the heart of his defense of Aulus Caecina, clearly shows that no one's property was safe (Frier 1985). In second place, and related to the first, the allegation made by the prosecution in Caecina's case that he was not a Roman and was therefore unable to inherit under the *ius civile* shows that the Roman legal order was struggling to come to terms with the fact that it was no longer a small Republic situated on the Italian mainland, but instead a much more significant power with overseas territories (Cicero, *Caecina* 95–103). Finally, from Cicero's own life, one could mention the confiscation of his property and the destruction of his house following his banishment and the great problems he encountered in trying to recover said property as an indication that property and politics were very closely allied towards the end of the Republic.

Thus, if we were to reflect back upon the "clusters of social phenomena" identified for the archaic period, we can see that they are all still present by the end of the Republic. In each case, though, the scope of the phenomenon has changed. In the political sphere, for example, the "struggle of the orders" within Roman society has replicated itself on a much larger scale to become the struggle between citizen and non-citizen. This affects every other phenomenon (e.g., economic or social) and has a profound impact on the development of the legal concepts of ownership and possession.

"LEGAL CULTURE" IN THE EMPIRE

In constructing the narrative of "Roman legal culture" in relation to ownership and possession in the Empire, a number of larger issues need to be borne in mind. First we are well informed about Roman law due to the writings of the Roman jurists and their preservation in the compilation of Justinian. Thus, legal sources will necessarily loom large. With that said, one may assume, given what is known about the selection procedures of the Justinianic commissions, that we have only the bare minimum of what must have existed concerning Roman property law during this period. There is much that has fallen by the wayside, especially regarding the practical side of things. Related to this are issues of intellectual focus. Depending on the view taken about the activities of the jurists and whether one believes that they were largely involved in an intellectual (rather than a practical) discourse concerning the law, the issues debated by them in the remaining Roman legal texts might only represent "reality" (whatever that means in this context) to a limited extent. The relationship between the Roman legal discourse about ownership and possession during this period and the larger socio-political currents dominating the Roman Empire remains problematic (Kehoe 2015).

The second issue to be borne in mind is one of periodization. The "classical period" of Roman law maps onto the period between the reigns of Augustus to Diocletian. As any scholar of Roman history will appreciate, this is a very large and (yet again) turbulent period that includes a number of costly wars, provincial problems, especially in Palestine, problems on the eastern frontiers with "barbarians," the whole of the "crisis of the third century" as well as various Germanic invasions (*c.* 259–270) in which Rome had to concede certain territories. It seems somewhat unlikely that these events did not impact on the Roman legal concepts of ownership and possession during this period, though they rarely seem to feature in modern dogmatic accounts of the classical Roman law on these topics.

It is not my intention to set out a comprehensive and systematic account of the state of ownership and possession during the classical period of Roman law. Modern textbooks reveal that (a) legal concepts such as *dominium* and *possessio* are "defined" in the legal sources and discussed at length; (b) the original distinction between *res mancipi* (a group of objects important for agriculture in early Roman society) and *res nec mancipi* (everything else) appears to have been pushed into the background by a more recent distinction between movable (i.e., chattels) and immovable property (i.e., land) (related to the decline of *mancipatio* and the rise of *traditio* as a mode of acquisition of ownership); (c) the classification of different modes of acquisition of ownership according to whether they derive from the *ius civile* or the *ius gentium* occurs in the sources; and finally (d) an increase in the number of limited real rights over the property of another with specific attention being paid to servitudes is visible.

Since law is to some extent a reflection of society (even if not a direct mirror), the question remains how to link the largely internally focused Roman law narrative with the larger contexts in which they existed. In my view, the starting point should be the "definitions" of the concepts as found in Roman legal literature:

D. 41, 2, 1, Paul. 54 ad ed. [Paul, book 54 *ad Edictum*]

Possessio appellata est, ut et Labeo ait, a sedibus quasi positio, quia naturaliter tenetur ab eo qui ei insistit, quam Graeci κατοχήν dicunt.

Possession is so called, according to Labeo, from "*sedes*," as it were "*positio*," because there is a natural holding, which the Greeks call κατοχή, by the person who stands on it. [Own translation]

D. 41, 2, 1, 1 Paul. 54 ad ed. [Paul, book 54 *ad Edictum*]

Dominiumque rerum ex naturali possessione coepisse Nerva filius ait eiusque rei vestigium remanere in his, quae terra mari caeloque capiuntur: nam haec protinus eorum fiunt, qui primi possessionem eorum adprehenderint. item bello capta et insula in mari enata et gemmae lapilli margaritae in litoribus inventae eius fiunt, qui primus eorum possessionem nanctus est.

And Nerva the younger says that *dominium* of property arose out of natural possession and that a vestige of this remains in relation to those things captured on earth, in the sea or in the heavens: for they become immediately the property of those who first took possession of them. Similarly, goods captured in war, an island arising in the sea as well as gems, stones and pearls found on beaches, become the property of those who first take possession of them. [Own translation]

Much has been made of these two definitions and it is not my intention to enter into a full exegesis of all of the conceptual complexities associated with these two texts (Piccinelli 1980). For the moment I wish to make only two points about them. First, although both texts are attributed to the third-century jurist Paul, it is clear (from the internal references to other jurists) that the "definitions" of ownership and possession occurred in the early to mid-first century CE (Labeo and Nerva filius in chronological order). While one may question the veracity of Labeo's etymological history of the term possession, it is clear that (in the minds of the Roman jurists) possession preceded ownership and that ownership was initially based on some primordial act of possession. In the past, these two statements have provided proof to scholars like Kaser who have sought to trace the origins of Roman ownership in customary law prevalent in the earliest period of Rome's history (Kaser 1956; Diósdi 1970). While this seems plausible, evidence remains scant. It seems more likely that the jurists here are inventing a tradition that links ownership and possession, no doubt owing to the legal significance of possession of land in the provinces (which, as we have seen above, was already at issue during the mid-to-late Republic). The practical significance of possession of movables in the context of proving ownership during a legal dispute using the formulary procedure may also have played a role in their reasoning, since, under the formulary system, the person who was not in possession of the object of the lawsuit carried the burden of proof of ownership (Santucci 2014b).

As mentioned above in relation the position in the mid-to-late Republic, Roman law was not yet a territorially based legal system. Access to Roman law depended on whether an individual either had Roman citizenship or had been granted the *ius commercii* (the right of commerce with Romans). How this relates to ownership and possession is complex and it may be that the focus on movable and immovable property, as well as the discussions of the different modes of acquisition of ownership of property and whether these originated from the *ius civile* or the *ius gentium*, are manifestations of this complexity. In its most basic form, someone could only exert *dominium* over an object [whether movable or immovable] if they had Roman citizenship or had been granted the *ius commercii*. Of course, matters of access to Roman courts could be resolved through fictions of citizenship, but the main principle was one of limited access to the Roman *ius civile* (Ando 2015a). As far as the ownership of land is concerned, matters are complicated. Take the following statements by Gaius from his textbook for law students, written in the latter part of the second century CE:

Gaius 2.27

solum Italicum mancipi est, provinciale nec mancipi est ...

Italian land is *res mancipi*, provincial land is not. [Own translation]

Gaius 2.7

Sed in provinciali solo placet plerisque locum religiosum non fieri, quia in eo solo dominium populi Romani est vel Caesaris, nos autem possessionem tantum vel usumfructum habere videmur; utique tamen, etiamsi non sit religiosum, pro religioso habetur. item quod in provinciis non ex auctoritate populi Romani consecratum est, proprie sacrum non est, tamen pro sacro habetur.

But in the case of land in the provinces most people accept that it is not made religious because ownership of such land is held by the Roman people or by the Emperor; we are regarded as having only possession or a usufruct; all the same, although not in fact religious, it is treated as religious. Again, anything in the provinces is not consecrated by authority of the Roman people and is not sacred properly speaking, yet it is treated as sacred. [Gordon Robinson translation]

The first passage originates from a heavily damaged section of the manuscript and is therefore fragmentary. The important point, though, is that according to Gaius, only Italic land [not provincial land] is *res mancipi*. To this may be added the statement in the next passage in which Gaius, in the context of his discussion of "religious land," notes that land in the provinces falls under the *dominium* of the Roman people or of the emperor and persons are only allowed to possess it or to hold a limited real right such as usufruct over it.

The importance of these two passages for our understanding of ownership and possession cannot be underestimated. Assuming that Gaius is accurately stating the law of his time, it would therefore mean that *dominium* of land could only ever be exercised over Italic land by Roman citizens or those with the *ius commercii*, while in the provinces (except for those cities that had been granted the privilege of Italic soil), the only entitlements available to these people were possession and limited real rights (Bleicken 1974; Kantor 2017). This, in my view, goes a long way towards explaining why possession and limited real rights feature so prominently in the legal sources of the classical period. It may also account for the decline of *mancipatio* as a mode of acquisition of ownership and the related rise of *traditio* (delivery—a mode of acquisition of ownership used for things that were not *res mancipi*). In reality, *traditio* was a much more prevalent legal transaction in large parts of the Empire than *mancipatio*.

One source often marginalized in discussions of the Roman law of ownership and possession is the corpus of writings of the Roman land surveyors. This collection of texts, spanning the first to the fifth centuries CE provides a unique snapshot of some of the more technical aspects of land surveying (an important aspect of centuriation mentioned above) and how the law of property (especially in the provinces) related to it. To understand the importance of land surveyors for our understanding of ownership and possession, let us take our cue from the work of Dilke with a statement about the late Republic and early Empire:

> The period following the civil war, when the Second Triumvirate had to provide land for thousands of discharged soldiers, was one of enormous expansion for surveying ... Some land was apportioned on a personal basis (*viritim*), but more often colonies were founded. It was under Augustus that the first steps leading eventually to a large and elaborate bureaucracy were taken. Only from his principate onwards do we find organisation of centuriated land in a truly civil service manner. (1971: 37)

Land surveyors are known to have acted in court cases where the parties disputed the extent or the location of property (Maganzani 2007). They were also instrumental in providing a record of their work to the authorities. Dilke summarizes it thus:

> It was part of the duty of a land surveyor to make a map (*forma*) of any land he had divided up. These maps were normally on bronze, and unfortunately none survives ... We can, however, form a reasonably good idea of these maps from the Corpus [of the Land Surveyors] and its illustrations, from the Orange tablets and from the Forma Urbis Romae ... The maps were drawn up in two copies. One of these remained in the local community, while the other was lodged in the Emperor's record office, the *tabularium*, built in 78 BC. (1971: 111–112)

Given the importance of provincial land, it would be wrong to assume that records were only kept of public land (Figure 6.3) (Figure 6.4). It would appear that these records also included land allocated to individuals, since an accurate record was required to establish liability for land tax, one of the main sources of income of the Roman state throughout its existence.

For a full account of these complexities, I refer the reader here to the translation and commentary by Campbell (2000) whose astute notes capture many of them. For the moment, I wish to use one aspect as an example. In the treatise of Frontinus, a land surveyor active towards the end of the first century CE, he reveals:

> Innumerable disputes arise concerning sacred and religious places. (Campbell 2000: 9)

The comment by Gaius, just over half a century later, cited above concerning the existence of "religious land" in the provinces, compliments Frontinus's statement nicely. If, as Gaius says, land cannot legally be "sacred" or "religious" in the provinces, and yet are treated as such, it is bound to give rise to legal ambiguities, especially when occupied illegally. It seems quite likely that this is what Frontinus (and for that matter Gaius above) is referring to here. To this may be added an observation from the commentary of pseudo-Agennius Urbicus, dating from the end of the fourth/start of the fifth century CE (or possibly later) on this very matter:

> Now, in Italy, as the most holy Christian religion increases, many people have taken over pagan groves or sites attached to temples, and now sow them. I thought that

FIGURE 6.3. Cadastre D'Arausio. Source: © Culturespaces / Christophe Recoura.

FIGURE 6.4. *Forma Urbis Romae*. Source: Wikimedia/Ptyx/CC BY-SA 4.0.

this should be stated, so that if a surveyor wishes to display his learning, he can point out that area that was granted to the shrine. Religious places are in a similar category. (Campbell 2000: 71)

So what should one take from this single example? First, it shows clearly that the dogmatic concepts of ownership and possession discussed by the Roman jurists during this period functioned within a larger context where land surveyors and their records engraved on bronze and stone existed. Furthermore, the distinction between Italic and provincial land gave rise to a complex legal scenario that must have caused problems in practice. As pseudo-Agennius Urbicus shows, the advent of Christianity as the state religion in the Roman Empire after the miraculous conversion of the Emperor Constantine added another element into the mix. What had formerly been "religious land" was now of uncertain legal status and people took advantage of the ambiguity.

Having already set out how, in my view, the legal rules relate to the larger socio-political circumstances of the period, two further "clusters of social phenomena" deserve a mention. The first is the economic component of ownership and possession. Many goods in the Roman Empire, whether movable or immovable were taxed when sold and, in certain cases, also when moved across internal or external frontiers (port taxes). A good example is the various taxes levied on the movement of slaves as is visible in the *lex portorii asiae* (a *lex* setting out a variety of rules, including custom duties on goods, payable when brought into the Roman province of Asia) (Cottier and Corbier 2008). Much more significant, though, were the taxes on land. One of the main consequences of the division between Italic and provincial land was that the former was exempt from taxation, while the latter was taxed. Thus, the economic environment in which the Roman law of ownership and possession matured intellectually, was one in which possession of land was an important provincial reality and provided a significant tax base for the Roman state (Delorme et al. 2005). Revenue gathered from these provinces went either to the senate or to the imperial coffers, depending on the type of province. While this might seem like an equitable division at first glance, it should be remembered that this division did not remain static (Lo Cascio 1997; Lo Cascio 2015).

One last issue that remains to be discussed is the change to the Roman legal system brought about by the enigmatic *Constitutio Antoniniana* [thereafter CA] of 212 CE.[13] Traditionally, Roman law scholarship has viewed this imperial enactment, which seems to have granted Roman citizenship to most free people living within the boundaries of the Roman Empire, as having a profound effect upon the application of Roman law in the sense that after the enactment of the CA, Roman law became "Reichsrecht" and therefore obliterated all non-Roman customs and practices operative in the Empire (Mitteis 1891). This view, based on late nineteenth-century German scholarship, has since become the focus of an intense and protracted debate, not only about the effect of this imperial enactment, but also about the continued existence of local legal orders post-212 CE. The debate has focused primarily on the Roman province of Egypt where new discoveries in papyrology, specifically examples of court reports and records of court decisions, have called into question the traditional view concerning the effect of the CA on local non-Roman customs and law (Dolganov n.d.).[14] To that extent, this comment by Agennius Urbicus also deserves a mention:

> Many different cases occur, which relate to the normal legal process, because of the diversity of the provinces. For instance, in Italy no small dispute is provoked over keeping out rain water, whereas in Africa a dispute on the same matter takes quite

a different direction; because it is a very dry region, a person has no greater reason for complaint than if someone prevents rainwater from flowing onto his property. (Campbell 2000: 21)

Not only do scholars need to be sensitive to legal diversity, but they also need to take into account the fact that the Roman Empire was a diverse entity geographically and that this must have affected legal practice.

This survey will, for various reasons, not progress past the ascent of Diocletian to the imperial throne. The two main reasons for this are the following. First, it was during the reign of Diocletian that the exemption from land taxes enjoyed by Italy was abolished. The significance of this step cannot be underestimated. As we have seen above, taxation was a core feature of any entitlement over provincial land. By removing this key distinction, Diocletian chipped away at one of the cornerstones of Roman property law. Even if the distinction between Italic and provincial land were only formally abolished during the reign of Justinian, it is this event, more than any other that affected the Roman law of property. The second issue relates to the central theme of this chapter, namely "legal culture."[15] The division of the Empire and the eventual demise of the Western Empire brought about certain fundamental changes in Roman legal culture. These include issues such as the rise of the colonate,[16] a specialist form of tenancy that tied tenants to the land, the interaction between Roman law and Germanic customary law after the fall of the Western Empire as well as the narrative of "decline"[17] historically associated with this period. It also bears repeating that the Justinianic restoration of "classical Roman law" was an artificial attempt to turn back the clock. The relationship between the law as stated in the Justinianic compilation and the realities on the ground has become an important theme in the study of Byzantine law.

CONCLUSION: TOWARDS A "CULTURAL HISTORY" OF OWNERSHIP AND POSSESSION

In the end, as with most things, what appeared to be a pretty straightforward brief turned out to be much more complicated. One theme which has emerged very clearly from this discussion, however, is that ownership and possession are neither static nor solely intellectual constructs existing in the "heaven of legal concepts." Jakab has recently argued this point forcefully in her survey of Roman property law (2015: 131). This insight bears reinforcing. Neither the structures, nor the content of the Roman law of ownership and possession were ever static. Rather, they were dynamic and took account of the political, social, and economic circumstances of the period. These circumstances form the "clusters of social phenomena" that shaped ownership and possession in Roman law and deserve closer scrutiny. A full history of the Roman law of ownership and possession has yet to be written. I hope to have provided merely a potential route map for such an investigation.

CHAPTER SEVEN

Wrongs

JACOB GILTAIJ

INTRODUCTION

In this chapter, I will focus on two types of wrongs, exemplified by two criminal transgressions in Greek and Roman Antiquity: "abuse" (ὕβρις, *iniuria*) and "adultery" (μοιχεία, *adulterium*). Merely hypothetically speaking, the reason to specifically single out these two transgressions is that they represent violations of moral or ethical norms above anything else. Of course, strictly speaking all crimes and delicts are in a sense moral transgressions as well, meaning that whatever a society deems punishable is always determined by the ethical norms that that society upholds. However, as we will see, these two transgressions seem have been thought of especially as moral violations by the members of the societies involved. Consequently, the purpose of this chapter lies beyond only describing the procedure surrounding the transgressions in the legal texts, and its instances in the literary sources: the goal is to see if a cultural norm – or a set of cultural norms – can be distilled from the manner in which abuse and adultery are valued as violations of this norm.

With this in mind, I have structured the chapter as follows: in the first two sections, I will offer a brief introduction to the criminal law systems of ancient Athens and Rome by means of two famous trials, those of Socrates and Jesus Christ, and the forensic speeches of Demosthenes and Cicero. Next, I will look at the transgressions of abuse and adultery in the context of the penal procedures they were punished in. Finally, I shall attempt to employ the transgressions of abuse and adultery to say something about Greek and Roman culture in general, and the relationship between criminal law and popular morality in Antiquity in particular.

PHILOSOPHERS, ORATORS, LAWYERS AND THE MESSIAH

Many famous trials have been handed down to us from Antiquity. Among those, the most prominent are undoubtedly the trials of Socrates and Jesus Christ. Due to the status of their protagonists, both trials are relatively well documented, and thus provide us with the first insight into ancient criminal proceedings. As is common knowledge, Socrates was a

---

Post-doctoral researcher at the University of Helsinki. The author wishes to thank Ms. Heta Björklund for her editorial prowess and kind assistance, and Mr. Robert Whiting for proofreading the text. This chapter is written in the context of the ERC-project "Reinventing the foundations of European legal culture" (no. 313100).

Greek philosopher, living in fifth-century BCE Athens. He was alleged to have committed two wrongs: corrupting the youth, and impiety to the gods. The trial took place in 399 BCE. A jury of Athenian citizens drawn by lot from a group of volunteers found Socrates guilty, and eventually, by majority vote, sentenced him to death, the penalty proposed by the prosecution. Instead of fleeing the city, which he was apparently expected and even implored to do, Socrates carried out his own execution by drinking hemlock.[1] Some five hundred years later, in the Roman province of Judea, Jesus Christ was arrested and led before the Sanhedrin, a council of Jewish religious authorities. There, according to the biblical sources, he was mocked and beaten for claiming he was the son of God and king of the Jews. Subsequently, Jesus was arraigned before the administration in Jerusalem for sedition against the Roman rule, but the Roman governor of Judea, Pontius Pilate, publicly announced his innocence. The gathered crowd outside the government building, however, insisted on capital punishment. The governor acquiesced, and Jesus Christ was crucified on Golgotha.[2]

Although there are obviously vast differences between the two proceedings, the trials of Socrates and Jesus Christ also have some things in common. Whereas in modern criminal law a judge would be bound by precedent and the penal code, in the cases of Socrates and Jesus these do not seem to matter at all.[3] The citizens of Athens appear to be completely free in their decision to convict Socrates, lacking a judge instructing them in legal criteria to be satisfied or specific matters to be proven before a verdict can be reached (Sealey 1994: 51; Lanni 2006: 25; Waterfield 2009: 27–31). Pontius Pilate even reverses his verdict in the face of the disapproval of the Jerusalem crowd. As a result, at first sight, the relationship between criminal trials in particular and moral wrongs is much more direct in ancient societies than in modernity. Both Socrates and Jesus Christ seem to have been convicted because they had transgressed a fundamental (political, religious) cultural norm of their respective eras. These norms are not directly embedded in law codes or legal rules; rather, they are expressions of the world view of those involved in the trial, and consequently the societies they are a part of (Figure 7.1).

Yet a further result of the possible relationship between criminal trials and moral wrongs in Antiquity is the importance of orators and rhetoricians in the proceedings. These kinds of forensic speeches are our main sources of ancient criminal legal systems. Only in later Antiquity would something resembling a law school emerge: all those involved in a Greek or Roman trial including judges, prosecutors and lawyers were essentially laymen (Sealey 1994: 51; see Tuori in this volume). If there was such a thing as an education fit for the courts, it was through studying rhetoric and oratory, something obviously reserved only for the Greek and Roman elite. The oratory of Demosthenes, living in fourth-century BCE Athens some decades after the death of Socrates, was a product of such self-study. His transmitted work also shows that in ancient Athens the difference between forensic and political speeches is only fleeting. As is evident from the trial of Socrates, in general there was no clear dividing line between criminal legal trials and political proceedings in classical Athens. Demosthenes, however, started off as what would now be termed a law clerk, writing speeches for others and handling fairly mundane matters of private law—contracts, inheritances, etc. The grander stage of political-criminal trials like that of Socrates was seemingly out of his reach, possibly due to a speech impediment.[4] Yet, through rigorously applying himself, Demosthenes overcame the problem and became a prolific officer of the court, with the speeches handed down to us giving us much of our information on ancient Greek culture and the workings of the Athenian legal system.

FIGURE 7.1. Fresco from the Sala di Grande Dipinto, Scene II in the Villa de Misteri (Pompeii). Source: Wikimedia / The Yorck Project / GNU Free Documentation License.

Not just for modern students of rhetoric is Demosthenes still the archetypical orator. Several centuries after the death of Demosthenes, a Roman lawyer named Marcus Tullius Cicero would name him as one of his great examples (Cicero, *Brutus* 35). Cicero himself had pursued a career similar to that of Demosthenes—practicing oratory in the public law courts and making a name for himself, eventually holding some of the most prestigious offices of the Roman Republic (Rawson 1983: 12–59). As in ancient Athens, Republican Rome did not have any formal training requirements for court functions. Private tutoring, self-study, authority in the field and, of course, a background in the Roman elite all were factors in obtaining a successful career in the legal profession (see Tuori in this volume). However, the fact that Cicero was a "new man" from the provinces proves that outsiders could be successful and rise to power. In classical Athens and ancient Rome there was a significant difference between what we would now term "private law" and "public law," a difference much greater than between penal proceedings and political speeches. Large-scale criminal trials, often with a political background, were publicly held at the Forum Romanum, with orators trying to win the jeering crowds for their cause (Rawson 1983: 22–24). It was at these kinds of proceedings that Cicero excelled, delivering many of his best-preserved defenses and indictments, and giving us our knowledge of Roman criminal law in the late Republic.

Socrates, Demosthenes, Cicero, Jesus Christ—all living in ancient societies, all legendary figures, all having something to do with the public criminal law systems of their respective times. Also, the trials of Socrates and Christ and the court speeches of Demosthenes and Cicero seem to confirm this close relationship between criminal law and popular morality. It seems someone who was convicted in a criminal trial was not primarily found guilty of breaking the law, but rather of acting against what was generally deemed proper behavior, with a cross-section of the populace acting as arbiters rather than a judge or the law on the books. The problem with this assumption, however, is the extraordinary character of the proceedings themselves:[5] given the prominence of the protagonists already in their own times, in what measure are the trials of Socrates and Christ really representative of the day-to-day punishing of wrongs in Antiquity? Is this not like comparing the Nuremberg trials to the prosecution of a parking violation? And what, therefore, does this say about the context in which Demosthenes and Cicero gave their speeches?

ANCIENT LAWS AND ANCIENT WRONGS

Let us return to the trial of Socrates, look at how it was structured, and see in what measure it was representative of the criminal legal order in classical Athens as a whole. In the trial itself, there were multiple stages: first, it had to be determined whether there was a case to answer and the accusers sworn in. Second, a jury was assembled by lot, and the accusers held their opening speeches. Then, the accused was allowed to defend himself, which Socrates did in his famous apology.[6] After witness testimonies were heard and the jury had reached a verdict, in the third stage again by the jury, not the judge, the punishment was set (Waterfield 2009: 7–19). In addition to the lack of the presence of a judge in the proceedings, two other absences are noteworthy: Socrates did not have a lawyer, although this may well have happened by choice, conducting the cross-examination of the accusers himself (Waterfield 2009: 8–19). Furthermore, even though he is accused of two well-defined offenses—impiety and corrupting the youth of Athens—it remains unclear what criteria needed to be fulfilled and proven before a guilty verdict could be reached by the jury.

For the content of specific transgressions in ancient Athens, there are two main sources of information: the laws of Athens and the speeches delivered primarily in its courts. Classical Athens around the time of Socrates actually did have a set of laws, set up first by Draco—which is where the proverbial notion of Draconian legislation comes from—and subsequently altered and redacted by and after Solon (Sealey 1994: 43–49).[7] However, even though this set of regulations has been reconstructed, (Ruschenbusch 2010: 57–63), generally speaking Athenian criminal law lacked clear legal definitions, particularly with regard to certain "subjective" transgressions (Hitzig 1899: 35–36; Sealey 1994: 53; Lanni 2006: 68, 118). Thus, written laws only summarily covered punishable transgressions, leaving a considerable amount of discretion for juries in particular (Sealey 1994: 54–55). For example, as is evident from the trial of Socrates, being found guilty of a specific crime did not always result in a specific punishment: this was still up to the jury to determine. Hence the important role of orators in these types of trials; the accusers in the trial of Socrates or someone like Demosthenes had multiple occasions to sway a jury for instance, obtaining a more severe or a milder punishment even after a jury had already condemned the accused. When we think of serious crimes, we think of manslaughter, various types of theft, rape or physical abuse, and in these cases we expect our government to punish those that are found guilty of committing them. From the trial of Socrates, it is already apparent that ancient societies differed somewhat in their perception of what constitutes a serious crime. Of course, matters such as theft and rape were brought before the courts, and corrupting the youth or impiety could be construed to constitute punishable offenses in a modern sense. However, rather than a dichotomy between private and public law as such, in ancient Athens a distinction was made between popular and private claims. The difference between the two claims is primarily that popular claims can be instituted by any citizen, whereas private claims were privy to the actual victim of the transgression. Moreover, popular claims tended to be limited to transgressions either committed against the common good, i.e., political crimes such as treason or against people lacking legal standing (Krause 2004: 17–18). This means that in ancient Athens prosecutions for manslaughter were probably strictly limited to private claims instituted by family members aimed at compensation (Krause 2004: 33–34). Vice versa, when we look at the criminal law speeches of Demosthenes handed down to us, they tend to concern popular claims with a political character: e.g., among his extant orations there are four instances of the popular claim regarding the enactment of unsuitable laws (MacDowell 2009: 153–206).

Whereas the trial of Socrates can to a large degree be seen as exemplifying the classical Athenian criminal legal system as a whole, in the case of the trial of Jesus Christ there is a complicating factor. The drama took place not in Rome, but in one of the provinces of the budding Empire. This means that whatever we know about the situation in Rome may not be relevant for Judea. Then again, one of our main sources for the application of Roman criminal law outside of Rome is a speech of Cicero. In his orations against Verres, made in 70 BCE, Cicero prosecutes the governor of the Roman province of Sicily for corruption (Figure 7.2). Taking place in Rome, the trial was one in the context of the large public proceedings held at the Forum Romanum, in front of a large crowd. The trial was held under a law regarding corruption enacted a decade before by the dictator Cornelius Sulla. Cicero states explicitly he was asked to prosecute the case on behalf of the residents of Sicily, with one of the more serious charges being the abuse of the judicial powers of the governor by Verres. As is evident from the trial of Jesus Christ, Roman governors in the provinces had the supreme judicial authority with the obligation for lower judicial bodies to bring more serious crimes like sedition before his court, as the religious council did with Christ. Moreover, Roman governors were very free to enjoy this power as they pleased, even though the prosecution of Verres by Cicero shows it was by no means unfettered. After Cicero's second oration, Verres did not await the outcome of the trial, and went into voluntary exile (Rawson 1983: 40–43). At this juncture a word needs to be said about the relationship between Roman law—or more accurately the legal rules of the Romans— and the local laws of the communities they conquered or otherwise came into contact with. Whereas there is barely such a thing as "ancient Greek law" since the laws are so peculiar to the separate city-states, Roman law was spread throughout the growing Empire over a period of three hundred years. The discussion on the measure in which the law of the Empire supplanted local laws goes back to a work of the Roman law scholar Ludwig Mitteis (Mitteis 1891; Höbenreich 1992: 547–551). But despite new information in the form of archaeological finds, we still do not know how Roman and local laws actually related to one another. From the trial of Jesus, however, it is clear the Roman governor had a superior jurisdiction in specific types of cases, particularly those involving political crimes.

FIGURE 7.2. Fresco from the Sala di Grande Dipinto, Scene VI in the Villa de Misteri (Pompeii). Source: Michele Falzone / Getty Images.

Returning to Verres, another thing his trial shows us about the Roman criminal law system is that specific trials were set up under specific laws. As in Athens, the distinction between crimes committed against the common good that were prosecuted on the basis of a popular claim, such as governmental corruption in the case of Verres, and claims stemming from someone's private interest is much more relevant than that between private and public criminal law, particularly in the course of the Roman Republic. For instance, manslaughter was for a long time seen as a private matter, just like theft and physical abuse (Kunkel 1962: 97–130). This changed somewhat with two sets of laws, the first enacted by the dictator Sulla to which the law regarding corruption also belongs. This set certainly included a public criminal law regarding manslaughter as well as physical abuse, but also several political transgressions. The second set then came into force several decades later after the death of Cicero, and is one of the hallmarks of the demise of the Republic and the rise of the Roman Empire. This set of laws, often replacing or building on those of Sulla, was enacted during the reign of Augustus between 27 BCE and 14 CE. Augustus did not replace the Sullan laws regarding manslaughter or physical abuse, but did formulate new ones concerning most political crimes, for example, the law regarding treason. Moreover, the emperor attempted to create some order in the chaos that was the Roman legal system at the time by abolishing some redundant procedures and making laws to streamline private and public criminal trials.[8]

Augustus had good reasons to do this. There is a definite measure of disarray to the manner in which transgressions were punished under Roman law from the later Republic until the later Empire. As stated, much of what we would see as typically falling under public criminal law, such as physical abuse, was deemed a private matter that remained primarily subject to claims in private law courts even after the enactment of the Sullan law regarding physical abuse. Only aggravated forms of theft, like the theft of cattle, were made a part of public criminal law. Otherwise, theft was punished by means of a private law action (Harries 2007: 43–58). Generally speaking, public criminal law was centered on single laws made for singular crimes that concerned transgressions of the common good: treason, corruption, sedition, public violence, et cetera. In this, there is another factor that determined how and under what circumstances a transgression was to be punished: status. Of course, both ancient Athens and ancient Rome were societies of slaveholders, and slaves did not enjoy equal treatment under the law to say the least. However, in classical Rome specifically, the division between citizenship and non-citizenship may have been even more important than that between slaves and free men, taking into account that slaves, by definition, did not have Roman citizenship. A Roman provincial governor had much more freedom to punish culprits when the defendant did not have Roman citizenship.[9] This leads one to question, for example, whether Jesus Christ was crucified, a harsh penalty even by Roman standards and usually reserved for slaves, because he lacked Roman citizenship or on the basis of the political seriousness of the crime of sedition.

In any case, with a multitude of possibly applicable laws to a particular transgression, again the role of orators in the public criminal trial needs to be highlighted here. Even in the rhetorical manuals written by Cicero himself, the importance of choosing the right procedure on the basis of a myriad of factors like the status of the prosecutors or defendants is emphasized. It seems that the notion of "playing the system" is not limited to modernity. Contrary to the situation in Athens, however, criteria more or less derived from legal texts or precedent do seem to have played a part in determining the proper procedure for specific transgressions. An interesting example of this is Cicero's defense of Milo, who was accused of killing Clodius in a clash between two rival gangs just outside Rome. The trial was held under a law regarding public violence, but Cicero argues primarily on the basis of the Sullan law regarding manslaughter. The problematic criterion is the fact that Milo was armed in public, making him automatically liable for a charge of public violence. However, if Cicero could manage to convince the jury that Milo did not bring his weapon with the intent of killing Clodius, a plea for self-defense might exonerate him under the law regarding manslaughter (Cicero, *For Milo* 14; Cahen 1923: 127–136). Scholars have argued that similar separations of legal criteria from popular morality form the essence of the development of legal science in Rome and account for the lack of such a development in Athens earlier (Schulz 1954: 13–17; Schulz 1963: 54–55, 60–71). In Rome, there is a difference between what is illegal and what is immoral. It may not be a coincidence that the development of Roman legal science coincided with the growth of the Roman sphere of influence in the Mediterranean. Early scientific treatments of law are primarily to be found in the context of the law of contracts (Cicero, *On duties* 3.69–70: Giltaij 2011: 31–36; Fiori in this volume). Yet, even though principles of fair dealing surely had a moral dimension, the law of contracts would not be the first place to look for a relationship between legal practice and ancient popular morality. To examine this relationship, I will focus on two transgressions to be found in the public criminal law of both classical Athens and Rome: abuse and adultery.

CRIMES AS TRANSGRESSIONS OF CULTURAL NORMS: ABUSE AND ADULTERY

Like so many others, the regulation punishing the crime of abuse in ancient Greece is transmitted mainly through the speeches of Demosthenes (Demosthenes, *Speeches* 21.47; Hitzig 1899: 34; Thalheim 1916 col. 31; Ruschenbusch 1965: 302). The character of the crime of abuse in fourth century BCE Athens is discussed in his speech against Meidias, who had punched Demosthenes in the face in a packed theater while the orator was there serving in an official capacity at a festival (Demosthenes, *Speeches* 21; Lanni 2006: 124–125). From the speech, it becomes clear there had been a long-standing rivalry between Demosthenes and Meidias, but the orator is at pains to include other instances of the misbehavior of Meidias, presenting him as a bully and an all-round bad seed (Demosthenes, *Speeches* 21.95–107; MacDowell 2009: 248–252). The affair then came to a head in the theater, with Meidias attempting to obstruct and derail the proceedings, resulting in the severe faux pas of putting his hands on an official during a public ceremony (Demosthenes, *Speeches* 21.36–55; MacDowell 2009: 245–247). As such, these fragments indicate abuse was seen in ancient Athens as the greater crime compared to mere physical assault, carrying, for instance, a serious penalty compared to the latter's compensatory damages.[10] Irrespective of whether the case itself actually involved abuse as such, Demosthenes provides examples in the speech where the public character of a physical assault amounted to abuse (Demosthenes, *Speeches* 21.71–76; Lanni 2006: 125).

Also, already from this text alone, the multitude of offenses the transgression covered become apparent. The transgression could be both physical and verbal, but was primarily aimed at dishonoring someone[11]: thus, the transgression is closely related to the Greek concepts of shame and honor (Hitzig 1899: 36–39; Cohen 1991: 83, 208; Krause 2004: 26; Lanni 2006: 28–30, 64–65) (Figure 7.3). A noteworthy aspect of the wording of the regulation on abuse as it appears in the law adapted by Solon is the explicit mention of children, women and slaves as victims (Hitzig 1899: 43–45; Thalheim 1916: col. 31; Sealey 1994: 129). In such cases, the legal guardian would lodge the complaint. The complaint generally speaking was therefore a popular claim, i.e., open to everyone, not just the victim (Hitzig 1899: 45; Guettel Cole 1984: 9; Krause 2004: 27). Lacking a statutory or otherwise singular definition, the exact meaning of the transgression has to be distilled from the extant relevant texts and few individual cases. Typical perhaps is the prosecution of Conon by Ariston as related by once again Demosthenes. Allegedly, Ariston was not only jumped and beaten, but also insulted by Conon.[12] Similar to the case against Meidias, it is not strictly speaking abuse that is being prosecuted. Yet, Demosthenes refers to the transgression of abuse to emphasize the dishonorable aspects of the matter at hand: it is employed to show the generally bad character of the culprit, his abusive personality rather than the act itself (Demosthenes, *Speeches* 54.24–37: Mirhady 2000: 199–200).

There are interesting points of overlap between abuse and adultery as transgressions in ancient Athenian law. For one thing, Aristotle mentions both as instances of transgressions lacking a singular legal definition; also, both are included in his list of public complaints (Aristotle, *Constitution of Athens* 59.2–4; Cohen 1991: 115, 122, but see 123); and committing abuse or adultery seems to have been prominent lawful grounds for being killed on the spot by the victim,[13] underlining the seriousness of the offenses as such. Cohen, stating "there are no 'sexual offenses', in the modern sense, in Athenian law," even suggests a material overlap with regard to various types of sexual misconduct.[14] Certainly, the crime of abuse as an affront to someone's honor appears closely related to

FIGURE 7.3. Fresco from the Sala di Grande Dipinto, Scene VIII in the Villa de Misteri (Pompeii). Source: De Agostini / L. Romano / Getty Images.

ancient Athenian notions of sexual deviancy (Cohen 1991: 183–185, 221–222; Krause 2004: 26); however, it is far from evident that adultery was actually punishable as a transgression with a specifically sexual character, i.e., aimed at sexual moral wrongness, but rather as the act of entering someone's house uninvited and making use of something that does not belong to one.[15] In this, it does not help matters that there are even fewer instances, such as relevant court cases, of adultery than abuse handed down to us. Yet, adultery does not seem to amount to dishonoring the victim any less than abuse (Cohen 1991: 123), and the importance of punishing adultery should not be underestimated (Krause 2004: 42). Leaving this complex problem aside, even though its text has not been transmitted, there is a long-standing consensus on the main features of the Athenian law punishing adultery[16]: what is punished is the act of seducing—in any case—the wife of an Athenian citizen.[17] It is thus the male adulterer that is primarily the object of punishment in the statute, either being lawfully killed by the victim on the spot or incurring the death penalty, whereas the adulteress would have been divorced and rejected by her house as well as all of the city's religious ceremonies, effectively making her an outcast (Cohen 1991: 107, Krause 2004: 41).

Before going into the Roman versions of the crimes of abuse and adultery, it may be interesting to note that in the Republic a single office came to be charged with upholding moral standards, namely the censor. Even though his function of keeping the lists of citizens and holding the census goes back as far as 443 BCE,[18] from 312 BCE on the censor is charged with the preservation of ethical norms. As appears from various later sources, the censors could punish moral transgressions by means of a censorial note (Mommsen 1877: 385, n. 2; Schmähling 1938: 38, 49, 84; Kunkel and Wittmann 1995: 416). Possibly, the censors formulated these ethical norms in edicts preserved or adapted by their successors (Mommsen 1877: 373, Schmähling 1938: 2). When a rule on equitable grounds was deemed to have been broken (Schmähling 1938: 2ff), a censorial note was inscribed in the archive and made public after the census.[19] The dishonorable conduct in question could lead to the penalty of ignominy or infamy (Cicero, *On duties* 3.115; Cicero, *For Cluentius* 121; Mommsen 1877: 382–383), or even disbarment from the senate or deprivation of Roman citizenship (Mommsen 1877: 384–387; Schmähling 1938: 13ff.; Kunkel and Wittmann 1995: 409). However, although they most likely did have jurisdiction,[20] due to the lack of credible source material (Mommsen 1877: 382; Greenidge 1894: 41f.; Schmähling 1938: 13f.; Suolahti 1963: 49) coupled with the presumed extra-legal, random and unwritten character of the procedure (Cicero, *For Cluentius* 117; Kunkel and Wittmann 1995: 407, 409), there is not much we know with certainty about the nature of the maintenance of norms by the censor. The sources simply do not provide enough information.

Contrary to the jurisdiction of the censor, the existence of a crime of abuse is well attested in the Roman sources. In the law of the XII Tables of 450 BCE, abuse originally only covered physical violence against free persons as well as slaves (Pugliese 1941: 1–38, Hagemann 1998: 40–48). However, the transgression came to encompass a myriad of offenses, ranging from verbal insult to sexual harassment, certainly primarily aimed at vindicating affronts to one's honor.[21] In this, there are remarkable similarities between the historical development of the crime of abuse in Greek and Roman law (Hitzig 1899: 55). For example, from a later compilation of Roman legal texts composed between 100 BCE and 250 CE known as the Digest, it appears that as in Greek law treating a free man as a slave constituted an act of punishable abuse (Hitzig 1899: 55–56; *Digesta* 47.10.11.9; *Digesta* 47.10.12, etc.). In another source, the Roman jurist Labeo, writing in the time of Augustus, even explicitly refers to the Greek transgression—in Greek no less—in his discussion of the notion of abuse.[22] Then again, whereas the type of abuse we have hitherto focused on was considered a public action in Athens to be instituted by any citizen, abuse as it is described in the extant Roman sources mainly was a private delict, meaning the victim alone could pursue the remedy primarily via the private procedure under the office of the *praetor*, the Roman magistrate charged with the distribution of legal remedies. Yet, there actually existed a public type of regulation against abuse, namely a law enacted by the late-Republican dictator Cornelius Sulla. The literature compares this regulation to the legal notion of abuse in ancient Greece since both may have been dealt with in a public criminal trial.[23]

In a similar vein, adultery was described and prohibited by a specific Roman statute, namely the law of Augustus regarding adultery.[24] The literature tends to treat the law in conjunction with two scandals that had affected Augustus himself. The first took place some time before his reign in 62 BCE and involved the wife of Julius Caesar, his adoptive father. An ally of Caesar had intruded into a religious ceremony overseen by the wife of

Caesar with the aim of seducing her. Attendance at the ceremony was strictly limited to women, and the ally was thus prosecuted. Even though he was eventually acquitted, the affair did heavy damage to the reputation of Caesar. He was forced to divorce his wife due to her perceived impiety as well as his function as a high priest, responsible for the proper execution of religious rituals (Rawson 1983: 93–105; McGinn 1998: 24). Augustus, having taken up the office of high priest himself, may have taken the scandal as a cue for his moral legislation. The second affair concerned the household of Augustus even more directly. During his reign in 2 BCE, his own daughter was convicted of adultery under her father's law and exiled to a desert island. In both cases, the trials may have been politically motivated. However, in Roman culture the notion of the *exemplum* is paramount: the necessity of "leading by example" and showing that no one is exempt from the norms Roman society upholds, even when it concerns one's own family (Bauman 1996: 53–55; McGinn 1998: 168–169; Harries 2007: 103) (Figure 7.4).

Another interesting aspect of the law of Augustus regarding adultery is the similarity to the transgression in ancient Athens. As in the case of abuse, a Roman jurist compares the transgression in his day to a notion in the relevant Greek legislation.[25] But there are more points of contact: like the Athenian law, the text of the regulation lacks a clear definition of adultery (McGinn 1998: 144), and, as in the Athenian law, there seems to have been a type of privileged accusation for the alleged victim, even though in principle it was a public one, i.e., open to every citizen (McGinn 1998: 145).[26] Moreover, the penalties in both legal orders for the adulterous women are somewhat comparable, being forms of expulsion from civil society, e.g., treated as a prostitute in Rome (McGinn 1998: 156–171). Finally, the principal aim of the law is described by McGinn as "the repression of those forms of non-marital sexual relations considered unacceptable by Roman society, particularly adultery" (McGinn 1998: 140). As such, there is a definite moral connotation to the law of Augustus: Schulz even goes so far as to ascribe to the emperor the motive of population control, coupling the law regarding adultery to various other Augustan legislative measures in the field of manumission and the extension of Roman citizenship (1954: 82). Be that as it may, a further similarity to the Greek development consists of the possibility that the statute limited the previously unfettered right of the husband (or father) to kill both the adulterer and the adulteress on the spot rather than confirming that right (McGinn 1998: 146–147). The motive of the legislator should then rather be sought in curbing self-help in the context of the family, or maintaining public order against violations of "private property," than a strictly moral purpose.

To summarize, the transgressions of abuse and adultery occur in both Greek and Roman law. Moreover, in both legal orders, these seem to be very closely connected to popular morality, by virtue of the context in which they are prosecuted, their content matter and their "subjective" character. The Romans even tended to refer to the earlier Greek iterations, leading to the question of whether the underlying societal norms were actually similar, and if so, what did these societal norms then entail?

THE SCOPE OF ABUSE AND ADULTERY AS MORAL TRANSGRESSIONS

Looking at the relevant legal sources, in an unexpected turn of events the best case for abuse and adultery in Roman law as specifically moral transgressions seems to be various forms of abuse of slaves. The analogy between adultery among the free and the sexual abuse of female slaves, even as a violation of the moral integrity of the female slave

FIGURE 7.4. Roman fresco showing a dancing menad from the Villa dei Misteri in Pompeii (Sala del Grande Dipinto, scene V). Source: Superstock / Getty Images.

herself, is made clear by the Roman jurists Papinian[27] and Ulpian.[28] Excessive beating of slaves was punished in the context of the crime of abuse as "morally wrong."[29] Even though generally speaking beating a slave was punishable only when this entailed an insult to the master, there is textual evidence that Roman jurists under certain circumstances also regarded the act as a criminal act against the slave proper (Buckland 1908: 80–82).[30] Moreover, it seems that, at least in the context of the abuse of slaves, it is stated in the legal sources as a specifically moral transgression. Finally, it should be mentioned that it is the master himself who is punished for committing these moral transgressions. For example, Ulpian states that a master's excessive cruelty towards his slave by forcing him into a life of shame and vice is to be punished. Furthermore, relief from cruelty, hunger or intolerable outrage should not be refused to those that cry out (*Mosaicarum et Romanarum legum collatio* 3.3.1, Hyamson 1913: 71). Similar statements can be found in other legal texts from the same era and later (Gai. *Inst.* 1.53, *Dig.* 1.6.2; *Dig.* 1.12.1). Leaving aside the many difficulties regarding the concrete procedure (Hagemann 1998: 63–64, 86–87, 116–126; Gamauf 1999), the main issue at hand is the jurist Ulpian seeing these acts against slaves as primarily and explicitly moral transgressions, violations of predetermined ethical norms.

Several scholars have connected a development towards a more humane treatment for slaves in legal texts from the time of Ulpian to the rise and spread of Christianity throughout the Empire (Schulz 1963: 297–299, 311–315; Gaudemet 1967: 715–718). Although as far as I can ascertain there is no direct evidence for this relation, in a later collection of Roman legal texts punishing abuse (and manslaughter) of slaves by their own masters is subsumed under the commandment "Thou shalt not kill" (Liebs 2015: 239–242, 253). Similarly, we still possess a wealth of information on the transgression of adultery in Roman law because compilations of Roman legal sources from the late Republic and early Empire were made under the auspices of Christian emperors, primarily Justinian's Digest in the sixth century CE. It seems that the commandment "Thou shalt not covet thy neighbours wife" and the transgression of adultery as it occurs in Roman public criminal law were to a degree seen as compatible (Liebs 2015: 91–96, 118–122), even though the underlying set of morals is fundamentally different; something signalled by Church Fathers like Ambrose as well (Colish 2008: 42–43). As such, when looking at Roman criminal law as an expression of ancient societal norms, the question can be posed in what measure we are actually seeing a Christianized version of these morals, due to later selections of texts that have been transmitted to us. The transgressions of abuse and adultery both have complicated later histories that long surpass the fall of the Roman Empire, up until the Enlightenment and arguably today. In this sense, it is perhaps impossible to look beyond two thousand years of Christian ethics and attempt to say something about ancient morality itself by means of the Roman legal texts (Figure 7.5).

On the other hand, Ulpian was not the first to refer to forms of legal protection for slaves against abuse in the early third century CE. The philosopher Seneca, writing about two hundred years before Ulpian, poses basically the same tripartite division of normatively charged notions in his treatise *On benefits* (3.22.3) that the jurist would make later. Apart from Seneca's more direct allusion to sexual abuse as such, the fascinating thing

FIGURE 7.5. Full fresco at one of the walls of the house: Roman fresco in the Villa dei Misteri at Pompeii, triclinium wall. Source: Iberfoto / Superstock.

about the text is not that the philosopher relates legal and moral-ethical considerations to one another, but his particular formulation of the legal institution as a demonstration of the ethical norm. First of all, this raises the question: where does the law come from? As regards the crime of abuse, we have seen there is some reason to assume a degree of similitude between specific Greek and Roman types of legal regulations dealing with this transgression, the peculiar structure of the complaint in particular.[31] Also, both were seen as similar by the Roman jurists themselves, and lastly to some degree appeared to have been applicable to criminal acts against slaves. It is therefore tempting to view the procedure as described in Seneca's text as the one based on the Sullan law regarding abuse, the creation or interpretation of which had, in turn, been to some degree influenced by the earlier Greek provisions. Scholars of Greek and Roman law have asked themselves the same questions, but, despite being fairly positive about the possibility, they do stress that there is simply not enough proof to assume that any of this supposed influence actually occurred (Pugliese 1941: 39–79). Besides that, there are other obstacles: for one, the Sullan law seems to deal exclusively with (apparently non-sexual) physical forms of abuse.[32]

As for adultery, the literature sometimes relates the application and even enactment of the Augustan law on the matter to his usurpation of the aforementioned censorial jurisdiction (Cassius Dio 54.6.6; Volkmann 1969: 80–81, 194–197; McGinn 1998: 79, fn 109, 90). However, this assumption is mostly based on a passage in Cassius Dio, who writes about two hundred years after Augustus. Then again, Dio is not the only source for the office of the censor dealing with familial matters: the historian Dionysius of Halicarnassus, writing as a contemporary of Augustus, portrays cruelty of masters to their slaves and unjust acts of the husband towards his wife as falling under censorial oversight, contrasting this with the earlier situation in Athens.[33] Composing his works a short time after Augustus, Valerius Maximus (8.2.3) provides an example of a woman guilty of adultery being punished by the censors by losing a portion of her dowry (McGinn 1998: 141). Finally, a noteworthy source is Augustus himself reading the speech of a Republican censor as regards family matters in the senate, possibly to justify his policies and laws (Suetonius, *Augustus* 89.2; McGinn 1998: 79). The point of citing these examples is not so much to show Augustus assuming the powers of the office of the censor, or that laws may have been drawn up with this office in mind, but rather that the crimes of abuse and adultery were the primary conduits of punishing violations of a preexisting moral code. This might be the reason for Augustus upholding the Sullan law regarding abuse[34] and enacting his law regarding adultery, whether or not actually connected to the office of the censor. For someone who ostensibly wanted to be seen as restoring Republican values, references to the censor may have served a propagandistic purpose as well. But the mere mention of the office suggest the laws were seen against a moral background by the Romans,[35] even if the references themselves served a political purpose and irrespective of whether the censors in the Republic in reality had the power or jurisdiction to punish abuse and adultery.

In his work on prostitution in Roman law, McGinn raises the question of the social purpose of the law of Augustus regarding adultery (McGinn 1998: 213, 246). Surely, public criminal prosecutions of abuse and adultery appear to be out of character with a division between public crimes with a political character, openly prosecuted before a jury of citizens, and private transgressions as matters of compensation between individuals and families. However, both in ancient Athens and Rome abuse and adultery were prosecuted publicly, as matters against the common good. Consider that Socrates and

Jesus, who were perceived as having transgressed fundamental societal norms, had been prosecuted in types of trials that were to a great extent similar to those applicable to abuse and adultery. So what was that fundamental societal norm the punishment of abuse and adultery in Athens and Rome aimed to protect? And are they indeed comparable norms, seeing the relationship between the notions of abuse and adultery in ancient Greek and Roman society? At first glance, seeing their subject matter, prosecutions of abuse and adultery seem to primarily protect against acts of sexual deviancy. But the sources provide a multitude of other considerations and motives. With ancient Greek and Roman societies being deeply patriarchal, it seems both abuse and adultery were also aimed at infringements of another man's household, be it his wife, his children, or his slaves. In this sense, punishing abuse and adultery is presented as an explicit alternative to self-help and private vengeance.

But further motives could be at play as well. As shown by the criminalization of the abuse of slaves by their own masters in Rome, the power of the pater familias over his household was protected on the one hand, but on the other some legal limits were imposed on it, specifically under the jurisdiction of the censor in the Republic and criminal proceedings for abuse in the course of the Empire. It is debatable whether the law of Augustus regarding adultery actually aimed at placing limits on the power of the pater familias in a similar fashion: seeing its character as an alternative to private vengeance, it could have been aimed at obliging the victim to request government aid rather than killing the culprits himself (McGinn 1998: 203–206; Harries 2007: 97–98). If this is the case, the marriage legislation of Augustus was an impressive feat of social engineering, making a symbolic and significant attempt to intrude into the Roman bedroom on a scale that was vast compared to what the government was capable of enforcing in practice. A fourth and final possible motive concerns the similarities between the Greek and Roman prosecutions for abuse and adultery, especially with the explicit references of the Roman jurists to the legislation of ancient Athens. In fifth and fourth century BCE Greece, prosecutions of abuse and adultery appear to be comparably structured by means of a popular claim and motivated as an alternative to private vengeance. Does this mean there was a more direct relationship between ancient Greek and Roman laws? And is then the fundamental societal norm at the basis of these laws comparable, notwithstanding the large cultural differences between classical Athenian and Roman society?

CONCLUSION

The trials of Socrates and Jesus Christ supply striking cultural insights into the prosecution of wrongs in ancient Athens and the Roman Empire. It appears both the philosopher and the Messiah were not primarily convicted for breaking a law, but rather for transgressing certain preexisting fundamental societal norms. Laws and legal criteria only carry a secondary role in their respective trials. The guilty verdicts in both instances are rendered almost without any recourse at all to legal criteria or precedents. Instead, juries of citizens seem to have been completely free to render their verdicts based on the evidence presented to them; thus, there is a close relationship between popular morality and the prosecution of wrongs committed in Antiquity. As such, the primary sources for ancient criminal legal systems are those presenting or refuting this evidence in court, in particular the speeches of the orator Demosthenes as regards Greece and the lawyer Marcus Tullius Cicero for Rome.

FIGURE 7.6. Dancing satyr (second style) from the cubiculum next to the Sala del Grande Dipinto in the Villa de Misteri (Pompeii). Source: DEA / A. DAGLI ORTI / Getty Images.

Looking at Demosthenes and Cicero, in classical times many of the transgressions we would now classify as serious crimes such as theft and manslaughter were subject to a private complaint instead of a public prosecution. Rather, public criminal law concerned crimes against the common good, often of a political nature, such as treason, sedition, and governmental corruption. These were prosecuted very openly and publicly, in front of large crowds, in central areas in Athens and Rome. However, in the course of their development, transgressions that were not primarily political by nature came to be a part of both criminal legal orders. In Athens, the crime of abuse is attested and described in several of the speeches of Demosthenes as a publicly prosecuted transgression. Similarly, adultery is counted among the public crimes. In Rome, only in the late Republic was legislation passed making abuse a crime against the common good. Some decades later, Augustus enacted the first law regarding adultery in ancient Rome, establishing it likewise as a public crime.

If the manner in which some ancient offenses are prosecuted says something about the way they are viewed by the societies involved, what then made abuse and adultery crimes against the common good, subject to a public prosecution? Without doubt, the transgressions have a moral character and were in all instances strongly related to ancient notions of shame and honor (Figure 7.6). Moreover, the examples the sources provide tend to involve the property of the victim, i.e., the wife, family members, or slaves of the pater familias, suggesting it is not the sexual deviancy in itself that is punished, but the culprit interfering with something that is not his. On the other hand, the treatment of abuse and adultery as public crimes could actually be seen as limiting the powers of the pater familias over his family, inasmuch as the cases often refer to their prosecution as an alternative to self-help, i.e., the victim enacting private vengeance on the culprit. In Roman law, this is taken to the extreme of the master incurring a criminal liability for the maltreatment, sexually or otherwise, of his own slave.

What does it then say about ancient societies that abuse and adultery were prosecuted publicly as serious crimes, in trials similar to those against Socrates and Jesus Christ? Obviously, this does suggest that victimizing another man's family amounted to a serious infringement on the rights of the pater familias as affecting the common good. In patriarchal cultures made up of slaveholders, this should not surprise us. However, abuse and adultery only became public crimes in Athens and Rome when the scope of these societies was expanding—the upshot of Hellenism in the former, the budding Empire in the latter case. With this, it seems reasonable to assume the criminalization of abuse and adultery, which formerly had been matters between citizens exclusively, was the result of an abstraction from the tribal, close-knit relations as they existed earlier. Punishing abuse and adultery developed into government responsibilities—particularly with a view to limiting the consequences of the continuous back and forth of forms of private vengeance. Finally, it is interesting, considering their references to the Athenian laws, to ask whether the Greek experience was explicitly taken into account by the Roman jurists in their practice and Augustus in his policies.

CHAPTER EIGHT

Legal Profession

KAIUS TUORI

INTRODUCTION

To speak of the legal profession in the context of the ancient world is an anachronism. Even in the most legally engaged of ancient cultures, such as classical Rome, there was no legal profession as it is currently understood. The modern groupings that now constitute the legal professions of the Western world, such as judges, advocates, prosecutors, lawyers, defense attorneys, administrative lawyers, or business lawyers, were conspicuously absent. What there was, in nearly every ancient culture from which we have enough sources to base any conclusions (e.g. Egypt, Mesopotamia, Greece and Rome, all complex societies that have left us a plethora of written sources), was a legal culture in which the settling of disputes was managed through some level of specialization. In most Greek city-states, trials were conducted in front of large panels of juries, whose composition was often based on random selection among citizens. The most important skill for these advocates was rhetoric, the capacity to sway the argument with persuasion that appealed to the feelings of the audience rather than cold facts (Crook 1995: 30–34). In ancient Rome, litigants were represented in court by persons skilled in the law and the judges, who were not necessarily lawyers, were often aided by legal specialists. Romans such as Cicero would often look down upon the Greeks, who took their legal advice from lowly court clerks (*pragmatici*), while among the Romans, legal knowledge was vested with the authority of the most eminent of citizens (Cicero, *De oratore* 1.253). With the lack of a uniform system of training or professional degrees, what constituted a legal professional or a person skilled in the law was a matter of common understanding among the group so distinguished. Likewise, they determined what counted as legal knowledge (in Rome, this encompassed not only knowledge of the statutory law, but also knowledge of legal customs and practices). What, then, formed this common understanding?

The purpose of this chapter is to explore the concept of the legal profession within the ancient world as a part of what is conceptualized as a social imaginary. Taylor's idea of the social imaginary has recently been revisited by Ando in an interesting essay on how to grasp the background assumptions behind practices and shared common understandings that legitimate them in the ancient world (Ando 2015b: 4). The concept of social imaginary thus encompasses not only what we know and how we know something, but also why we think that something is right and proper the way it is. In this chapter, the aim is to use the framework of social imaginaries to grasp the deep structure of how a legal profession was conceptualized socially. Instead of looking at the various groupings of persons involved in the legal world, in this chapter our aim will be one particular example, the social ties and shared cultural understanding that united the Roman legal profession. People involved in the same profession tend to form a particular sub-culture, where certain values and presuppositions are shared. The chapter explores the themes of friendship and enmity, networks of politics and friendship, the shifting borders of professional and personal, and the difficult definitions of students and friends.

The nature of the Roman legal profession has been the subject of growing controversy among classicists and Roman legal historians. During the last decades, the importance of kinship and social networks has been increasingly acknowledged and may yet lead to an unprecedented transformation of our views on lawyers and their role in Roman society (Crook 1995; Harries 2006). This chapter charts a more nuanced middle passage in the so-called professionalization debate (*Fachjuristenstreit*) in juristic prosopography, between the orthodoxy of W. Kunkel (2001) and R. A. Bauman (1983, 1989) and the challenges of Tellegens (most recently Tellegen-Couperus and Tellegen 2013: 31–50). Of those, the first argued for a minimalist view, they wanted to see legal professionals or lawyers as specialists defined by a rigid core competence and distinct from rhetoricians or politicians speaking in courts, the latter claimed that no such distinctions existed and rhetorical training was extended also to the so-called legal experts (on that, see especially Leesen 2010).

This chapter offers a new reading of the changes in the relationships between the actors on the juridical stage, the lawyers, orators, clients, and friends. It is argued that even though the inner dogmatic coherence of the law appears to continue, the social and political networks of the legal profession undergo a profound change during the first century BCE. This change was not limited to a rupture in the relationship between the political and legal sphere, it also involved the way lawyers interacted with their *familiares*, students, allies, friends, and clients. As always, it is most interesting to examine a situation during a time of change, as change allows the unspoken assumptions and underpinnings to emerge within the cultural landscape. It is equally necessary to question how the internal coherence of law was both constituted and maintained.

The argument is substantiated using material from two cases, first the esteemed legal family of Mucii Scaevolae, second the Augustan jurists Labeo and Capito and their rivalry. The conventional image of Republican jurisprudence is dominated by the Ciceronian account of the tasks of the lawyer as *respondere cavere agere*, the idea that lawyers had three main tasks: to respond to legal queries (*respondere*), to draft legal documents and thus to prevent issues beforehand (*cavere*) and to advance legal claims in court (*agere*). The emphasis of the importance of *communis opinio* and collegiality on the one hand, and the acquisition of gratitude (*gratia*) by means of responding to legal queries (*respondere*) on the other (Bauman 1983), have disguised the very competitive nature of the profession during the late Republic. The idealized image of the Mucii Scaevolae is contrasted with the intense juxtaposition of Labeo and Capito, the main figures of Augustan jurisprudence and the founders of the first schools of law.

WHY LAWYERS LOST THEIR FRIENDS

The English word "friendship" brings to mind deep emotional connections between like-minded individuals. The Latin word *amicitia*, which is often awkwardly translated as friendship, had many varied meanings. Not only did it mean friendship in the modern sense, it also denoted ties of political, social and economic alliance, cooperation and even subservience. These alliances were highly ritualized and formed lasting connections that manifested themselves in many ways (Mustakallio and Krötzl 2010). One did not necessarily like one's friends.

The reason why friendship was so important to the legal profession has to do with both the external role of the jurists (defined as the *iuris prudentes*, the persons skilled in the law) in their relationship with Roman society as well as the internal dynamics of the legal profession in the face of political change. The process we will be examining here is the gradual change in the meaning and importance of *amicitia* for lawyers. The vanishing significance of *amicitia*, clients and alliances, during the early Principate is best demonstrated by looking at the indexes of Richard A. Bauman's three books on Roman jurists in their political setting: in the first book, about the Republic, there are numerous references under the heading *amicitia*. In his two books about the Empire, however, there is nothing between the entries "alimenta" and "Annaeus" (Bauman 1983, 1985, 1989).

The ancient Roman sources demonstrate that during the Republic, nearly every lawyer of some worth participated actively in politics and had numerous clients (the earliest form of legal representation was the patron's duty to defend his clients in court, as Plautus testifies) (Kunkel 2001). Social status and esteem were highly important in all public activities, both in political debates as well as in legal cases. What this meant was that in order to prevail in a court case, the gravity of the advocate's person and lineage were of utmost importance for the argument. An argument or a speech in court made by a person with low social standing and thus little respect among the Roman elite could even be harmful for his client, while a noted jurist, whose ancestors had performed great services to the state, could convince the audience, and with it the judges, using the power of name recognition (Bablitz 2007). The court sessions took place in the political administrative center of Rome, the Forum Romanum, and watching trials was a favorite pastime (Figure 8.1).

FIGURE 8.1. The Roman Forum and the Comitium on 44BC, a reconstruction. Source: Wikimedia / Public Domain.

Lawyers crafted alliances with the ties of *amicitia*, which were so amply present in the history of the Republic. Lawyers came, for the most part, from the oldest ranks of the aristocracy, who were focused on an ongoing battle for supremacy within the Republic (Gruen 1995). These alliances were mostly political and social, but they were also mirrored in the workings of legal literature and legal science. The legal opinions of one's friends were quoted with reverence. As is known, legal opinions of private lawyers were the vehicle of legal development during the Republic in the absence of meaningful legislation. These opinions were, by their very form, a demonstration of the social nature of the profession: they were primarily known through custom and oral tradition. A legal opinion or *responsa* of a jurist was initially simply an oral response to a legal query by a client or magistrate. These were sometimes written down and collected, but the collections were of secondary importance to the oral pronouncements they recorded. The number of friends a jurist had was thus a determinant in how important he was and the esteem that his colleagues placed on him. A lawyer's friends would thus decide on the impact that he could have on law (Schulz 1946; Bauman 1983; Harries 2006).

In contrast, during the early years of the Principate and thereafter, lawyers and law oriented themselves towards the emperor and the imperial bureaucracy. Lawyers ceased to talk about friendship, unless they were talking about friends in high places. The system of clients paying homage was turned into a system of clients paying money. What happened? Two competing theories can be produced to explain this change: first the profound change in the social and political setting from the late Republic to the Principate and, second, the professionalization of lawyers (Bauman 1983; Kunkel 2001).

The underlying legal point about the position of the jurists and their relationships with each other stems from the concept of jurist's law: the content of the law was primarily created and defined by jurists, not legislators or judges. In a legal culture like Rome, where the development of private law was in the hands of the consulting jurists, legislation by popular assemblies or imperial edicts and court practice played only a negligible role in how the doctrine of law was formulated. The sources of law were thus primarily the works of jurists, where they comment upon the edicts or each others' opinions. In the words of an esteemed author and one of the great American scholars of Roman law, A. Arthur Schiller:

> Given *auctoritas prudentium*, the view of one jurist was as valid as that of another. It was the respect and confidence in the ability of a jurist, in the knowledge that his services were dedicated to the well-being of the Roman state, that gave his views legal force, not their adoption by a state official or even another jurist. (Schiller 1971: 1236)

Cicero himself would ask the rhetorical question: "Who truly deserved the name of a lawyer?" and immediately answers it: "I should say that he deserves it who is learned in the laws" (Cicero, *De oratore* 1.212). What this meant is that the law was a self-referential system, where the lawyers would define among themselves whose mastery of the tradition was such that he would be a worthwhile authority to quote. Knowledge of the tradition, gained through apprenticeship (as there were before Late Antiquity no formal schools of law), brought authority. The interesting point here is that Cicero himself was a rhetorician, a speaker, who maintained that there was a strict separation between the legal profession and the learned speaker. This distinction and the conviction that antagonism existed between the two groups has long been established in scholarship (Schulz 1946), but whether it exists anywhere else than in the writings of Cicero is questionable. It is often forgotten that the statement by jurist Aquillius Gallus that "this has nothing to do with law, it is a matter for Cicero" (Cicero, *Topica* 51), meaning the issue at hand was not legal but rhetorical, was repeated by Cicero himself. Cicero would thus define himself both as an outsider—a rhetorician in oppositional terms with the legal profession—but equally as someone who is knowledgeable in the tradition and the profession (Figure 8.2).

The understanding of the legal culture as a cumulative process built upon the written works of earlier generations is evident in the way Pomponius, the mid-first-century BCE

FIGURE 8.2. Cicero, from a bust at the Capitoline Museum, Rome. Source: Flickr / Library of Congress.

author of a textbook containing the only extant history of Roman law written by Romans themselves, describes the creation of the legal profession:

> Very many very great men have professed knowledge of civil law. But the ones of whom an account must be given in the present work, to let it be clear by whom—by what quality of men—legal principles have been developed and passed down. As to that, tradition has it that of all those who mastered this knowledge, none earlier than Tiberius Coruncanius made a public profession of it. (Digest of Justinian 1.2.2.35, tr. Watson et al.)

Pomponius continues that the profession has deeper roots, as the first person to possess the skill of a lawyer was Publius Papirius, who lived during the reign of the last king of Rome (perhaps in the sixth-century BCE) and compiled a collection of the laws of the kings. For Pomponius, the willingness to be publicly consulted marked a crucial turning point, a move from private knowledge to the public service. A good example of Pomponius' turn to publicity is the reference to Gaius Scipio Nasica, who from public funds was given a house on the Via Sacra in the center of Rome so that he could be more easily consulted on legal matters (Digest of Justinian 1.2.2.35–7) (Figure 8.3).

FIGURE 8.3. Fresco representing Terentius Neo and his wife discovered in Pompeii, Italy. (Neo was initially a baker but the portrait shows him with the official toga signifying that he is a magistrate or lawyer and a document roll, symbolizing his social advancement). Source: Wikimedia / Jebulon / CC0 1.0.

However, for Pomponius, the *iuris periti* (those knowledgeable of the law) were a cohesive social group, both horizontally and vertically. Though he mentions many names—nineteen noted jurists during the centuries before Quintus Mucius—the legal profession is for him a single unit, where individuals are defined not only by their connections with each other but also by the citations they give to each other. The legal mode of communication was both written and oral. The juristic writings, of which Pomponius often mentions only the number of books (only some titles, e.g., the *Tripertita* were mentioned) were the primary vertical way of transmission and also the method through which jurists could achieve immortality. Equally important was consultation in person, where answers to legal issues were given not only to the public but also to other lawyers (Digest of Justinian 1.2.2.35–43).

The point was that in a legal culture based on jurist's law, the friendships between jurists would have a significance in the formation of the law through the acceptance of their opinions as valid and an accurate definition of the law or a successful solution to a legal problem. How this acceptance worked is quite elusive and hard to define. By the classical period, there was no real test of whether someone's opinion was accepted and counted as law, and the late antique way of counting the opinions of classical jurists was based on a wholly different, mechanical logic. Does the vanishing of the importance of friends then mean the demise of jurist's law? Consequently, does that reflect the vanishing importance or the transformation of the legal profession?

The dramatic nature of this change can be demonstrated by juxtaposing two examples two generations apart: Quintus Mucius Scaevola Pontifex and his Late Republican friends against the friendlessness of M. Antistius Labeo and C. Ateius Capito during the Augustan period.

THE FRIENDS OF MUCIUS

Q. Mucius Scaevola Pontifex (*c.* 140–82 BCE), consul for the year 95 BCE, was a scion of the illustrious Mucii Scaevolae family, which produced numerous lawyers as well as priests (Behrends 1976; Bauman 1983: 340–421; Tuori 2007: 22–36). The family could trace its lineage back to the quasi-mythical hero Gaius Mucius Scaevola, who was apprehended in 508 BCE while trying to assassinate the Etruscan king Porsenna and, to prove his bravery, burned his right hand in a fire (hence the family name Scaevola, "left-handed") (Figure 8.4). He was also a teacher and a friend of Cicero, which is the main reason we know so much about him (Cicero, *Laelius* 1.1). Most of our knowledge of Quintus Mucius is based on Cicero, who forms a sort of cosmos on his own due to his voluminous writings about his contemporaries.[1]

As a jurist, Quintus Mucius is one of the most influential early Roman legal scholars, whose main achievement was summarized by Pomponius in the second century CE as:

> Quintus Mucius, son of Publius and a *pontifex maximus*, became the first man to produce a general compendium of the civil law by arranging it into eighteen books. (Digest of Justinian 1.2.2.41, tr. Watson et al.)

Based on this, he has been named the founding father of jurisprudence as a scientific scholarly exercise (Frier 1985: 168–171; Tuori 2007: 36–52). What this actually entails is something of a mystery, because we know very little about the content of these books and how they were organized. What is more important for our purposes is that he had also taught law to Cicero and a number of other prominent men, including many leading Roman lawyers.

FIGURE 8.4. Scaevola confronts Porsenna. Rubens and Van Dyck (before 1628). Source: Heritage Images / Getty Images.

For Cicero, Quintus Mucius became a stereotypical example of an old Roman nobleman devoting his life to public service and striving for justice and virtue. From other historical sources, we know that he belonged to the politically conservative part of the Senatorial elite, which opposed the popular party that sought to overturn the oligarchy in favor of a more democratic system. Quintus Mucius went through the whole of the career structure of the Roman upper classes, starting from the office of the tribune of the plebs in 106 BCE (Cicero, *Brutus* 43.161), becoming a curule edile in 103 BCE (Cicero, *Against Verres* 4.59.133; *De officiis* 2.16.57), and finally reaching the consulate in 95 BCE (Cicero, *Brutus* 64.229; *Against Verres* 2.49.122). Becoming consul, the highest magistrate of the

Republic, was the pinnacle of a political career, followed usually by a governorship in the provinces: for Quintus Mucius, this was the province of Asia. In the case of Quintus Mucius, his final magistracy was that of the supreme pontiff, the *pontifex maximus*, the leader of the pontifical college who led the rites of the official state religion. For a lawyer, being a chief pontiff was not as uncommon as might appear, for the pontifical college had a central role in the early development of law. During the early Republic they were charged with the task of interpreting the law and drafting legal formuls—the writs that were used to initiate legal claims in courts (Digest of Justinian 1.2.2.6). The formulas were simple sentences: the first part defined the conditions and the second outlined the consequence (if something, then something).

During the late Republic it was common that friendships, alliances, and clients were nurtured in the practice of law. The legal practice would entail not only representation in lawsuits, but even more importantly giving legal advice and drafting legal documents such as contracts. It could be said that legal advice and representation was a commodity that brought influence and friends. Though legal advice was given on an honorary basis, it did not mean that debts would not be incurred in social capital that amounted to clienthood (David 1992):

> To protect a man in his legal rights [, to assist him with counsel,] and to serve as many as possible with that sort of knowledge tends greatly to increase one's influence and popularity. Thus, among the many admirable ideas of our ancestors was the high respect they always accorded to the study and interpretation of the excellent body of our civil law. And down to the present unsettled times the foremost men of the state have kept this profession exclusively in their own hands; but now the prestige of legal learning has departed along with offices of honor and positions of dignity; and this is the more deplorable, because it has come to pass in the lifetime of a man [Servius Sulpicius Lemonia Rufus] who in knowledge of the law would easily have surpassed all his predecessors, while in honor he is their peer. Service such as this, then, finds many to appreciate it and is calculated to bind people closely to us by our good services. (Cicero, *De officiis* 2.65, tr. Miller)

A system of ritualized friendship, the *clientela*, was a central component in the functioning of Roman society. This friendship consisted of a quasi-sacred bond between a patron and a client, where the patron was usually older, wealthier and of a higher status than the client. These bonds formed an interlinked pyramidal structure where clients would have their own clients; patrons would, in turn, be clients to someone else. Only in the very highest echelons of society were there relatively few people (*principes*, or "first men") who might have considered themselves to be without a patron or two. Even they formed alliances among each other, which were conceptualized as friendships (*amicitia*). As explained earlier, what the notion of friendship meant was not as much a sentimental tie rather than an alliance where the client (who was not referred to as *cliens*, as the term was understood to be derogatory, but as an *amicus*) sought support from the patron, be it economic (a loan), social (advice and help in marrying of a daughter) or political (support in the coming elections) (Cicero, *De oratore* 3.133).

An important part of the assistance was legal aid. The ancient Roman legal system was conceptually very different from a modern one as the role of the families was large and the state had little interest in the execution of legal rulings. Until fairly late in the Republic or even the Empire, things that self-evidently belonged to the state responsibility such as apprehending a robber or a murderer and bringing them to justice were a task for private initiative. For a person of modest means, apprehending someone and bringing a suit in court meant turning to their family and kin for support. To provide legal representation in court was understood to be the patron's duty, from which he could not shrink. That meant that for a person of high status or nobility (such as Quintus Mucius or Cicero), knowledge of the law was vital (Gaughan 2010; Fuhrmann 2012).

Accordingly, it was not surprising that Cicero became a student of Quintus Mucius. It was, on the contrary, an expected part of elite education. There was no legal training per se, no schools where one could enroll. This was true in most skills; only philosophy and rhetoric had dedicated educational institutions, especially in Greece, where upper-class Roman youths might travel to complete their formal education. The traditional system of learning was through apprenticeship. Through familial, social and political connections one could gain the opportunity to follow the teaching of a respected authority. This would mostly take the form of following the teacher around as he went about his business giving legal advice and attending court cases. In many ways, the legal aspect of the education was quite indistinguishable from the general education of an upper-class Roman. Much like knowing how to fight in the army, one was expected to know how to manage public affairs and to command. As part of their duties as magistrates, they were also expected to sit as a judge in legal cases. Cicero became the student of Quintus Mucius at the age of eighteen, after Publius Mucius Scaevola had died. How long this education lasted or what it comprised is not clear, but Cicero appears to have used his legal teachings in the composition of his provincial edict (Cicero, *Laelius* 1.1; *Atticus*. 6.1.15; Behrends 1976: 268–269).

For Cicero, Quintus Mucius was an idealized character, who embodied the true Roman virtues of moderation, justice, and wisdom. Cicero would mention him repeatedly as an exemplum, also adding him as one of the characters in the dialog of *On the Laws* (*de legibus* 2.19.47). Quintus Mucius had a number of other pupils, among them such famous lawyers as Aquillius Gallus, Balbus Lucilius, Sextus Papirius and Gaius Juventius (Digest of Justinian 1.2.2.41–42).

The nature of legal science at the time was cumulative. To make a valid argument, one had, in most cases, to cite opinions favorable to one's case. The objective was to make it apparent that what one said was a reflection of the *communis opinio* of respected lawyers, not just the opinion of a single lawyer. The precedent favored was, in the Roman case, not judicial precedent but legal opinions or *responsa* given by other lawyers. How this worked can be to some extent deduced from Republican literature, for example where L. Crassus cites the opinion of Mucius Scaevola to overturn Scaevola himself (Cicero, *De oratore* 1.57). Even Pomponius, the second-century CE jurist who wrote the partially known history of Roman law, mentions how the writings of the pupils of Mucius Scaevola are hardly ever read, but are known through the works of Servius Sulpicius, who quoted them at length (Digest of Justinian 1.2.2.42; Stein 1966).

Servius Sulpicius, however, was a close friend of Cicero's. He was also a pupil of Quintus Mucius, though he was not as successful. In the history of Pomponius he is mentioned as being scolded by Quintus Mucius for not understanding the teaching he was given and the legal opinions that they contained. According to Quintus Mucius, "it was disgraceful for a patrician of a noble family who regularly appeared as advocate in courts to be ignorant of the law on which his cases turned." This insult supposedly led him to study law harder (Digest of Justinian 1.2.2.43). Again, ignorance was here defined as the state of being outside the tradition itself and being thus unable to understand the arguments made.

Within legal scholarship, the importance of general agreement and support from the community meant that having the support of one's peers was fundamental. The opinions of respected predecessors were cited, but more important were those of contemporaries. These lawyers were mentioned by other lawyers as friends. Lawyers, like other upper-class Romans, formed alliances that varied in their binding nature. In the Republican legal culture these ties of alliance were an integral part of the formation of legal culture and the functioning of legal scholarship. What the tangled web of alliances between Cicero and leading lawyers, scholars, and speakers demonstrates is the interconnectedness of the areas of learning and elite politics. Like the Greek trials, where the speakers would make moral, political, and ethical arguments, in the late Republican Rome the cases of the elite, especially those of political notables, were surrogate arenas for battles between different political factions and alliances. What these alliances had in common was that they were primarily lateral groups of extended families and their allies, who considered themselves to be more or less equal. In the following, we will explore the change that takes place when the political, legal, and cultural arena is transformed by the emergence of the emperor as the overarching authority figure who dwarfed all other actors with his immense wealth and unlimited power.

FRIENDS IN HIGH PLACES

Our second example revolves around two jurists, M. Antistius Labeo and C. Ateius Capito (both thought to have died in 22 CE), the founders of the Proculian and Sabinian Schools of jurisprudence, respectively. The two schools were named after their first pupils, and they continued to dominate legal science until the second century.[2] During their lifetimes, Labeo and Capito struggled for supremacy in the field of law, but with different strategies. Labeo was politically a hardcore Republican, who never really accepted the Augustan takeover and the demise of the Republic. He won the respect of his peers for his independence of opinion and his creative thinking. Capito was a member of the new elite and bent over backward to appeal to Augustus, who reciprocated by appointing him consul. As a result, Labeo has traditionally been seen as a heroic figure, while Capito has been dismissed as a politically motivated upstart (the accepted view is summarized best by Schulz 1946: 101–102). This view has only rarely been challenged (e.g., by Bauman 1989: 26–55; Nörr 1994: 75).

Following the interest that lawyers during the early Empire had in gaining imperial favor (Liebs 2010), it is not surprising that Pomponius sees the creation of the schools of law as a reaction to imperial power and a change in legal culture and here Labeo and Capito had a central role:

> After him, the leading authorities were Ateius Capito, who was of Ofilius' school, and Antistius Labeo, who went to lectures of all the above, but who was a pupil of Trebatius. Of these two Ateius was consul. Labeo declined to accept office when Augustus made him an offer of the consulship whereby he would have become *consul suffectus* (interim consul). Instead, he applied himself with the greatest firmness to his studies, and he used to divide up whole years on the principle that he spent six months at Rome with his students, and for six months he retired from the city and concentrated on writing books. As a result, he left four hundred manuscript rolls (volumina) most of which are still regularly thumbed through. These two men set up for the first time rival sects, so to say. For Ateius Capito persevered with the line

which had been handed down to him, whereas Labeo set out to make a great many innovations on account of the quality of his genius and the trust he had in his own learning which had drawn heavily on other branches of knowledge (Digest of Justinian. 1.2.2.47, tr. Watson et al.)

What this meant is unclear. Should we understand that the schools were institutions of learning, or that they were simply schools of thought, or possibly a combination of the two? What is clear is that they had pupils with whom they discoursed in a somewhat more organized manner than that which occurred in a simple apprenticeship system. What is equally evident is that the form and structure of the pedagogical material was changing, perhaps as steps towards some kind of logic or systematization.

The historian Tacitus, a member of the senatorial aristocracy that had a distinctly negative view of imperial power, described the attitudes of Capito and Labeo through their relationship to the imperial house. He begins with the background of Ateius Capito:

By his eminence as a jurist he had won the first position in the state; but his grandfather had been one of Sulla's centurions, nor had his father risen above a praetorship. His consulate had been accelerated by Augustus, so that the prestige of that office should give him an advantage over Antistius Labeo, a commanding figure in the same profession. For that age produced together two of the glories of peace; but, while Labeo's uncompromising independence assured him the higher reputation with the public, the pliancy of Capito was more to the taste of princes. The one, because he halted at the praetorship, won respect by his ill-treatment; the other, because he climbed to the consulate, reaped hatred from a begrudged success. (Tacitus, *Annales* 3.75, tr. Jackson)

In addition to the advent of the emperor in the field of law and the importance of imperial political connections, the main change in the legal environment was the growing importance of legal writing. As mentioned, Labeo spent half of the year in Rome with his pupils and the other half on retreat, concentrating on writing his books (Digest of Justinian 1.2.2.47). Books became more important for attaining fame and influence in the legal sphere for a number of reasons. One was the sheer growth of Rome and its legal profession. With the expansion of Roman citizenship in the provinces, the number of people utilizing Roman law grew exponentially. If, during the early Republic, Rome could be defined as a face-to-face society, by the late Republic the city of Rome itself had hundreds of thousands of inhabitants and the total number of Roman citizens was in the millions. Having a very small and tight-knit group who interacted in a small area in the center of Rome as its legal profession was simply not sufficient.

While writing had always been important for law, both as a mode of communication and preserving information as well as in the symbolic acts of inscribing laws on bronze tablets or contracts on wax tablets (Meyer 2004), it was only the publication of introductory textbooks such as the Institutes of Gaius from the second-century CE, which facilitated the spread of legal knowledge and transformed legal culture. Information about law became generally accessible.

The new imperial court system was a hierarchical structure, in which it was possible to appeal against convictions, as opposed to the old Republican court system in which the only appeal was the possibility of *provocatio* in the case of the death penalty. This influenced the professionalization of legal representation as, in the new system, lawyers were able to collect fees for their efforts (Bablitz 2007: 142). Law became a career path and a way of gaining an income.

A part of this change was the enigmatic institution called the *ius respondendi*. According to Pomponius, it was an imperial privilege which gave its holder the power to issue legal opinions on the authority of the emperor:

> Massurius Sabinus was of equestrian rank, and was the first person to give state-certificated opinions (*publice respondere*). For after this privilege (*beneficium*) came to be granted, it was conceded to him by Tiberius Caesar. [49] To clarify the point in passing: before the time of Augustus the right of stating opinions at large was not granted by emperors, but the practice was that opinions were given by people who had confidence in their own studies. Nor did they always issue opinions under seal, but most commonly wrote themselves to the judges, or gave the testimony of a direct answer to those who consulted them. It was the deified Augustus who, in order to enhance the authority of the law, first established that opinions might be given under his authority. From that time this began to be sought as a favor. As a consequence of this, our most excellent emperor Hadrian issued a rescript on an occasion when some men of praetorian rank were petitioning him for permission to grant opinions; he said that this was by custom not merely begged for but earned and that he [the emperor] would accordingly be delighted if whoever had faith in himself would prepare himself for giving opinions to the people at large. [50] Anyway, to Sabinus the concession was granted by Tiberius Caesar that he might give opinions to the people at large. He was admitted to the equestrian rank when already of mature years and almost fifty. (Digest of Justinian 1.2.2.48–50, tr. Watson et al.)

This passage may be read as a sign of the rising influence of the emperor and showed how individuals sought to gain more power over their peers through their association with the emperor. What the passage underlines is that the emperors would perhaps grant their authority to the opinion of jurists, but that they would not begin selecting jurists so privileged, but rather left that to the jurists to decide on who, based on their learning and expertise, would be worthy of it. Whether these imperial seals of approval were given to many jurists and what it might have meant for their opinions and their validity has been hotly debated for hundreds of years. Because Pomponius' text is garbled and hard to decipher, an unequivocal conclusion is not to be expected (Tuori 2007: 71–134).

The nature of legal science became confrontational instead of cumulative, which was reflected in the relationships between lawyers. Instead of the Republican horizontal approach, where lawyers tended to be friends with their contemporaries, a vertical structure was applied. In it, lawyers had pupils and teachers in their near circle, i.e., men either older or younger than them.

A more pointed version of the same idea is the change in the use of the word "friend," especially in cases where the "friends" of lawyers were dead. For example, the late second early third-century CE jurist Ulpian refers to Maecianus and Salvius Julianus as his friends (Digest of Justinian 37.14.17). The trouble is, neither of them was alive at that time. Alexander Severus, for his part, refers to the urban praefect as *amicus noster* (Codex of Justinian 4.56.1). However, condemnation could equally travel beyond the grave. The third-century CE jurist Paulus refers to the opinion of Mucius Scaevola as being inept (*ineptissimum est,* Digest of Justinian 41.2.3.23).

Both the Republican friendship and the enmities of the Principate were highly ritualized forms of social interaction that had not only political or social, but also legal implications. It is difficult to say whether they had any sentimental grounding; did they, for example, even like their friends?

During the Empire it was no longer necessary to have a large entourage, it was actually necessary to have just one real friend, i.e., the emperor. In the imperial context, lawyers, far from relying on an informal system of friendship, were actually allowed, and almost expected, to hate each other. They began to overturn and contest each others' opinions instead of building on them. My claim is that the change was first and foremost a change in rhetoric, not in sentiment. In fact, we cannot know if it was just rhetoric in Cicero. The image one has from the Roman sources is that the political struggle for supremacy was intense during the late Republic, while the legal arena was more peaceful. During the Empire, the political avenues left no room for competition. However, this was only partly true. Behind the scenes, competition was intense in both legal and political arenas, though their forms changed. Members of the elite, who had previously been rivals on a level political playing field, where alliances were built to secure victories in voting, now needed to secure only the favor of the emperor for themselves and their allies to gain advancement in their careers. The emperor was, however, a dangerous friend. Successive power struggles wreaked havoc among the people in or near the imperial court. Any friendship with the emperor could cool and a misspoken word could mean sudden death (Romm 2014).

What was even more important was that though the emperor was nominally all-powerful and during the high Empire became increasingly regarded as "living law," such blanket statements were sometimes misleading. As commentators and authors as well as officials, it was the jurists who would finally decide if an opinion by an emperor (or, often, a lawyer drafting the opinion for the emperor) was worth remembering and thus whether it would continue to carry the force of law. This was ultimately how the content of the law was settled. Some opinions by emperors suffered a different fate. Not only were they forgotten, but they were sometimes actively censured after their death (Honoré 1994).

One of the possible reasons for the end of legal friendships was the end of "multitasking" by lawyers and the transformation of the practices of the legal profession. While Quintus Mucius did the whole *cursus honorum*, imperial lawyers were mostly just professional lawyers and only occasionally ventured into illustrious political careers. Even if they did, their election to, say, the consulship, depended solely on the emperor. There was not a similar need for extensive entourages of clients and alliances. This is naturally not to say that entourages would have become extinct, they were simply no longer vital to advancement in office.

There are even indications that the whole idea of having friends in a legal context was beginning to be seen as suspect. For example, Hadrian is mentioned to have included in his legal council not his friends, but the finest legal minds of the age, which were also approved by the Senate (Historia Augusta *Hadrian* 18.1). These "friends" (*amici*) of the emperor were a group of high-ranking former officials and trusted advisors, whom the emperor could use as his envoys, not necessarily his personal friends. These friends would aid the emperor in his interactions with the people, which could be very close, as is evident in the illustrations of the contemporary scenes of the emperor in the Forum, where he would be within touching distance of the crowd (Figure 8.5).

It has long been established that Republican jurists were not professional in the modern sense. They were more like all-round gentlemen who had acquired legal knowledge and used it as part of their skills as persons in public service and as part of the general interaction among their friends and allies. Law and legal knowledge was a good way to gain new friends and supporters, no doubt also to advance one's political career. Nobody, as far as we know, derived their livelihood from law (Harries 2006: 34–35).

FIGURE 8.5. A scene from the Forum, from the Plutei of Trajan, a stone balustrade built by Emperor Trajan, now at Curia Julia in Rome. Source: Wikimedia/Cassius Ahenobarbus/CC BY-SA 3.0.

However, this view is necessarily biased as our sources come from the highest echelons of Roman society. Whether there were salaried lawyers who remain invisible from our sources is possible, but due to the fact that legal representation demanded high status and respectability, it is doubtful that it would have been a major phenomenon.

While talking of lawyers, modern scholarship has either downplayed or overemphasized emotions. Change in the rhetoric of friendship was a combination of political, social, and professional factors. As legal writing was changed to a written exercise, it was no longer necessary to refer to living authorities. Books were, in any case, more practical, as they were not in the habit of changing their minds. Behind the rhetoric was fierce competition, which has often been obscured. Liking or disliking someone was, to some extent, quite irrelevant.

NOTES

Preface

1. Laurence Rosen, *Law as Culture: An Invitation* (Princeton: Princeton University Press, 2006), 199–200.
2. Pierre Legrand, *Fragments on Law-as-Culture* (Deventer: W E J Tjeenk Willink, Schoordijk Institute, 1999), 5.
3. Malcolm Andrews, *Landscape and Western Art* (Oxford History of Art) (Oxford: oxford University Press, 1999), 53.

Introduction

1. While Egypt remains outside our purview, the Pharaohs had international diplomatic correspondence with all the courts of the Near East in the fifteenth century BC (Bottéro 1992: 10).
2. India and China would have merited attention as part of a different study, which would call into question the periodization and analytical purchase of a term such as "antiquity." I thank Teemu Ruskola for pointing this out clearly to me.
3. Jean Bottéro describes his years of "overwhelming initiation rites" before he could move freely around ancient Mesopotamian sources, which he numbers in half a million intelligible documents (1992: 19–20).
4. The editor of one of the most impressive collective efforts to organize all known legal materials of the ancient Near East—in Mesopotamia, Syria, Anatolia, and Egypt—admits that "the lack of continuity in the sources mean that ... [a]t most, a series of snapshots, scattered at random in time and place, can be compiled" (Westbrook 2003a: 2).
5. Reflecting on the possibility that the story about the Christians supposed to have been crucified and burned alive by Nero may turn out to be fictional (a hypothesis raised by Shaw 2015), G. W. Bowersock (2015) writes: "it is both important and humbling to recognize that the history with which we have all grown up can change in the twinkling of an eye when a scholar as acute and deeply read as Brent Shaw detects cracks in an edifice we thought we knew well."
6. Westbrook suggests that these collections of "just verdicts" [*dînât mêšarim*] functioned pretty much like "a reference work for consultation by judges when deciding difficult cases" (2009: 10). The hypothesis has plausibility, although he has to contend with the fact that "[t]here is no direct evidence from cuneiform sources for the consultation of law codes as there is for the omen series" (id.).
7. Rather, it is a document explaining the historical development of Athenian society, how it came to be what it was in fourth century BCE.
8. Several authors since Finley have tried to retain the idea of Greek law bound together by some basic principles and ideals like *dike* ("law," "justice"), *blabē* (harm, injury), *hybris* ("insolence," "transgression"), *homologein* ("to agree"), *kyrios* ("master, in control of"). See discussion in Gagarin (2005b).

9. Finley, for example, followed H. L. A. Hart's distinction between law and custom and morality (1966: 121), and accepted the basic (though not undisputable) idea that "law is a system of rules" (1966: 139).
10. Within the positivist framework Burckhardt opposed, three schools of thought could be distinguished: first, the idea that historical narratives were built out of a succession of biases and preconceptions for historians to correct (associated to the work of classical historian B. G. Niebuhr); second, the schools that rediscovered the importance of archival work and documentary evidence to produce a history "as it really was" associated with Leopold von Ranke (1795–1886); and third, the historical school of Savigny which tried to find the origins of Germanic law in Roman law (Murray 1998: xx–xxi).
11. As David Nelken reminds us, "the purported uniformity, coherence or stability of given … cultures will often be no more than a rhetorical claim projected by outside observers or manipulated by elements within the culture concerned" (2004: 6).
12. For an attempt to reclaim Thucydides for the field of international relations, see Lebow (2003). Lebow's reading is indebted to White (1984: 59–92).
13. For Maine, feudalism supposes such discontinuity with the Greek and Roman "fountainheads" (Maine [1861] 1906: 14).
14. Chiba defines "legal postulates" as "the particular values and ideas … to ideationally found, justify and orient, or else supplement, criticize and revise the existing legal rules" (1993: 209).
15. Whether he succeeded or not is a different thing. For an overview of Hindu law, see Menski (2006: 196–278).
16. In the context of Greece, Rosalind Thomas suggests that the laws that went up in writing "were not the ones agreed by all, but the contentious ones, the rules which constantly caused trouble … " (2005: 54). For writing in the Roman context, see Wolf (2015) and Meyer (2015). For the relationship between orality and writing in Near Eastern cultures in contrast to Roman and Hebrew, see Westbrook (2003a: 12–13, 19–20).
17. See recently Clifford Ando (2011) on the role of legal fictions as a way to mediate between law-preservation and creation in the context of deep pluralism during the Roman Empire.
18. Twining argues that Glenn still needs an analytical concept of "the legal" to distinguish legal traditions and compare between them (Twining 2006: 113). However, because "the legal" is not a defined category of "things" or a "field," but a way of symbolizing human conduct (MacDonald 2006), a very thin understanding of what might potentially fall under law's field of vision suffices; one able to detect manifestations of law and of legal phenomena that we would not easily categorize as such in the modern world (see, e.g., the range of topics covered by Louis Gernet 1955). In this the legal scholar and the anthropologist are not far apart.
19. During the Athenian plague (430 BCE), in the midst of the war between Athens and Sparta, an old prophecy was remembered according to which war with the Dorians would also bring death. There had been controversy as to whether the word in the oracle was "dearth" (*limos*) rather than "death" (*loimos*). Thucydides adds ironically that were a future situation of famine to arise, the alternative interpretation would be surely reactivated (Thucydides 1972: 156, ii. 54).
20. The genuine problem of comparison must be distinguished from *extrapolation* and *reconstruction*. Extrapolation is the mechanism by which we rely on information we possess to fill in the gaps of other places where information is lacking, e.g., to use information about Athens to speculate about other city-states (criticized by Finley 1951; Cohen 2005). A related procedure is reconstruction. Raymond Westbrook, one of the

foremost experts in Near Eastern law—extending into biblical law and the Greco-Roman world—considers there is enough similarity between them to postulate a shared legal culture, despite differences (Westbrook 2003a and 2009). He relies on this basic premise to complete the pieces of once a unitary whole of which we have just lost the full picture. Since the hypothesis is one of a common root, "the theory ... is not one of comparative law but of an actual connection between the ancient Near Eastern Codes and the Twelve Tables" (Westbrookd 2009: 54) as well as the Hebrew Bible (2009: 104).

21. The law is thus quoted in Demosthenes 23.53: "If somebody kills a man after finding him next to his wife or mother or sister or daughter or concubine kept for producing free children shall not be exiled as a killer on account of this" (Gagarin 2011: 75–76).
22. This trial would presumably take place before the Court of the Delphinium—not the Areopagus (Gagarin 2011: 75).
23. Husa (2007) argues that, in theory, functionalism recognizes the importance and relevance of context, but in practice fails to live according to these high standards.
24. The consideration of texts is not the same in all cultures of antiquity. While the text is central to the Jewish tradition, it is less so in the oral context of Near Eastern law, where legal documents had no independent evidentiary evidence until the first millennium BCE (Westbrook 2003a: 13). Further, while in the Hellenistic and Roman periods the exact words of the statute are analyzed and taken as the basis of judgments, in the ancient Near East the participants did not engage in a word-by-word reading of legal precepts, which were not regarded as autonomous or exhaustive (Westbrook 2003a: 19–21).
25. See, for example, his reading of the Garden of Eden, where he singles out the literary technique of *mise an abyme*, a self-referential structure by which the text presents an image of itself in one of the details of the plot (Levinson 2008: 40–47). Levinson also acknowledges that "scholarship that is attentive to the synchronic interpretation of a text need not be harmonistic ... " (2008: 198).
26. The Pentateuch embeds in its narrative three separate legal collections: The Covenant Code (Exod. 21:1–23:29), The Holiness Code (Lev. 17–26) and the laws of Deuteronomy (chapters 12–26) (Levinson 2008: 33). According to Levinson, these originally independent legal corpora, heavily influenced by Near Eastern law collections, began to be collected by Judean scribal editors during the Babylonian exile, confronted with the threat to their national existence (Levinson 2008: 33).
27. That the story of Deuteronomy would precede Exodus is not conceivable, for it would entail a move from a problem-free to a problematic text in matters of substantive importance (Levinson 2008: 66 fn 36).
28. For the political stakes of reading strategies, including a gendered perspective, see Boyarin (1990).
29. See the discussion on the (im)pertinence of "resonance" for dating biblical texts between Levinson and Stackert (2013) and Joshua Berman (2013).
30. The objection resembles that of the "new historicism" against conventional historicism, which impoverishes texts by reducing them to instantiations of their contexts. The situation may have slightly improved since the time LaCapra wrote—though not as to moot the argument. For a reappraisal, see Surkis (2014).
31. There might be a tension here between "new historicists" and "cultural historians," as new historicist "literary scholars set their texts a-wobbling while historians nail theirs to the ground" (Maza 2004: 265).
32. As different from abstract concepts, *keywords* aim to touch upon the texture and cultural fabric of historical experience (Williams 1976; Antaki 2014: 63–64). The chosen keywords

(justice, constitutions, codes, agreements, arguments, property and possession, wrongs, legal profession) are not dogmatic categories valid for all times or places (cf. Rupprecht 2005), but entry points into the respective legal traditions; small windows that open to the ancient cultures which, in continuous back and forth movement, allow us to *think through* them.

Justice

1. This and other passages cited from the *Law Stele of Hammurabi* are my translations, after the edition of Roth 1997: 76–142. Passages are identified, according to Assyriological convention, by column (xlvii) and line number (59–78).
2. After Keller 2012.
3. After Clark 2012: 142.
4. Scholars recognized structural and detailed similarities between Mesopotamian and biblical law "codes" as soon as Hammurabi's Law Stele was discovered in ancient Susa (modern day Iran) in 1901. For studies arguing for a shared legal tradition, see, for example, Raymond Westbrook (1988) and numerous articles written by Westbrook and collected (posthumously) in Wells and Magdalene eds. (2009); Westbrook 2009d. For a compelling argument that biblical writers specifically re-worked the inscription of Hammurabi's Law Stele, see Wright 2009: esp. 91–110.
5. Hammurabi ruled as king of Babylonia from around 1792 to around 1750 BCE. His reign is distinguished for political consolidation of territories neighboring his city-state of Babylon, which he brought under control through a combination of successful military engagements and the calculated making and breaking of diplomatic treaties. Historically, his kingship marks the end of a centuries-long pattern of rival city-states, and the beginning of a kingdom in southern Mesopotamia that became known as Babylonia, after its capital city Babylon, a political entity that would last down to its conquest by the Persian King Cyrus in 539 BCE, marking the end of indigenous Mesopotamian rule.
6. Known law collections from that precede Hammurabi's *Stele* are the Laws of Ur-Namma, (*c.* 2100 BCE), the Laws of Lipit-Ishtar (*c.* 1930 BCE), and the Laws of Eshnunna (*c.* 1770 BCE). Hammurabi's Laws are followed by the Middle Assyrian Laws (*c.* 1076 BCE), the Neo-Babylonian Laws (*c.* 700 BCE). From Anatolia, we have the comparable Hittite Laws, first written down *c.* 1650–1500. For translations and some commentary, see Roth 1997. For an important new manuscript of the Laws of Ur-Namma, see Miguel Civil (2011): 221–310. For a discussion of ancient Near Eastern law collections, see Raymond Westbrook (2009a) (originally published in *Revue Biblique* 92 (1985): 247–265).
7. See also Westbrook 2009(b).
8. In the twelfth century, an Elamite raiding party plundered several cities in northern Babylonia, and king Shutruk-Nahhunte carried home and erected in his god's temple, together with a number of other Babylonian trophy monuments, Hammurabi's *Stele*.
9. For a consideration of the role of the scribal curriculum and royal monuments in shaping and spreading royal ideology in Mesopotamia, including specifically the Law Stele of Hammurabi, see Michalowski (1990): esp. 62–65. See also Cooper (1993). For a discussion of different levels of cuneiform literacy in the ancient Near East, see Veldhuis (2011).
10. For a summary of the history of the editing of the inscription and challenges to restoring the inscription in full, see Roth (1997): 73–76.

11. Stone was rare in Mesopotamia, and kings regularly boasted in their inscriptions of having acquired it from foreign lands. For stone monuments as an explicitly royal prerogative, see Slanski (2003a): 237–245.
12. See, for example, the essays of Raymond Westbrook collected in Wells and Magdalene eds. (2009); Westbrook (2009d).
13. For an illustrated survey of Western visual representations of justice in explicitly public and state contexts, see Resnik and Curtis 2011.
14. For the icononography of the god, see also the entry "Utu (Shamash)" in Black and Green eds. (1992).
15. For a discussion of visual markers of masculinity and their significance in Near Eastern royal monumental art, see Winter (1996).
16. See also Robson (2007): 246–247.
17. See Jacobsen (1987). For the same performative power of divine images extended as well to royal images, see Winter (1992). For application of contemporary semiotic theory to the Mesopotamian concept of performative images, see Bahrani (2003): 121–148. For the application of the Akkadian term *tsalmu* "image" to relief sculptures as well as to sculptures in the round, see Slanski (2003b).
18. E.g., Exodus 20:4–5 ("The Ten Commandments"), Isaiah 40:18–29.
19. For a famous example, see the *Epic of Gilgamesh*, when Gilgamesh promises his dying companion, Enkidu, to have goldsmiths fashion "your image of gold beyond measure" (tablet VII, 48, after the edition of Foster ed. (2001): 54).
20. The very act of reciting a name is the heart of ancient Near Eastern rituals for the dead, customarily the responsibility of a surviving family member or descendant. For an introduction to rituals and belief concerning the dead, see Scurlock (1995): 1883–1893.
21. In the original Babylonian, the lines rendered here in bold, are marked as direct speech to be spoken out loud.
22. For a recent evaluation of the complexity of measuring literacy in ancient Mesopotamia, and the arguments against very restricted literacy in the second millennium, see Charpin (2010): 53–67.
23. For an additional discussion of the inter-relationship between the inscription and the relief sculpture, see Slanski (2007): 52–4.
24. Mankind's inability ever to fully fathom divine justice is perhaps most deeply explored in the biblical book of Job.
25. In addition to royal decrees of *misharu*, two additional means existed to ameliorate the effects of agrarian debt on the farming families: the possibility to redeem, or buy back, family land and/or family members pledged and seized as surety for loans, and time limits on the length of servitude. See Westbrook 2009c.
26. Dating the works credited to Homer and Hesiod is a large scholarly enterprise. For simplicity's sake, I rely here on the editions of the works cited in the References: R. Lamberton's introduction to Hesiod *Works & Days, Theogony* (Hesiod 1993: 1), and B. Knox's introduction to *The Iliad* (Homer 1990: 19). Knox's essay also provides a good introduction to questions of composition and authorship.
27. In addition to ancient myths from Mesopotamia about the creation of mankind, see, of course, Genesis 1–2.
28. See, for example, Herington (1973).
29. See also Hesiod (1993): *Theogony* 185, 477; *Works & Days* 900.
30. It is, in fact, the only surviving scene from Attic painting to show the death of Agamemnon (Vermeule 1966: 1).

31. Vermeule argues that details from the painting suggest the vase be seen as an "illustration" of Aeschylus' *Oresteia*, rather than expressing general knowledge of the myth (pp. 6–7, 19–21).
32. The Melian Dialogue is Thucydides' only use of dialogic form outside of the exchange between king Archidamus of Sparta and the delegation from Plataea (Book 2.71–4; Connor 1984: 148). Even so, that exchange is much shorter and author explanations interrupt the exchanges of direct speech, giving a greater sense of narration than performance.
33. For more on the juxtaposition of the Melian episode and the Sicilian expedition and its impact, see Connor (1984): 147–157 and 19, fn. 28.

Constitution

1. The date of Herodotus' *History* is contested, but there is agreement about the anachronistic presence of mid-to-late-fifth-century references in the constitutional debate it stages: see Lane (2014: 69–70).
2. On Ismene as speaking for the common law, see Frank (2006). On the importance of the play's minor characters, especially the chorus, see Atkison (2016).
3. I leave to one side the claim Athena makes on behalf of "the male" (736–741) for I think it is and is meant to be taken as specious: Athena, after all, does have a mother, Metis, as Aeschylus' audience would have been well aware.
4. For a different appreciation of Creon, see Honig (2013).
5. On Creon and also Antigone as *auto-nomoi*, see Frank (2006) and Allen (2005).
6. This mutual conditioning between individual psychology and political environment is the backdrop for the analogy between soul and city that appears across the writings of Plato and Aristotle, on which, see Ferrari (2005).
7. For my treatment of this theme in Aristotle, see Frank (2005).
8. In his *Histories*, second-century Roman historian Polybius sees things similarly, criticizing both tyranny (5.11) and unbridled democracy, calling the latter "mob-rule," *ochlokratia* (6.57).
9. On the "powerful, yet ambiguous, cultural symbol" of tyranny in antiquity, see Forsdyke (2009).
10. On Solon, see Mossé (2004: 242–259).
11. *Statesman* is to be included in this grouping as well but I leave this dialog to one side for the purposes of this chapter. On the importance of reading the *Laws* alongside other dialogs of Plato, see Rowe (2010: 29–50).
12. On the legislation of the *kallipolis*, see also Pradeau (2005: 100–123).
13. For discussion of this passage, see Laks (2010: 217–231).
14. See also Popper [1944] (2013).
15. For one of many examples, see Menn (2006: 24), "the Athenian stranger serves as a stand-in for Plato himself, the good Athenian by contrast to the usual products of the democracy, who has the philosophical and mathematical knowledge which the Spartans and Cretans are sadly lacking" (footnote omitted). For a thorough discussion of theories that take characters in Plato's dialogs to speak for Plato, see Nails (1999: 15–26) and Press (2007).
16. It is to be noted that Adeimantus in the *Republic* and Megillus in the *Laws* withhold their acquiescence more frequently than do Glaucon and Cleinias.
17. On the resemblances between the constitutions of Magnesia and Sparta, see Menn (2006).
18. I do so in relation to the *Republic* in Frank (2018).

19. Nightingale (1993: 293) argues that insofar as "they issue from a lawgiver who is accorded almost divine status," and are "inscribed monologues that cannot be questioned or challenged by the citizens," the preludes, like the laws, do not so much persuade as command obedience. I entirely agree. Where we disagree is in what is to be made of this. Where Nightingale takes the Athenian to stand for Plato, I see Plato as giving his readers every reason to see what Nightingale sees and therefore to take a critical distance from what the Athenian appears to stand for.
20. The same idea appears in Pericles' funeral oration.
21. Smith Pangle (2014) argues there is an inevitable need for coercion in politics. I agree. But there are differences in kind and degree of coercion. I believe that the laws Plato has the Athenian propose exhibit coercion of an enslaving kind and degree.
22. For discussion of the "parallel between the Athenian's treatment of the interlocutors and the lawgiver's handling of the citizens of Magnesia," see also Nightingale (1993: 295–296).
23. For elaboration, see Frank (2018).
24. For the argument that the early education orients not to virtue but to war, see Frank (2007).
25. McIlwain is citing *Arthur Young's Travels in France during the Years 1787, 1788, 1789*, ed. Matilda Betham-Edwards (London: George Bell and Sons, 1909), para. 4.32.
26. Lane (2013b: 59) notes that Plutarch is the only source to "present a Lycurgean prohibition on written law" and that Plato's *Laws* (858e) and *Phaedrus* (258c) imply, on the contrary, that Lycurgus did promulgate written laws for Sparta.
27. There is much more to be said about Plato and writing: see Nightingale (1993); Lane (2013b); Frank (2018).

Codes

1. Works on "law and literature" and "law and society" have been instrumental in producing this kind of scholarship. One of the most thorough overviews of the intersection between legal and cultural meaning can be found in Binder and Weisberg (2000).
2. The foundational work in this regard is Cover (1992). Two important works that attempt to further this agenda are Kahn (1999) and Rosen (2006). See also Mezey (2001).
3. This chapter works within the hermeneutic assumption that legal text qua text is subject to the same interpretive challenges as other texts but operates within a framework of communally agreed upon assumptions and practices. See Fish (1980) and Fish (1989).
4. Examples of this kind of activation can be found with respect to Talmudic legal stories in Wimpfheimer (2011).
5. Some of these cultures have spawned multiple academic fields. The Israelite/Jewish tradition includes materials from the Hebrew Bible, from the Dead Sea Scrolls and from rabbinic literature. These are generally studied by different subfields of scholars. In the Greek and Roman contexts, legal materials are studied by scholars who specialize in law, but they are also treated by classicists.
6. These are: 1: Ur-Nammu (~2100 BCE); 2: Lipit-Ishtar (~1925 BCE); 3: Eshnunna (~1850 BCE); 4: Hammurabi (1680 BCE); 5: Hittite (thirteenth century BCE); 6: Assyrian (twelfth century BCE); 7: Neo-Babylonian (sixth century BCE).
7. Some might want to follow Westbrook in adding the biblical codes to the Mesopotamian grouping. There are benefits to this grouping as well.
8. These include the *Manual of Discipline, The Damascus Document, The Community Rule, Some Precepts of the Law* (4QMMT) and several other smaller codes or fragments of codes. For a recent consideration of the code qualities of this set of texts, see Schiffman (2010).

9. All of rabbinic literature was originally produced orally and only reduced to writing at a later period.
10. J. J. Finkelstein importantly resisted the comparative lens that viewed Mesopotamian legal codes as negative moral models for later biblical codes (Finkelstein 1958; Finkelstein 1966; Finkelstein 1981).
11. Consider the Thibault–Savigny debate about German codification in the nineteenth century in this light. While there was tremendous admiration for the code as an ideal, Savigny felt that the Roman code was itself only a result of weak jurists.
12. The unique legal codes of the Dead Sea Scrolls (as opposed to the scrolls that are copies of biblical codes) are primarily concerned with matters of cult and membership. There isn't a strong legacy of theorization of private law, for example. For more on this, see Schiffman (2010).
13. Scholars believe that *Avot* needs to be dated slightly later than the rest of Mishnah.
14. Within scholarship on ancient law, a common trope is the discovery of deep structure within the arrangement of the code. See e.g., literature cited at Paul (1970); Eichler (1987); Kristensen (2004).
15. For a related notion of degrees of narrativity, see Simon-Shoshan (2012).
16. For more on the casuistic form as narrative, see Bartor (2010).
17. On the distinction between script and narrative see Bruner (1991).
18. Much of the articulation of New Criticism against authorial intent transpired within the context of writing about meaning in poetry. See e.g., Wimsatt (1954).
19. In light of Hurowitz (1994) it might be more correct to say that the laws were produced to provide content for the narrative claims of prologue and epilogue.
20. For a review of attempts to find the prologue/epilogue format in the Bible, see Hurowitz (1994).
21. I thank Simeon Chavel for convincing me of this perspective. For a recent reexamination of the role of Moses as both prophet and voice of the law see Stackert (2014).
22. See e.g., Exodus 21:13; Leviticus 19. For deeper literary analysis of this eruption, see Bartor (2010).
23. For an overview of midrash and the violence with which it regularly reads the biblical corpus see the essays collected in Hartman and Budick (1986).
24. Compare the biblical narrative of Amnon and Tamar in 2 Samuel 13.
25. This case is famously central to Robert Cover's "Nomos and Narrative" (Cover 1992).
26. The narrativization developed by Rashi is hinted at in rabbinic literature at BT Sanhedrin 107a attributed to R. Dostai, a second-century CE Palestinian rabbi. It is also referenced, though not worked out, at Tanhuma Deuteronomy 21. Midrash Tannaim, a work of tannaitic midrash that is often unreliable in its presentation of second-century rabbis (some of the views are as late as the twelfth century) also mentions the general idea that the rebellious son occurs because of marriage to an inappropriate woman (Stern 1998).
27. The notion of Torah as subject is a common feature of early rabbinic midrash. For an articulate theorization of this phenomenon see Yadin-Israel (2004).
28. Moshe Halbertal includes the case of the rebellious son as one of several biblical passages that force rabbinic reinterpretations out of ethical critique (1997).
29. One could add the next case of the need to hang an executed body as a continuation of the sequence.
30. Note 22 above noted that this identification of the divine as the lawgiver is present in various biblical legal code contexts.
31. The rabbinic Foucauldian assertion of power has been a common thesis over the last decade. In this vein see Berkowitz (2006); Rosen-Zvi (2008); Wimpfheimer (2011).
32. And this ambivalence is echoed in the divisions among biblical interpreters. See Stern (1998).

Agreements

1. An excellent history of these problems in Prodi (2000). However, he does not distinguish between the Jewish and the Christian concepts; see also Schneewind (1998).
2. With reference to Roman religion, see Scheid (1981: 117 and esp. 150).
3. With reference to the law of contracts, see especially Gordley (1991: 40–45),whom, however, I cannot follow in the idea that the civil law jurists of the Middle Ages had arrived at the conclusion that all contracts were binding by consent.
4. A well-known exception was the *lex Aquilia* on damages. For a convincing defense of the traditional view on this problem see Santucci (2014a).
5. See the paradigmatic case of Lab. 4 *Posthumous works*, D. 19.1.50 as interpreted by Talamanca (1997).
6. On *varṇāśramadharma* see for all Hiltebeitel (2011: 215–227); on its origins see Olivelle (1993: 73–111).
7. On this passage and on its relationship with Greek theogonic models, see Fiori (1996: 107–110).
8. For the sake of simplicity, in the following paragraphs I will use the terms "archaic," "classical," and "late" in a quite general sense, according to the three main periods of the development of Roman law as depicted—with an emphasis on their socio-economic value—by Serrao (2006). Other handbooks use more nuanced distinctions, tend to undervalue the importance of the archaic period, and are mostly concentrated on classical law, pictured as a "system."
9. The best presentation of the private law of this period is in Serrao (2006). As for public law, see De Martino (1972). An excellent introduction, in English, to the historical period is Cornell (1995).
10. While Roman clientship is a well-known institution, the *sodalitates* have been studied less (Fiori 1999a).
11. Paul Diacon, epitome to Sextus Pompeius Festus', *On the Meaning of Words*, s.v. *pelices* (Lindsay 248).
12. On the *addictio* and its nature of slavery of a Roman in Rome—usually denied by the scholars—see Fiori (2001) and Masi Doria (2012: 321–325).
13. In the XII Tables, *pacisci* is mentioned as a remedy to avoid the talion in case of an injury consisting in tearing one's limb (tab. 8.1). On *pacisci* during the trial see tab. 1.6.
14. These rules are set down by the XII Tables: see tab. 3, 5 (*pacisci* after the trial and declaration *in comitio* of the debt). That the declaration was aimed at finding someone to take on the debt, is a shared guess (see for all Pugliese 1962; Albanese 1987).
15. On the sharing of legal and religious beliefs with the peoples of Italy see Catalano (1965). The parallels between international and private law have been lucidly seen by Watson (1993) (whose idea that the gods were judges both in private and international controversies, however, I cannot share).
16. For a general introduction to this period, Schulz (1951) is, in the English language, a classic. The standard reference book is Kaser (1972), but see also Talamanca (1990), which is among the best of the recent handbooks. An excellent study on the role of the agreement, particularly concentrated on this period, is Cascione (2003).
17. Pomponius 9 *On Sabinus*, Digest 18.1.20. For a detailed analysis of this fragment see Fiori 1999b: 190–206 (a shorter account in English is to be found in Fiori 2014b: 44–45).
18. They are the *lex Iulia de maritandis ordinibus* (18 BCE) and the *lex Papia Poppaea nuptialis* (9 BCE). On the importance of the *mores maiorum* in Augustus' matrimonial legislation see for all Nörr (1981).

19. For a general introduction to the law of this period see Kaser (1975); for contracts, see Levy (1956).

Arguments

1. Cf. Plato, *Phaedrus* 257c, Dinarchus 1.111, see Bonner (1926: 219–222) and Dover (1968: 155–157).
2. Cf. Carey (1994b: 181) understates the point: "it was probably very difficult to win a case without any supporting testimony or documentation at all. Rhetoric can only take you so far."
3. Carey (1994b: 96 fn 6) points out that Aristotle exaggerates the distinction between artful and artless proofs.
4. Schiappa (1999: 35–39) has argued against this view, which originates with Plato, *Phaedrus* 267a. I am not so sure that we can dismiss Plato's evidence.
5. See Calhoun (1919: 177–193). Lentz (1989: 72) sees a reluctance on the part of the Athenians to introduce writing into their pleadings: "the use of written evidence in the law courts of Athens is a popular reflection of the attitude towards writing Plato expresses in the Phaedrus." I would argue that the integration of writing followed as an integral part of the maturation of the democratic constitution.
6. See also Mirhady (2007: 48–59, 228–233). Harris (2013 :101–137) has argued against my view.
7. The translations of Demosthenes in this chapter are modified from Murray (1936–1939).
8. Jaeger (1938: 29–30) emphasizes that, unlike Antiphon and Andocides, none of the great speechwriters who immediately preceded Demosthenes, Lysias, Isaeus, or Isocrates, made a practice of delivering speeches in the Athenian courts. The first two were metics (resident non-Athenians), and Isocrates kept silent, circulating his "speeches" in written form only instead.
9. Certainly some allowance must be made for the fact that many cases in which the later orators engaged did not rely as much on information that could be supplied by witnesses.
10. I have sketched the similarities and the putatively common origins of these accounts in Mirhady (1991a: 5–28).
11. For the advice on laws, see Carey (1996: 33–46) and on challenges to oath and torture see Mirhady (1991b: 78–83; and 1996: 119–131).
12. Aristotle, *Rhetoric* 1.15, 1375b3-5: "That the just is something true and beneficial, but the apparently just is not, so that the written law (is) not (just); for it does not fulfill the function of law." Cf. D. Mirhady (1990: 393–410). It is important to recognize how the argumentation works within Aristotle's scheme. "True" (*alêthes*) and "beneficial" (*sumpheron*) represent for him two different vectors of argumentation, which he pursues throughout his account of the rhetoric of law. He associates truth with fairness (*to epieikes*), on one vector, and the beneficial with universal law (*koinos nomos*), in the sense of law that is universally beneficial, on the other. Truth and fairness are associated with what is "more just" (*dikaioteron*), the details of a particular case and of the particular individuals involved that make application of the general parameters of written law inappropriate. On the other hand, the beneficial and universal law are associated with unwritten laws, which serve the interests of the community or state. The former, for instance, may lead to forgiveness (*sungnomê*) of an individual's shortcomings; the latter to punishment that may serve as an example to the community as a whole.
13. Similar argumentation appears in Antiphon's homicide speeches (5.87 and 6.3, 5). Cf. Sommerstein and Bayliss (2013: 113 fn 175).

14. Cf. Demosthenes 20.114, 37.47, 41.14, 57.1; Isocrates 1.40; Lycurgus 1.20, 33; Lysias 23.16.
15. Cf. Aeschines 3.260; Demosthenes 25.11, 16, 75, 26.7.
16. Cf. Aeschin. 3.17; Dem. 18.298, 18.308.
17. They have been followed by Rubinstein (2005: 99–124). The explanation of Cohen (1995: 110–111) seems no more satisfactory: "witnesses are there to tell whatever needs to be told to support you." Carey (1994b: 184) points out that in classical Athens, the implicit view of the role of witnesses "places the emphasis on matters of fact."
18. The identities of the witnesses who provide testimony in Demosthenes 27.22, 26, 28, 33, and 39, for instance, are never stated.
19. It is embraced by Isocrates 15.27. I have traced some of the continuity in the use of the oath-challenge from Homer to the fourth century, in Mirhady (1991b: 78–80).
20. The authenticity of this speech has been challenged (Blass 1893: 232–234). Several parts are repeated from *Against Aphobus* 1.27. To me, the speech is undoubtedly by Demosthenes, although I am willing to believe that it was thoroughly worked through (by him) before reaching its current state.
21. For the procedures surrounding this situation Carey (1995: 114–119).
22. For a similar situation, see Isaeus 8.6–14. For other passages and discussion of this stock argument, see Mirhady (1991b: 80–81).
23. Gagarin (1996) has proposed that such challenges to torture (*basanos*) were only legal fictions: that torture rarely, if ever, occurred. In general, he follows the magisterial study of Thür (1977).
24. They may be the people who happened by and helped Ariston home afterwards, though it can only be Phanostratus who testifies to the beginning of the actual assault (9). Later in the speech, he identifies the passers-by by name (32).
25. A briefer version of this chapter appeared as Mirhady 2000.

Property and Possession

1. A good example is Diósdi (1970). This book, having been written during the height of communism, is also an interesting social artifact that deserves closer study in its own right.
2. A notable exception is Watson (1983a), although his general position on "legal transplants" seems not to take "legal culture" into account.
3. Magisterial surveys such as those of Heitland (1921) are no longer feasible.
4. Most recently Humbert (2005). Although the ideas of Raymond Westbrook, recently collected in Westbrook (2015), are tantalizing, his arguments concerning the supposed Near Eastern influences on the drafting of the XII Tables have never received widespread support. This volume is well worth reading, however, as he makes a number of compelling points about the continuing impact of nineteenth-century anthropological assumptions upon the study of ancient law more generally.
5. For a good account of the sources and a likely reconstruction, see Crawford (1996). It is worth noting that Crawford's reconstruction is very different from other, earlier attempts and should therefore be scrutinized when compared to earlier reconstructions.
6. Both Forsythe (2005) and Carandini (2011) provide good accounts of this period.
7. See also Forsythe (2005: 209–211). Thomas (2005) reaches broadly the same conclusions in relation to ancient Greek law.
8. For a thorough account, see Capogrossi Colognesi (1981). One may point here specifically to the importance of *Terminus*, the god of boundaries, in the Roman belief system.

9. Kaser (1956), remains an important early work on this topic, but should now be read in light of more recent contributions by Capogrossi Colognesi (2014: 126–132). See Forsythe (2005: 211–215).
10. It has been suggested by scholars such as Kaser (1956) that "ownership" was originally restricted to movables whereas land was owned in common. At some point, land came to be privately "owned," but ownership was restricted to the *pater familias*. This, presumably ties in with more general narratives about patriarchy and the legal restrictions visible in many areas of Roman property law over other members of the Roman *familia* and their ability to own property independently from the *pater familias*. While there is undoubtedly an element of truth in this account, much of the detail remains debatable and modern scholars should remain sensitive to the extent to which this narrative is founded upon nineteenth-century anthropology and the concept of "primitive law."
11. Indeed Jakab (2015: 115) has recently suggested that more attention needs to be paid to archaeology in order to uncover more information about property rights in the Republic.
12. For how all this relates to the rise of *latifundia*, see Harper (2015) and Launaro (2015).
13. Corbo (2013) is one of the latest monographs on this.
14. The recording of property holding in Egypt is vastly complicated by the existence of a central property archive. For all this, see Maresch (2002).
15. Harris (2012) provides a good general survey of the complexities of this term in Late Antiquity.
16. See generally Lo Cascio (1997). The importance of *longi* and *longissimi temporis praescriptio* in the development of later Roman property law should not be underestimated, see Nörr (1969).
17. The standard work here is Levy (1951), but should be read in light of Vandendriessche (2006).

Wrongs

1. The literature on the trial is immense; I have used Waterfield (2009: 3–19).
2. As in the case of the trial of Socrates, the amount of literature is enormous. I have employed Schrage (2003) for a legal-historical introduction from the *Ars Aequi* series on historical landmark cases, in Dutch.
3. Notwithstanding the use of analogous cases (Dover 1974: 218–219).
4. By speaking with pebbles in his mouth, though this is probably an embellishment in the later sources (Badian 2000: 15–16).
5. Leading to a myriad of problems from a legal-historical perspective (Schrage 2003: 262–263).
6. Handed down by Plato and Xenophon, see Waterfield (2009: 8–19).
7. The crime of "hubreos grafe" (ὕβρεως γραφή), "hubris" meaning abuse and "grafe" public criminal trial, was not defined in the Draconian or Solonic legislation (Ruschenbusch 1965: 303).
8. By means of the law of Augustus regarding private trials (*lex Iulia iudiciorum privatorum*) and the law of Augustus regarding public criminal trials (*lex Iulia iudiciorum publicorum*); see Giltaij (2013).
9. For a gruesome example of this, see Bauman (1996: 19); a governor decapitating a Gallic prisoner of war because one of his courtesans had never seen a man die before.
10. The death penalty (Krause 2004: 27; Lanni 2006: 65, 93). An estimated fine to be paid to the state (Hitzig 1899: 48–49).

11. Thalheim (1916: col. 31–32). Setting it apart from "aikias dike" (αἰκίας δίκη), the private complaint for abuse, which punished the physical injury foremost (Hitzig 1899: 1–22; Krause 2004: 24–25), often in the same case; the distinction is not sharp (Hitzig 1899: 39–40; Lanni 2006: 93). As an explicit sexual offense, see Guettel Cole (1984: 98).
12. Demosthenes, *Speeches* 54.1, 54.8–19 (the acts are described in 54.8–9); see Krause (2004: 27–28), Lanni (2006: 64–65), MacDowell (2009: 240–242). For other sources referring to a single act of insult and violence, see Hitzig (1899: 41–43).
13. In the case of adultery the victim being the cheated-upon husband (Cohen 1991: 82–83, 100–109, 123, 155; Krause 2004: 40; Lanni 2006: 94–95). The husband himself was allowed to cheat on his wife (Krause 2004: 41).
14. E.g., seduction of free married women, statutory rape of boys (Cohen 1991: 176–180, 227).
15. Cohen 1991: 123, 109: "violation of … the husband's claim to exclusive sexual access to his wife." The law concerning adultery then rather was aimed at curbing self-help, i.e., killing the adulteress (Guettel Cole 1984: 100–101; Cohen 1991: 124; compare Sealey 194: 110).
16. Cohen (1991: 99). Although the focus is on Athens, adultery was apparently seen as an abomination in all of Greece (Lanni 2006: 95).
17. Demosthenes, *Speeches* 23.53; Cohen (1991: 100, 107–108). Otherwise: Cantarella (1991: 295–296).
18. Kunkel and Wittmann (1995: 391), with bibliography. Also, Mommsen (1877: 331–469); Suolahti (1963), containing a list and descriptions of the successive holders of the office.
19. Kunkel and Wittmann (1995: 406); full procedure: Mommsen (1877: 384–387), Kunkel and Wittmann (1995: 420ff).
20. Mommsen (1877: 354), Greenidge (1894: 52–53): all the essential tenets of a court case are there.
21. For a comparative list in common law, see Ibbetson (2013: 36–37). The amount of literature is staggering; here I will just refer to Zimmermann (1996: 1050–1094, 1074–1077 for common law, and 1085–1094 for the modern German conception).
22. Hitzig (1899: 54); Pugliese (1941: 57–58); Hagemann (1998: 64–67); *Mosaicarum et Romanarum legum collatio* 2.5.1, a text by the third-century jurist Paulus. The text has been handed down to us in a peculiar but generally fairly trustworthy source, namely a fourth-fifth century CE comparison between various Roman regulations and the Pentateuch: Hyamson (1913: xxx); Schulz (1963: 297–299); Liebs (2015: 239–242). See however Pugliese (1941: 40–46 and 58).
23. The *lex Cornelia de iniuriis* (c. 81 BCE) (Hitzig 1899: 59–60, 72–80; Pugliese 1941: 42; Hagemann 1998: 62–64), although, weirdly, the introductory form probably was not a public criminal accusation but a private action (the *actio ex lege Cornelia de iniuriis*) (Kunkel 1974: 59–60), to be instituted by the victim alone (*Digesta* 47.10.6; Pugliese 1941: 122–123, 151).
24. The *lex Iulia de adulteriis* (c. 18 BCE) (Kunkel 1974: 91–92; McGinn 1998: 70, 140). This is probably the earliest and only Roman law regarding adultery despite the puzzling statement of the jurist Paul in *Mosaicarum et Romanarum legum collatio* 4.2.2 stating that there were many laws before it (McGinn 1998: 142).
25. Ulpian in *Digesta* 48.5.24 (Cantarella 1991: 291–292; Ruschenbusch 2010: 59). The reference is to a term in both the Draconian and Solonic laws, amounting to "at the moment of penetration," allowing the father to kill someone committing adultery with his daughter on the spot. Other direct references to Solon's laws occur in texts of a single

Roman jurist, namely Gaius: *Digesta* 10.1.13 (Ruschenbusch 2010: 127) and *Digesta* 47.22.4 (Ruschenbusch 2010: 145).

26. On this problem, see Pugliese (1941: 129), comparing it with the accusation under the Sullan law regarding abuse, and Ankum (1985: 153–205).
27. *Digesta* 48.5.6; McGinn (1998: 196–198). It is doubtful whether before the enactment of the Augustan law regarding adultery the adulterer could be punished by means of a legal remedy regarding abuse (Kunkel 1974: 121–122). As "immoral": *Digesta* 18.7.6 (McGinn 1998: 314). There were multiple legal remedies: compare Ulpian (in *Digesta* 47.10.25); Raber (1969: 169) and Gamauf (1999: 90, fn. 65–67).
28. *Digesta* 47.10.15.15: it does not amount to abuse to sexually harass women who wear the garb of prostitutes and slaves, i.e., togas, a punishment also given to adulterous women (McGinn 1998: 160–161).
29. *Adversus* or *contra bonos mores* (*Digesta* 47.10.15.35, 38–42), not just by Ulpian, but as a separate rubric in the edict of the praetor "regarding abuse of slaves" (Lenel 2010: 401). On the term, see Wittmann (1974: 343); Raber (1969: 7–8, 119–120); *Mosaicarum et Romanarum legum collatio* 2.5.8; Zimmermann (1996: 1058–1059); Ibbetson (2013: 42–43); *Digesta* 47.10.33.
30. Compare Gaius, *Institutes* 3.222 and *Digesta* 47.10.15.35 and 43. The sources, however, do not clarify if it is an actual insult to the slave himself, or a purely physical form of abuse.
31. It is mostly in the realm of public criminal law: the complaint has to primarily be lodged by the victim and the ensuing fine is forfeit to the state (Hitzig 1899: 80–81).
32. *Digesta* 47.10.5pr.; Hitzig (1899: 72); Pugliese (1941: 117); Hagemann (1998: 62), though flogging (*verberatio*) is one of the transgressions punished under the law, which also had a non-physical connotation as regards a slave, i.e., as an offense against the master's honor, see Hagemann (1998: 84).
33. Where the front door of a house marked the boundary behind which any man could live as he pleased (Dionysius of Halicarnassus 20.13.3); Schmähling (1938: 38); Kunkel and Wittmann (1995: 416). Critically: Watson (1983b: 53–65).
34. Only one of the few, apart from the Sullan law regarding homicide and the law regarding forgeries (Kunkel 1974: 90).
35. Compare McGinn 1998: 82: " … abstracted the norms it established … "

Legal Profession

1. Studying a person like Quintus Mucius Scaevola presents its own difficulties. Since the Mucii Scaevolae were not a family known for their innovativeness in naming their children, deducing whether an author meant one Quintus Mucius rather than another is a challenge, since their homonyms are legion (*quintus* means simply "the fifth"). For our purposes, the main distinction is between our Quintus Mucius, i.e., Quintus Mucius Scaevola Pontifex (consul in 95 BCE) and his relative Quintus Mucius Scaevola Augur (consul 117 BCE), who had also taught Cicero. The additions Pontifex and Augur are purely conventional and refer to their positions as magistrates. The latter's father was also called Quintus Mucius Scaevola (consul 174 BCE).
2. There is considerable difference of opinion regarding the doctrinal distinctions between them, but that does not interest us here (see Falchi 1981; Leesen 2010).

BIBLIOGRAPHY

1985. *JPS Hebrew-English Tanakh: The Traditional Hebrew Text and the New JPS Translation*. Philadelphia: Jewish Publication Society.
Aeschylus. 1991. *Oresteia*. Translated by Richard Lattimore. In David Grene and Richard Lattimore (eds.), *The Complete Greek Tragedies*, vol. 1. Chicago: University of Chicago Press.
Aeschylus. 2011. *The Complete Aeschylus*: Volume 1: *The Oresteia* (Greek Tragedy in New Translations). Translated and edited by Peter Burian and Alan Shapiro. Oxford: Oxford University Press.
Albanese, Bernardo. 1987. *Il processo privato romano delle legis actiones*. Palermo: Palumbo.
Allen, Danielle. 2005. "Greek Tragedy and Law." In Michael Gagarin and David Cohen (eds.), *The Cambridge Companion to Ancient Greek Law*. New York: Cambridge University Press.
Alt, Albrecht. 1966. *The Origins of Israelite Law: Essays on Old Testament History and Religion*. Translated by Robert A. Wilson. Garden City: Doubleday.
Amsterdam, Anthony and Jerome Bruner. 2000. *Minding the Law*. Cambridge, MA: Harvard University Press.
Ando, Clifford. 2011. *Law, Language, and Empire in the Roman Tradition*. Philadelphia: University of Pennsylvania Press.
Ando, Clifford. 2015a. "Fact, Fiction, and Social Reality in Roman Law." *Law and Philosophy Library*, 110: 295–324.
Ando, Clifford. 2015b. *Roman Social Imaginaries: Language and Thought in Contexts of Empire*. Toronto, Buffalo, and London: University of Toronto Press.
Ankum, Hans. 1985. "La *captiva adultera*. Problèmes concernant l'*accusatio adulterii* en droit Romain classique." *Revue Internationale des Droits de l'Antiquité*, 32: 153–205.
Annas, Julia. 2010. "Virtue and law in Plato." In Christopher Bobonich (ed.), *Plato's Laws: A Critical Guide*. New York: Cambridge University Press.
Antaki, Mark. 2014. "No Foundations?" *No Foundations: An Interdisciplinary Journal of Law and Justice*, 11: 61–77.
Arcangeli, Alessandro. 2012. *Cultural History: A Concise Introduction*. Abingdon and New York: Routledge.
Archi, Gian Gualberto. 1958. "Il concetto della proprietà nei diritti del mondo antico." *Rivista trimestrale di diritto e procedura civile*, fasc, 4(1): 1201–1216.
Aristophanes. 1978. *The Knights*. Translated by Alan Sommerstein. London: Penguin.
Aristotle. 1996. *The Politics and the Constitution of Athens*. Edited by Stephen Everson. New York: Cambridge University Press.
Aristotle. 2002. *Nicomachean Ethics*. Translated by Joe Sachs. Newburyport: Focus Publishing.
Atkison, Larissa M. 2016. "*Antigone*'s Remainders: Choral Ruminations and Political Judgment." *Political Theory*, 44: 219–239.
Bablitz, Leanne. 2007. *Actors and Audience in the Roman Courtroom*. Abingdon and New York: Routledge.
Badian, Ernst. 2000. "The Road to Prominence." In Ian Worthington (ed.), *Demosthenes: Statesman and Orator*. London: Routledge.

Bahrani, Zainab. 2003. *The Graven Image: Representation in Babylonia and Assyria*. Philadelphia: University of Pennsylvania.

Balkin, Jack M. 1994. "Understanding Legal Understanding: The Legal Subject and the Problem of Legal Coherence." *Yale Law Journal*, 103: 105–176.

Balot, Ryan. 2001. *Greed and Injustice in Classical Athens*. Princeton: Princeton University Press.

Bartor, Assnat. 2010. *Reading Law as Narrative: A Study in the Casuistic Laws of the Pentateuch*. Atlanta: Society of Biblical Literature.

Bauman, Richard A. 1983. *Lawyers in Roman Republican Politics: A Study of the Roman Jurists in their Political Setting, 316-82 BC*. Munich: C. H. Beck.

Bauman, Richard A. 1985. *Lawyers in Roman Transitional Politics: A Study of the Roman Jurists in their Political Setting in the Late Republic and Triumvirate*. Munich: C. H. Beck.

Bauman, Richard A. 1989. *Lawyers and Politics in the Early Roman Empire: A Study of Relations between the Roman Jurists and the Emperors from Augustus to Hadrian*. Munich: C. H. Beck.

Bauman, Richard A. 1996. *Crime and Punishment in Ancient Rome*. London and New York: Routledge.

Beard, Mary. 2015. *SPQR: A History of Ancient Rome*. New York: Liveright.

Behrends, Okko. 1976. "Die Wissenschaftslehre im Zivilrecht des Q. Mucius Scaevola pontifex." *Nachrichten der Akademie der Wissenschaften in Göttingen, Philologisch-historische Klasse*, 7: 263–304.

Behrends, Okko, Theodor Mommsen, Paul Krüger, and Peter Apathy, eds. 1995. *Corpus Iuris Civilis: Text und Übersetzung. Bd. 2, Digesten 1-10*. Müller: Heidelberg.

Berger, Harry Jr. 2015. *The Perils of Uglytown: Studies in Structural Misanthropology from Plato to Rembrandt*. New York: Fordham University Press.

Berman, Joshua. 2013. "Historicism and its Limits: A Response to Bernard M. Levinson and Jeffrey Stackert." *Journal of Ancient Judaism*, 4: 297–309.

Berkowitz, Beth A. 2006. *Execution and Invention: DeathPenalty Discourse in Early Rabbinic and Christian Cultures*. New York: Oxford University Press.

Binder, Guyora and Robert Weisberg. 2000. *Literary Criticisms of Law*. Princeton: Princeton University Press.

Birks, Peter and McLeod Grant. 1987. "Introduction." In Peter Birks and Grant McLeod (eds.), *Justinian's Institutes*. Ithaca: Cornell University Press.

Birks, Peter, Alan Rodger, and John S. Richardson. 1984. "Further Aspects of the 'Tabula Contrebiensis'." *The Journal of Roman Studies*, 74: 45–73.

Black, Jeremy and Anthony Green, eds. 1992. *Gods, Demons and Symbols of Ancient Mesopotamia: An Illustrated Dictionary*. Illustrated by Tessa Rickards. London: The British Museum Press.

Blass, Friedrich. 1893. *Die attische Beredsamkeit*, Book 3:1, *Demosthenes*. Leipzig: Teubner.

Bleicken, Jochen. 1974. *In provinciali solo dominium populi Romani est vel Caesaris: zur Kolonisationspolitik der ausgehenden Republik und frühen Kaiserzeit*. Frankfurt am Main: Johann Wolfgang Goethe-Universität.

Bonner, Robert J. 1905. *Evidence in Athenian Courts*. Chicago: University of Chicago Press.

Bonner, Robert J. 1926. *Lawyers and Litigants in Ancient Athens: The Genesis of the Legal Profession*. Chicago: University of Chicago Press.

Bottéro, Jean. 1992. *Mesopotamia: Writing, Reasoning, and Theogony*. Chicago: University of Chicago Press.

Bowersock, Glen W. 2015. "Inside the Emperor's Clothes." *New York Review of Books*, 62(20), December 17, 2015. Available online at www.nybooks.com/articles/2015/12/17/rome-inside-emperors-clothes/.

Boyarin, Daniel. 1990. "The Politics of Biblical Narratology: Reading the Bible like/as a Woman." *Diacritics*, 20(4): 31–43.

Bruner, Jerome. 1991. "The Narrative Construction of Reality." *Critical Inquiry*, 18: 1–21.

Bryen, Ari Z. 2013. *Violence in Roman Egypt: A Study in Legal Interpretation*. Philadelphia: University of Pennsylvania Press.

Buckland, William Warwick. 1908. *The Roman Law of Slavery*. Cambridge: Cambridge University Press.

Burckhardt, Jacob. [1860] 2004. *The Civilization of the Renaissance in Italy*. Translated by S. G. C. Middlemore with a new Introduction of Peter Burke and Notes by Peter Murray. London: Penguin.

Burckhardt, Jacob. [1872] 1998. *The Greeks and Greek Civilization*. Edited by Oswyn Murray and translated by Sheila Stern. New York: St. Martin's Press.

Burckhardt, Jacob. [1902] 1979. *Reflections on History*. Indianapolis: Liberty Classics.

Burke, Peter. 2004a. "Introduction: Jacob Burckhardt and the Italian Renaissance." In Jacob Burckhardt (ed.), *The Civilization of the Renaissance in Italy*. London: Penguin.

Burke, Peter. 2004b. *What Is Cultural History?* Cambridge, UK, and Malden: Polity Press.

Burke, Peter, Joan Pau Rubiés, Melissa Calaresu, and Filippo De Vivo. 2010. *Exploring Cultural History: Essays in Honour of Peter Burke*. Farnham, UK, and Burlington: Ashgate.

Cahen, R. 1923. "Examen de quelques passages du Pro Milone." *Revue des Études Anciennes*, 25(2): 119–233.

Calasso, Francesco. 1967. *Il negozio giuridico*. 2nd edn. Milan: Giuffrè.

Calhoun, Gorge M. 1919. "Oral and Written Pleading in Athenian Courts." *Transactions of the American Philological Association*, 50: 177–193.

Campbell, Brian. 2000. *The Writings of the Roman Land Surveyors: Introduction, Text, Translation and Commentary*. London: Society for the Promotion of Roman Studies.

Cantarella, Eva. 1991. "Moicheia. Reconsidering a Problem." In Michael Gagarin (ed.), *Symposion 1990*. Cologne, Weimar and Vienna: Böhlau.

Capogrossi Colognesi, Luigi. 1969. *La struttura della proprietà e la formazione dei "iura praediorum" nell'età repubblicana*, Book 1. Milano: Giuffrè.

Capogrossi Colognesi, Luigi. 1976. *La struttura della proprietà e la formazione dei "iura praediorum" nell'età repubblicana*, Book 2. Milano: Giuffrè.

Capogrossi Colognesi, Luigi. 1978. *Storia delle istituzioni romane arcaiche*. Roma: Ricerche.

Capogrossi Colognesi, Luigi. 1981. *La terra in Roma antica: forme di proprietà e rapporti produttivi*. Roma: La Sapienza.

Capogrossi Colognesi, Luigi. 2014. *Law and Power in the Making of the Roman Commonwealth*. Translated by Laura Kopp. Cambridge: Cambridge University Press.

Carandini, Andrea. 2011. *Rome: Day One*. Princeton: Princeton University Press.

Carey, Chris. 1994a. "Legal Space in Classical Athens." *Greece & Rome*, 41: 172–186.

Carey, Chris. 1994b. "Artless Proofs in Aristotle and the Orators." *Bulletin of the Institute for Classical Studies*, 39: 95–106.

Carey, Chris. 1995. "The Witness's *Exomosia* in the Athenian Courts." *The Classical Quarterly*, 45: 114–119.

Carey, Chris. 1996. "*Nomos* in Attic Rhetoric and Oratory." *The Journal of Hellenic Studies*, 116: 33–46.

Cascio, Elio Lo. 1997. "Dall'affitto agrario al colonato tardoantico: continuità o frattura?" In Elio Lo Cascio (ed.), *Terre, proprietari e contadini dell'impero romano: dall'affitto agrario al colonato tardoantico*. Rome: NIS, 1997.

Cascio, Elio Lo. 2015. "The Imperial Property and Its Development." In P. Erdkamp et al. (eds.), *Ownership and Exploitation of Land and Natural Resources in the Roman World*. Oxford: Oxford University Press, 2015.

Cascione, Cosimo. 2003. *Consensus. Problemi di origine, tutela processuale, prospettive sistematiche*. Naples: Editoriale Scientifica.

Catalano, Pierangelo. 1965. *Linee del sistema sovrannazionale romano*, vol. 1. Turin: Giappichelli.

Charpin, Dominique. 2010. *Reading and Writing in Babylon*. Translated by Jane Marie Todd. Cambridge, MA: Harvard University Press.

Chiba, Masaji. 1993. "Legal Pluralism in Sri Lankan Society: Toward a General Theory of non-Western Law." *Journal of Legal Pluralism*, 33: 197–212.

Cicero, Marcus Tullius. 2000. *On the Republic*. Translated by Clinton Walker Keyes. Cambridge, MA: Harvard University Press.

Civil, Miguel. 2011. "The Law Collection of Ur-Namma." In A. R. George (ed.), *Cuneiform Royal Inscriptions and Related Texts in the Schøyen Collection*. Bethesda: CDL Press.

Clark, Matthew. 2012. *Exploring Greek Myth*. Chichester, West Sussex, and Malden: Wiley-Blackwell.

Cohen, David. 1991. *Law, Sexuality and Society. The Enforcement of Morals in Classical Athens*. Cambridge: Cambridge University Press.

Cohen, David. 1995. *Law, Violence and Community in Classical Athens*. Cambridge: Cambridge University Press.

Cohen, David. 2005. "Introduction." In Michael Gagarin and David Cohen (eds.), *The Cambridge Companion to Ancient Greek Law*. New York: Cambridge University Press.

Colish, Marcia L. 2008. "Ambrose of Milan on Chastity." In Nancy Deusen (ed.), *Chastity: A Study in Perception, Ideals, Opposition*. Leiden and Boston: Brill.

Connerton, Paul. 1989. *How Societies Remember*. Cambridge: Cambridge University Press.

Connor, W. Robert. 1984. *Thucydides*. Princeton: Princeton University Press.

Cooper, Jerrold S. 1993. "Paradigm and Propaganda: The Dynasty of Akkade in the 21st Century BC." In Mario Liverani (ed.), *Akkad, The First World Empire. Structure, Ideology, Traditions*. Padova: Sargon.

Corbo, Chiara. 2013. *Constitutio Antoniniana: Ius Philosophia Religio*. Napoli: M. D'Auria editore.

Coriat, Jean-Pierre. 2014. *Les constitutions des Sévères. Règne de Septime Sévère*, vol. I. Rome: École Française de Rome.

Cornell, Tim. 1995. *The Beginnings of Rome: Italy and Rome from the Bronze Age to the Punic Wars (c. 1000-264 BC)*. London and New York: Routledge.

Cotterrell, Roger. 2006. *Law, Culture and Society: Legal Ideas in the Mirror of Social Theory*. Aldershot, England and Burlington: Ashgate.

Cotterrell, Roger. 2014. "A Concept of Law for Global Legal Pluralism?" In Seán P. Donlan and Lukas H. Urscheler (eds.), *Concepts of Law: Comparative, Jurisprudential and Social Science Perspectives*. Farnham: Ashgate.

Cottier, Michel, and Mireille Corbier. 2008. *The Customs Law of Asia*. Oxford and New York: Oxford University Press.

Cotton, Anne K. 2014. *Platonic Dialogue and the Education of the Reader*. Oxford: Oxford University Press.

Cover, Robert M. 1983. "The Supreme Court 1982 Term. Foreword: Nomos and Narrative." *Harvard Law Review*, 97(4): 4–68.

Cover, Robert M. 1992. *Narrative, Violence, and the Law: The Essays of Robert Cover*. Edited by Martha Minow, Michel Ryan and Austin Sarat. Ann Arbor: University of Michigan Press.

Crawford, Michael H. 1996. *Roman Statutes*. London: Institute of Classical Studies, School of Advanced Study, University of London.

Crook, J.A. 1995. *Legal Advocacy in the Roman World*. Ithaca, NY: Cornell University Press.

Cursi, Maria Floriana. 2013. "*Amicitia* e *societas* nei rapporti tra Roma e gli altri popoli del Mediterraneo." *Index*, 41: 195–227.

Cursi, Maria Floriana. 2014. "*Bellum iustum* tra rito e *iustae causae belli*." *Index*, 42: 569–585.

David, Jean-Michel. 1992. *Le patronat judiciaire au dernier siècle de la république romaine*. Rome: École Française de Rome.

Davies, John. 2005. "The Gortyn Laws." In Michel Gagarin and David Cohen (eds.), *The Cambridge Companion to Ancient Greek Law*. New York: Cambridge University Press.

Davis, Natalie Zemon. 1983. *The Return of Martin Guerre*. Cambridge, MA: Harvard University Press.

Dawson, Richard. 2014. *Justice as Attunement: Transforming Constitutions in Law, Literature, Economics, and the Rest of Life*. Abingdon: Routledge.

DeLorme, Charles D., Stacey Isom, and David R. Kamerschen. 2005. "Rent Seeking and Taxation in the Ancient Roman Empire." *Applied Economics* 37(6): 705–711.

De Martino, Francesco. 1972. *Storia della costituzione romana*, vol. 1. 2nd edn. Naples: Jovene.

De Martino, Francesco. 1973. *Storia della costituzione romana*, vol. 2. 2nd edn. Naples: Jovene.

Dening, Greg. 2002. "Performing on the Beaches of the Mind: An Essay." *History and Theory*, 41: 1.24.

Diesselhorst, Malte. 1959. *Die Lehre des Grotius vom Versprechen*. Cologne and Graz: Böhlau.

Dilke, Oswald A. W. 1971. *The Roman Land Surveyors: An Introduction to the Agrimensores*. Newton Abbot: David and Charles.

Diósdi, György. *Ownership in Ancient and Preclassical Roman Law*. Budapest: Akadémiai Kiadó, 1970.

Dolganov, Anna. n.d. "Reichsrecht and Volksrecht in Theory and Practice: Roman Law and Litigation Strategy in the Province of Egypt (P. Oxy. II 237, P. Oxy. IV 706, SB XII 10929)." Available online at www.academia.edu/5896267/Reichsrecht_and_Volksrecht_in_Theory_and_Practice_Roman_Law_and_Litigation_Strategy_in_the_Province_of_Egypt_P._Oxy._II_237_P._Oxy._IV_706_SB_XII_10929_. (Accessed November 5, 2015).

Dover, Kenneth J. 1968. *Lysias and the Corpus Lysiacum*. Berkeley: University of California.

Dover, Kenneth J. 1974. *Greek Popular Morality in the Time of Plato and Aristotle*. Oxford: Blackwell.

Dumézil, Georges. 1969. *Idées romaines*. Paris: Gallimard.

Eichler, Barry L. 1987. "Literary structure in the laws of Eshnunna." In Francesca Rochberg-Halton (ed.), *Language, Literature and History: Philological and Historical Studies Presented to Erica Reiner*. American Oriental Society: New Haven.

Etxabe, Julen. 2010. "The Legal Universe After Robert Cover." *Law & Humanities*, 4(1): 115–147.

Etxabe, Julen. 2013. *The Experience of Tragic Judgement*. Abingdon: Routledge.

Euben, J Peter. 1997. *Corrupting Youth: Political Education, Democratic Culture, and Political Theory*. Princeton: Princeton University Press.

Euripides. 1991a. *Orestes*. Translated by William Arrowsmith. In David Grene and Richard Lattimore (eds.), *The Complete Greek Tragedies*, vol. 4. Chicago: University of Chicago Press.

Euripides. 1991b. *The Suppliant Women*. Translated by Frank William Jones. In David Grene and Richard Lattimore (eds.), *The Complete Greek Tragedies*, vol. 4. Chicago: University of Chicago Press.

Ewald, William. 1998. "The Jurisprudential Approach to Comparative Law: A Field Guide to 'Rats'." *American Journal of Comparative Law*, 46(4): 701–707.

Falchi, Gian L. 1981. *Le controversie tra Sabiniani e Proculiani*. Milan: Giuffrè.

Ferrari, G.R.F. 2005. *City and Soul in Plato's Republic*. Chicago: University of Chicago Press.

Finkelstein, Jacob J. 1958. "Bible and Babel." *Commentary*, 26(431): 44.

Finkelstein, Jacob J. 1966. "Sex Offenses in Sumerian Laws." *Journal of the American Oriental Society*, 86(4): 355–372.

Finkelstein, Jacob J. 1981. "The Ox that Gored." *Transactions of the American Philosophical Society*, 71(2): 1–89.

Finley, Moses. 1951. "Some Problems of Greek Law: A Consideration of Pringsheim on Sale." *Seminar Jurist*, 9: 72–91.

Finley, Moses. 1966. "The Problem of the Unity of Greek Law." In *La Storia del Diritto nel Quadro delle Scienze Storiche. Atti del Primo Congresso Internationale della Società Italiana di storia del Diritto*. Florence: Leo Olshki, 129–142.

Fiori, Roberto. 1996. *Homo sacer. Dinamica politico-costituzionale di una sanzione giuridico-religiosa*. Naples: Jovene.

Fiori, Roberto. 1998–1999. "*Ius civile, ius gentium, ius honorarium*: il problema della 'recezione' dei *iudicia bonae fidei*." *Bullettino dell'Istituto di Diritto romano "Vittorio Scialoja,"* 101–102: 165–197.

Fiori, Roberto. 1999a. "*Sodales*. 'Gefolgschaften' e diritto di associazione in Roma arcaica (VIII-V sec. a.C.)." In *Societas-Ius. Munuscula di allievi a Feliciano Serrao*. Naples: Jovene.

Fiori, Roberto. 1999b. *La definizione della locatio conductio. Giurisprudenza romana e tradizione romanistica*. Naples: Jovene.

Fiori, Roberto. 2003a. "Il problema dell'oggetto del contratto nella tradizione civilistica." In *Modelli teorici e metodologici nella storia del diritto privato*, vol. 1. Naples: Jovene.

Fiori, Roberto. 2003b. *Ea res agatur. I due modelli del processo formulare repubblicano*. Milan: Giuffrè.

Fiori, Roberto. 2008. "*Fides* et *bona fides*. Hiérarchie sociale et catégories juridiques." *Revue historique de droit français et étranger*, 86: 465–481.

Fiori, Roberto. 2011a. *Bonus vir. Politica filosofia retorica e diritto nel de officiis di Cicerone*. Naples: Jovene.

Fiori, Roberto. 2011b. "La struttura del matrimonio romano." *Bullettino dell'Istituto di diritto romano Vittorio Scialoja*, 105: 197–234.

Fiori, Roberto. 2012. "The Roman Conception of Contract." In T. A. J. McGinn (ed.), *Obligations in Roman Law. Past, Present, and Future*. Ann Arbor: University of Michigan Press.

Fiori, Roberto. 2013. "La gerarchia come criterio di verità: *boni* e *mali* nel processo romano arcaico." In C. Cascione and C. Masi Doria (eds.), *Quid est veritas? Un seminario su verità e forme giuridiche*. Naples: Satura.

Fiori, Roberto. 2014a. "The *vir bonus* in Cicero's *de officiis*: Greek philosophy and Roman legal science." In *Aequum ius*. От друзей и коллег к 50-летию профессора Д.В. Дождева. Moscow: Statyt.

Fiori, Roberto. 2014b. "Rise and Fall of the Specificity of Contracts." In B. Sirks (ed.), *Nova ratione. Change of Paradigms in Roman Law*. Wiesbaden: Harrassowitz.

Fish, Stanley E. 1980. *Is there a Text in this Class? The Authority of Interpretive Communities*. Cambridge, MA: Harvard University Press.

Fish, Stanley E. 1989. *Doing What Comes Naturally: Change, Rhetoric, and the Practice of Theory in Literary and Legal Studies*. Durham: Duke University Press.

Forsdyke, Sara. 2009. "The Uses and Abuses of Tyranny." In Ryan Balot (ed.), *A Companion to Greek and Roman Political Thought*. Chichester: Wiley-Blackwell.

Forsythe, Gary. 2005. *A Critical History of Early Rome from Prehistory to the First Punic War*. Berkeley: University of California Press.

Foster, Benjamin. 1995. "Social Reform in Ancient Mesopotamia." In K. D. Irani and Morris Smith (eds.), *Social Justice in the Ancient World*. Westport: Greenwood Press.

Foster, Benjamin R., ed. and trans. 2001. *The Epic of Gilgamesh*. New York: Norton.

Fraistat, Shawn. 2015. "The Authority of Writing in Plato's *Laws*." *Political Theory*, 43: 657–677.

Frank, Jill. 2005. *A Democracy of Distinction: Aristotle and the Work of Politics*. Chicago: University of Chicago Press.

Frank, Jill. 2006. "The *Antigone*'s Law." *Law, Culture, and the Humanities*, 2: 336–340.

Frank, Jill. 2007. "Wages of War: On Judgment in Plato's *Republic*." *Political Theory* 35(4): 443–467.

Frank, Jill. 2015. "On *Logos* and Politics in Aristotle." In Thornton Lockwood and Thanassis Samaras (eds.), *Aristotle's* Politics: *A Critical Guide*. Cambridge: Cambridge University Press.

Frank, Jill. 2018. *Poetic Justice: Rereading Plato's Republic*. Chicago: University of Chicago Press.

Frankenberg, Günther. 1985. "Critical Comparisons: Re-Thinking Comparative Law." *Harvard International Law Journal*, 26(1): 411–455.

Frankenberg, Günther. 2014. "The Innocence of Method—Unveiled: Comparison as an Ethical and Political Act." *Journal of Comparative Law*, 9(2): 222–258.

Freedman, Lawrence. 1990. "Some Thoughts on Comparative Legal Culture." In David Clark (ed.), *Comparative and Private International Law: Essays in Honor of John Henry Merryman in his Seventieth Birthday*. Berlin: Duncker and Humblot, 49–57.

Frier, Bruce W. 1985. *The Rise of the Roman Jurists: Studies in Cicero's Pro Caecina*. Princeton: Princeton University Press.

Fuhrmann, Christopher J. 2012. *Policing the Roman Empire: Soldiers, Administration, and Public Order*. New York: Oxford University Press.

Gadamer, Hans-Georg. [1960] 1989. *Truth and Method*. 2nd and rev. edn. Translated by Joel Weinsheimer and Donald G. Marshall. New York: Continuum.

Gagarin, Michael. 1996. "The Torture of Slaves in Athenian Law." *Classical Philology*, 91: 1–18.

Gagarin, Michael. 2005a. "The Unity of Greek Law." In Michael Gagarin and David Cohen (eds.), *The Cambridge Companion to Ancient Greek Law*. New York: Cambridge University Press.

Gagarin, Michael. 2005b. "Early Greek Law." In Michael Gagarin and David Cohen (eds.), *The Cambridge Companion to Ancient Greek Law*. New York: Cambridge University Press.

Gagarin, Michael (ed.). 2011. *Speeches from Athenian Law*. Austin: University of Texas Press.

Gagarin, Michael and David Cohen, eds. 2005. *The Cambridge Companion to Ancient Greek Law*. New York: Cambridge University Press.

Gagarin, Michael and Paul Woodruff, eds. 1995. *Early Greek Political Thought from Homer to the Sophists*. New York: Cambridge University Press.

Gamauf, Richard. 1999. *Ad statuam licet confugere*. Frankfurt am Main: Peter Lang.

Gantz, Timothy. 1993. *Early Greek Myth*, vol. 1. Baltimore: Johns Hopkins University Press.

Garnsey, Peter. 1970. *Social Status and Legal Privilege in the Roman Empire*. Oxford: Oxford University Press.

Gaudemet, Jean. 1967. *Institutions de l´Antiquité*. Paris: Sirey.

Gaughan, Judy E. 2010. *Murder Was Not a Crime: Homicide and Power in the Roman Republic*. Austin: University of Texas Press.

Geertz, Clifford. 1973. *The Interpretation of Cultures*. New York: Basic Books.

Geertz, Clifford. 1983. *Local Knowledge: Further Essays in Interpretive Anthropology*. New York: Basic Books.

Gernet, Louis. 1955. *Droit et société dans la Grèce Ancienne*. Paris: Sirey.

Gill, Christopher. 2006. *The Structured Self in Hellenistic and Roman Thought*. Oxford: Oxford University Press.

Giltaij, Jacob. 2011. *Mensenrechten in het Romeinse recht?* Nijmegen: Wolf.

Giltaij, Jacob. 2013. "The Problem of the Content of the *lex Iulia iudiciorum publicorum*." *Tijdschrift voor Rechtsgeschiedenis*, 81(3/4): 507–529.

Glanert, Simone, ed. 2014. *Comparative Law: Engaging Translation*. Abingdon: Routledge.

Glenn, Patrick H. 2010. *Legal Traditions of the World: Sustainable Diversity in Law*, 4th edn. Oxford and New York: Oxford University Press.

Goldhill, Simon. 2000. "Civic Ideology and the Problem of Difference: The Politics of Aeschylean Tragedy, Once Again." *Journal of Hellenic Studies*, 120: 34–56.

Goodrich, Peter. 2014. *Legal Emblems and the Art of Law: Obiter Depicta as the Vision of Governance*. New York: Cambridge University Press.

Gordley, James. 1991. *The Philosophical Origins of Modern Contract Doctrine*. Oxford: Oxford University Press.

Gordon, Peter. 2014. "Contextualism and Criticism in the History of Ideas." In Darrin McMahon and Samuel Moyn (eds.), *Rethinking Modern European Intellectual History*. Oxford and New York: Oxford University Press.

Gordon, William M. and O. F. Robinson. 1988. *The Institutes of Gaius*. Ithaca, NY: Cornell University Press.

Green, Anna. 2008. *Cultural History: History and Theory*. New York: Palgrave Macmillan.

Greenberg, M. 1960. "Some Postulates of Biblical Criminal Law." In Menahen Haran (ed.), *Yehezkel Kaufmann Jubilee Volume*. Jerusalem: Magnes Press.

Greengus, Samuel. 1995. "Legal and Social Institutions of Ancient Mesopotamia." In Jack Sasson (ed.), *Civilizations of the Ancient Near East*. New York: Scribner's.

Greenidge, Abel Henry Jones. 1894. *Infamia: Its Place in Roman Public and Private Law*. Oxford: Clarendon.

Grimme, Hubert. 1907. *The Law of Hammurabi and Moses: A Sketch*. Translated by William T. Pilter. London: Society for Promoting Christian Knowledge.

Grossi, Paolo. 1973. "La proprietà nel sistema privatistico della Seconda Scolastica." In P. Grossi (ed.), *La Seconda Scolastica nella formazione del diritto privato moderno*. Milan: Giuffrè.

Gruen, Erich. 1995. *The Last Generation of the Roman Republic*. Berkeley: University of California Press.

Gualandi, Giovanni. 1963. *Legislazione imperiale e giurisprudenza*, vol. 2. Milan: Giuffrè.

Guettel Cole, Susan. 1984. "Greek Sanctions against Sexual Assault." *Classical Philology*, 79(2): 97–113.

Hagemann, Matthias. 1998. *Iniuria. Von den XII-Tafeln bis zur Justinianischen Kodifikation*. Cologne, Weimar, Vienna: Böhlau.

Hahm, David. E. 2009. "The Mixed Constitution in Greek Thought." In Ryan Balot (ed.), *A Companion to Greek and Roman Political Thought*. Chichester: Wiley-Blackwell.

Halbertal, Moshe. 1997. *Mahpekhot parshaniyot be-hithavutan: 'arakhim ke-shikulim parshaniyim be-midreshe halakhah*. Jerusalem: Magnes Press.

Halliwell, Stephen. 2009. "Theory and Practice of Narrative in Plato." In Jonas Grethlein and Antonios Rengakos (eds.), *Narratology and Interpretation: The Content of Narrative Form in Ancient Literature*. Berlin and New York: Walter De Gruyter.

Hammer, Dean. 2014. *Roman Political Thought: From Cicero to Augustine*. Cambridge: Cambridge University Press.

Hansen, Mogens H. 1991. *The Athenian Democracy in the Age of Demosthenes*. Oxford: Oxford University Press.

Harper, Kyle. 2015. "Landed Wealth in the Long Term: Patterns, Possibilities, Evidence." In Paul Erdkamp, Koenraad Verboven, and Arjan Zuiderhoek (eds.), *Ownership and Exploitation of Land and Natural Resources in the Roman World*. Oxford: Oxford University Press.

Harrell, Hansen C. 1936. *Public Arbitration in Athenian Law*. Columbia: University of Missouri.

Harries, Jill. 2006. *Cicero and the Jurists: From Citizen's Law to the Lawful State*. London: Duckworth.

Harries, Jill. 2007. *Law and Crime in the Roman World*. Cambridge: Cambridge University Press.

Harries, Jill. 2012. "Roman Law and Legal Culture." In Scott Johnson (ed.), *The Oxford Handbook of Late Antiquity*. Oxford: Oxford University Press.

Harris, Edward M. 1993. "*Apotimema*: Athenian Terminology for Real Security in Leases and Dowry Agreements." *The Classical Quarterly*, 43: 73–95.

Harris, Edward M. 1994. "Law and Oratory." In Ian Worthington (ed.), *Persuasion: Greek Rhetoric in Action*. London: Duckworth.

Harris, Edward M. 2013. *The Rule of Law in Action in Democratic Athens*. Oxford: Oxford University Press.

Hartman, Geoffrey H. and Sanford Budick, eds. 1986. *Midrash and Literature*. New Haven: Yale University Press.

Heitland, William Emerton. 1921. *Agricola: A Study of Agriculture and Rustic Life in the Greco-Roman World from the Point of View of Labour*. Cambridge: Cambridge University Press.

Hendry, Jennifer. 2014. "Legal Comparison and the (Im)possibility of Translation." In Simone Glanert (ed.), *Comparative Law: Engaging Translation*. Abingdon: Routledge.

Herington, C.J. 1973. "Review: *The Justice of Zeus* by Hugh Lloyd-Jones." *The American Journal of Philology*, 94(4): 395–398.

Herodotus. 1987. *The History*. Translated by David Grene. Chicago: University of Chicago Press.

Hesiod. 1993. *Works and Days; and Theogony*. Translated by Stanley Lombardo; Introduction by Robert Lamberton. Indianapolis and Cambridge: Hackett Publishing.

Hiltebeitel, Alf. 2011. *Dharma. Its Early History in Law, Religion, and Narrative*. Oxford: Oxford University Press.

Hitz, Zena. 2009. "Plato on the Sovereignty of Law." In Ryan Balot (ed.), *A Companion to Greek and Roman Political Thought*. Chichester: Wiley-Blackwell.

Hitzig, Hermann Ferdinand. 1899. *Injuria. Beiträge zur Geschichte der injuria im griechischen und römischen Recht*. Munich: Ackermann.

Höbenreich, Evelyn. 1992. "À propos 'Antike Rechtsgeschichte': einige Bemerkungen zur Polemik zwischen Ludwig Mitteis und Leopold Wenger." *Zeitschrift der Savigny-Stiftung für Rechtsgeschichte: Romanistische Abteilung*, 109: 547–562.

Homer. 1990. *The Iliad*. Translated by Robert Fagles; Introduction by Bernard Knox. New York: Penguin.

Homer. 1996. *The Odyssey*. Translated by Robert Fagles; Introduction by Bernard Knox. New York: Penguin.

Honig, Bonnie. 2013. *Antigone, Interrupted*. Cambridge and New York: Cambridge University Press.

Honoré, Tony. 1994. *Emperors and Lawyers: With a Palingenesia of Third-Century Imperial Rescripts 193-305 AD*. Oxford: Clarendon Press.

Hudson, Michael. 1993. "The Lost Tradition of Biblical Debt Cancellations." Available online at http://michael-hudson.com/wp-content/uploads/2010/03/HudsonLostTradition.pdf. (Accessed August 29, 2015).

Hudson, Michael. 2002. "Reconstructing the Origins of Interest-Bearing Debt and the Logic of Clean Slates." In Michael Hudson and Marc Van De Mieroop (eds.), *Debt and Economic Renewal in the Ancient Near East*. Bethesda, MD: CDL Press.

Humbert, Michel. 2005. *Le dodici tavole: dai decemviri agli umanisti*. Pavia: IUSS Press.

Humphreys, Sally C. 1985. "Social Relations on Stage: Witnesses in Classical Athens." *History and Anthropology*, 1(2): 313–369.

Hurowitz, Victor. 1994. *Inu Anum *s*irum: Literary Structures in the Non-Juridical Sections of Codex Hammurabi*. Philadelphia: University Museum.

Husa, Jaakko. 2007. "About the Methodology of Comparative Law: Some Comments Concerning the Wonderland." *Maastricht Faculty of Law Working Paper Series*, 5: 1–20.

Hyamson, Moses. 1913. *Mosaicarum et Romanarum legum collatio*. Oxford: Oxford University Press.

Ibbetson, David J. 2013. "Iniuria, Roman and English." In Eric Descheemaeker and Helen Scott (eds.), *Iniuria and the Common Law*. Oxford and Portland: Hart.

Jackson, John. 1937. *Tacitus: Annals. With An English Translation*. Cambridge, MA: Harvard University Press (Loeb Classical Library 312).

Jacobsen, Thorkild. 1987. "The Graven Image." In Patrick D. Miller, Paul Hanson and S. Dean McBride (eds.), *Ancient Israelite Religion: Essays in Honor of Frank Moore Cross*. Philadelphia: Fortress.

Jacotot, Mathieu. 2013. *Question d'honneur. Les notions d'honos, honestum et honestas dans la République romaine antique*. Rome: École Française de Rome.

Jaeger, Werner. 1938. *Demosthenes: The Origins and Growth of His Policy*. Berkeley: University of California.

Jakab, Eva. 2015. "Property Rights in Ancient Rome." In Paul Erdkamp, Koenraad Verboven, and Arjan Zuiderhoek (eds.), *Ownership and Exploitation of Land and Natural Resources in the Roman World*. Oxford: Oxford University Press.

Kahn, Paul W. 1999. *The Cultural Study of Law: Reconstructing Legal Scholarship*. Chicago: University of Chicago Press.

Kantor, Georgy. 2017. "Property in Land in Roman Provinces." In Kantor, Georgy, Tom Lambert, and Hannah Skoda (eds.), *Legalism: Property and Ownership*. Oxford: Oxford University Press.

Kaser, Max. 1956. *Eigentum und Besitz im älteren römischen Recht*. Cologne: Böhlau.

Kaser, Max. 1972. *Das römische Privatrecht*. I. *Das altrömische, das vorklassische und klassische Recht*. 2nd edn. Munich: C. H. Beck.

Kaser, Max. 1975. *Das römische Privatrecht*. II. *Die nachklassischen Entwicklungen*. 2nd edn. Munich: C. H. Beck.

Kaser, Max and Karl Hackl. 1996. *Das römische Zivilprozessrecht*. Munich: C. H. Beck.

Kehoe, Dennis P. 2015. "Property Rights over Land and Economic Growth in the Roman Empire." In Paul Erdkamp, Koenraad Verboven, and Arjan Zuiderhoek (eds.), *Ownership and Exploitation of Land and Natural Resources in the Roman World*. Oxford: Oxford University Press.

Keller, Timothy. 2002. "What is Biblical Justice?" Available online at www.relevantmagazine.com/god/practical-faith/what-biblical-justice.

King, Leonard W. 1910. *A History of Sumer and Akkad: An Account of the Early Races of Babylonia from Prehistoric Times to the Foundation of the Babylonian Monarchy*. London: Chatto & Windus.

Kleinhans, Martha-Marie and Roderick. MacDonald. 1997. "What is a *Critical* Legal Pluralism?" *Canadian Journal of Law and Society*, 12: 25–46.

Koselleck, Reinhart. 1981. *Preußen zwischen Reform und Revolution. Allgemeines Landrecht, Verwaltung und soziale Bewegung von 1791 bis 1848*. 2nd edn. Stuttgart: Klett-Cotta.

Kraus, Fritz R. 1984. *Königliche Verfügungen in Altbabylonischer Zeit*. Leiden: Brill.

Krause, Jens-Uwe. 2004. *Kriminalgeschichte der Antike*. Munich: C. H. Beck.

Kristensen, Karen R. 2004. "Codification, Tradition and Innovation in the Law Code of Gortyn." *DIKE Rivista di storia del diritto greco ed ellenistico*, 7: 135–168.

Krygier, Martin. 1986. "Law as Tradition." *Law and Philosophy*, 5: 237–262.

Kunkel, Wolfgang. 1962. *Untersuchungen zur Entwicklung des römischen Kriminalverfahrens in vorsullanischer Zeit*. Munich: C. H. Beck.

Kunkel, Wolfgang. 1974. "Quaestio." In Hubert Niederländer (ed.), *Kleine Schriften. Zum römischen Strafverfahren und zur römischen Verfassungsgeschichte*. Weimar: Böhlau. 33–110.

Kunkel, Wolfgang. 2001. *Die Römischen Juristen. Herkunft und soziale Stellung*. Cologne, Weimar, Vienna: Böhlau Verlag.

Kunkel, Wolfgang and Roland Wittmann. 1995. *Staatsordnung und Staatspraxis der römischen Republik*, vol. 2. Munich: C. H. Beck.

LaCapra, Dominick. 1983. "Rethinking Intellectual History and Reading Texts." In *Rethinking Intellectual History: Texts, Contexts, Language*. Ithaca, NY: Cornell University Press.

Laks, André. 2010. "Plato's 'Truest Tragedy': *Laws* Book 7, 817a-d." In Christopher Bobonich (ed.), *Plato's Laws: A Critical Guide*. New York: Cambridge University Press.

Lane, Melissa. 2013a. "Founding as Legislating: The Figure of the Lawgiver in Plato's *Republic*." In Noburu Notomi and Luc Brisson (eds.), *Dialogues on Plato's Politeia (Republic): Selected Papers from the Ninth Symposium Platonicum*. Sankt Augustin: Academia Verlag.

Lane, Melissa. 2013b. "Platonizing the Spartan *Politeia* in Plutarch's *Lycurgus*." In Verity Harte and Melissa Lane (eds.), *Politeia in Greek and Roman Philosophy*. Cambridge: Cambridge University Press.

Lane, Melissa. 2014. *The Birth of Politics: Eight Greek and Roman Political Ideas and Why They Matter*. Princeton: Princeton University Press.

Langlands, Rebecca. 2006. *Sexual Morality in Ancient Rome*. Cambridge: Cambridge University Press.

Lanni, Adriaan. 2006. *Law and Justice in the Courts of Classical Athens*. Cambridge: Cambridge University Press.

Launaro, Alessandro. 2015. "The Nature of the Villa Economy." In Paul Erdkamp, Koenraad Verboven, and Arjan Zuiderhoek (eds.), *Ownership and Exploitation of Land and Natural Resources in the Roman World*. Oxford: Oxford University Press.

Lebow, Richard Ned. 2003. *The Tragic Vision of Politics: Ethics, Interests and Orders*. Cambridge: Cambridge University Press.

Leesen, Tessa G. 2010. *Gaius Meets Cicero: Law and Rhetoric in the School Controversies*. Leiden and Boston: Martinus Nijhoff Publishers.

Legrand, Pierre. 1995. "Comparative Legal Studies and Commitment to Theory." *The Modern Law Review*, 58: 262–273.

Legrand, Pierre. 2014. "Withholding Translation." In Simone Glanert (ed.), *Comparative Law: Engaging Translation*. Abingdon: Routledge.

Legrand, Pierre. 2016. *Le Droit Comparé*. 5th edn. Paris: Presses Universitaires de France.

Lenel, Otto. 2010. *Das edictum perpetuum*. 3rd edn. Aalen: Scientia.

Lentz, Tony. 1989. *Orality and Literacy in Hellenic Greece*. Carbondale: Southern Illinois University Press.

Lepschy, Giulio. 1992. "Subject and Object in the History of Linguistics." *Journal of the Institute of Romance Studies*, 1: 1–15.

Levin, B. M., ed. 1921. *Iggeret Rav Sherira Gaon*. Haifa: Golda-Itskovski.

Levinson, Bernard. 2008. *"The Right Chorale": Studies in Biblical Law and Interpretation*. Tübingen: Mohr Siebeck.

Levinson, Bernard and Jeffrey Stackert. 2013. "The Limitations of 'Resonance': A Response to Joshua Berman on Historical and Comparative Method." *Journal of Ancient Judaism*, 4: 310–333.

Levy, Ernst. 1951. *West Roman Vulgar Law: The Law of Property*. Philadelphia: American Philosophical Society.

Levy, Ernst. 1956. *Weströmisches Vulgarrecht. Das Obligationenrecht*. Weimar: Böhlau.

Liebs, Detlef. 2010. *Hofjuristen der römischen Kaiser bis Justinian: vorgetragen in der Sitzung vom 14. November 2008*. Munich: Verlag der Bayerischen Akademie der Wissenschaften.

Liebs, Detlef. 2015. *Das Recht der Römer und die Christen*. Tübingen: Mohr Siebeck.

Lintott, Andrew William. 1992. *Judicial Reform and Land Reform in the Roman Republic: A New Edition, with Translation and Commentary, of the Laws from Urbino*. Cambridge: Cambridge University Press.

Lintott, Andrew William. 2009. "The Theory of the Mixed Constitution at Rome." In Richard Brooks (ed.), *Cicero and Modern Law*. Burlington: Ashgate.

Liverani, Mario. 2003. *Oltre la Bibbia. Storia antica di Israele*. Rome and Bari: Laterza.

Lloyd-Jones, Hugh. 1983. *The Justice of Zeus*. 2nd edn. Berkeley: University of California Press.

Loraux, Nicole. 2002. *The Divided City: On Memory and Forgetting in Ancient Athens*. Translated by Corinne Pache with Jeff Fort. New York: Zone Books.

MacDonald, Roderick. 2006. "Here, There ... And Everywhere: Theorizing Legal Pluralism; Theorizing Jacques Vanderlinden." In Nicholas Kasirer (ed.), *Étudier et enseigner le droit: Hier, aujord'hui et demain. Études offertes à Jacques Vanderlinden*. Montréal: Éditions Yvon Blais.

MacDowell, Douglas M. 2009. *Demosthenes the Orator*. Oxford: Oxford University Press.

McGinn, Thomas A. J. 1998. *Prostitution, Sexuality and the Law in Ancient Rome*. Oxford: Oxford University Press.

McIlwain, Charles Howard. 1940. *Constitutionalism: Ancient and Modern*. Ithaca: Cornell University Press.

Mackenzie, Roderick A. F. 1964. "The Formal Aspect of Ancient Near Eastern Law." In W. Stewart McCullough (ed.), *The Seed of Wisdom: Essays in Honor of TJ Meek*. Toronto: University of Toronto Press.

Maganzani, Lauretta. 2007. *Land Surveying for Legal Disputes: Technical Advice in Roman Law*. Naples: Jovene. Available online at http://hdl.handle.net/10807/28616.

Maine, Henry Sumner. [1861] 1906. *Ancient Law: Its Connection with the Early History of Society and its Relation to Modern Ideas*. 10th edn with Introduction and notes by Frederick Pollock. London: John Murray.

Maine, Henry Sumner. 1871. *Village-Communities in the East and West: Six Lectures Delivered at Oxford*. London: John Murray.

Maine, Henry Sumner. 1886. *Dissertations on Early Law and Custom: Chiefly Selected from Lectures at Oxford*. New York: Henry Holt.

Manthe, Ulrich. 2003. *Die Rechtskulturen der Antike: vom alten Orient bis zum Römischen Reich*. Munich: C. H. Beck.

Mara, Gerald. 1997. *Socrates' Discursive Democracy: Logos and Ergon in Platonic Political Philosophy*. Albany: SUNY Press.

Maresch, Klaus. 2002. "Die Bibliotheke Enkteseon Im Römischen Ägypten Überlegungen Zur Funktion Zentraler Besitzarchive." *Archiv Für Papyrusforschung Und Verwandte Gebiete*, 48(1): 233–246.

Martino, P. 1986. *Arbiter*. Rome: CNR e Università di Roma "La Sapienza."

Masi Doria, Carla. 2012. "*Libertorum bona ad patronos pertineant*: su Calp. Flacc. *decl. exc.* 14." *Index*, 40: 313–325.

Maza, Sarah. 2014. "Stephen Greenblatt, New Historicism, and Cultural History, or, What We Talk about When We Talk about Interdisciplinarity." *Modern Intellectual History*, 1(2): 249–265.

Menn, Stephen. 2006. "On Plato's *Politeia*." In John Cleary and Gary Gurtler (eds.), *Proceedings of the Boston Area Colloquium in Ancient Philosophy*, vol. 21. Leiden: Brill Academic Publishers.

Menski, Werner 2006. *Comparative Law in a Global Context: The Legal Systems of Asia and Africa*. New York: Cambridge University Press.

Merry, Sally Engle. 1998. "Law, Culture, and Cultural Appropriation." *Yale Journal of Law & the Humanities*, 10: 575–603.

Meyer, Elizabeth A. 2004. *Legitimacy and Law in the Roman World: Tabulae in Roman Belief and Practice*. Cambridge: Cambridge University Press.

Meyer, Elizabeth A. 2015. "Writing in the Roman Legal Contexts." In David Johnston (ed.), *The Cambridge Companion to Roman Law*. New York: Cambridge University Press.

Mezey, Naomi. 2001. "Law as Culture." *Yale Journal of Law & the Humanities*, 13: 35–67.

Michaels, Ralf. 2006. "The Functional Method of Comparative Law." In Mathias Reimann and Reinhard Zimmermann (eds.), *The Oxford Handbook of Comparative Law*. New York: Oxford University Press.

Michalowski, Piotr. 1990. "Early Mesopotamian Communicative Systems: Art, Literature and Writing." In Ann Gunter (ed.), *Investigating Artistic Environments in the Ancient Near East*. Washington: Smithsonian Institution.

Miller, Walter. 1913. *M. Tullius Cicero: On Duties. With An English Translation*. Cambridge, MA: Harvard University Press (Loeb Classical Library 30).

Mirhady, David C. 1990. "Aristotle on the Rhetoric of Law." *Greek, Roman, and Byzantine Studies*, 31: 393–410.

Mirhady, David C. 1991a. "Non-Technical *Pisteis* in Aristotle and Anaximenes." *American Journal of Philology*, 112: 5–28.

Mirhady, David C. 1991b. "The Oath-Challenge in Athens." *Classical Quarterly*, 41: 78–83.

Mirhady, David C. 1996. "Torture and Rhetoric in Athens." *The Journal of Hellenic Studies*, 116: 119–131.

Mirhady, David C. 2000. "Demosthenes as Advocate: The Private Speeches." In Ian Worthington (ed.), *Demosthenes: Statesman and Orator*. London: Routledge.

Mirhady, David C. 2002. "Athens' Democratic Witnesses." *Phoenix*, 56: 255–274.

Mirhady, David C. 2007. "The Dikasts' Oath and the Question of Fact." In A. Sommerstein and J. Fletcher (eds.), *Horkos: The Oath in Greek Society*. Bristol: Bristol Classical Press.

Mitteis, Ludwig. 1891. *Reichsrecht und Volksrecht in den östlichen Provinzen des Römischen Kaiserreichs mit Beiträgen zur Kenntniss des griechischen Rechts und der spätrömischen Rechtsentwicklung*. Leipzig: Teubner.

Mommsen, Theodor. 1877. *Römisches Staatsrecht*, vol. 2, part 1. Leipzig: Hirzel.

Mommsen, Theodor, Paul Krueger, and Alan Watson, eds. 1985. *The Digest of Justinian*, in 4 vols. Philadelphia: University of Pennsylvania Press.

Monoson, S. Sara. 2000. *Plato's Democratic Entanglements: Athenian Politics and the Practice of Philosophy*. Princeton: Princeton University Press.

Morgan, Kathryn, ed. 2003. *Popular Tyranny: Sovereignty and its Discontents in Ancient Greece*. Austin: University of Texas Press.

Morrow, Glenn R. 1960. *Plato's Cretan City: A Historical Interpretation of the* Laws. Princeton: Princeton University Press.

Mossé, Claude. 2004. "How a Political Myth Takes Shape: Solon, 'Founding Father' of the Athenian Democracy." In P.J. Rhodes (ed.), *Athenian Democracy*. New York: Oxford University Press.

Munn, Mark. 2000. *The School of History: Athens in the Age of Socrates*. Berkeley: University of California Press.

Murray, Augustus T., trans. 1936–39. *Demosthenes III–V*. Cambridge, MA: Harvard University Press.

Murray, Oswyn. 1998. "Introduction." In Jacob Burckhardt (ed.), *The Greeks and Greek Civilization*. New York: St. Martin's Press.

Mustakallio, Katariina and Christian Krötzl, eds. 2010. *De Amicitia: Friendship and Social Networks in Antiquity and the Middle Ages*. Rome: Institutum Romanum Finlandiae.

Nagy, Gregory. 1995. "Images of Justice in Early Greek Poetry." In K. D. Irani and Morris Smith (eds.), *Social Justice in the Ancient World*. Westport: Greenwood Press.

Nails, Debra. 1999. "Mouthpiece Schmouthpiece." In Gerald A. Press (ed.), *Who Speaks for Plato?* Lanham: Rowman & Littlefield.

Nelken, David. 2004: "Using the Concept of Legal Culture." *Australian Journal of Legal Philosophy*, 29: 1–26.

Nelken, David. 2007. "Defining and Using the Concept of Legal Culture." In Esin Örücü and David Nelken (eds.), *Comparative Law: A Handbook Comparative Law*. Oxford: Hart.

Nelken, David. 2012. *Using Legal Culture*. London: Wildy, Simmonds & Hill.

Nightingale, Andrea. 1993. "Writing/Reading a Sacred Text: Writing/Reading a Sacred Text: A Literary Interpretation of Plato's *Laws*." *Classical Philology*, 88(4): 279–300.

Nörr, Dieter. 1969. *Die Entstehung der longi temporis praescriptio; Studien zum Einfluss der Zeit im Recht und zur Rechtspolitik in der Kaiserzeit*. Cologne: Westdeutscher Verlag.

Nörr, Dieter. 1981. "The Matrimonial Legislation of Augustus: An Early Instance of Social Engineering." *The Irish Jurist*, 16: 350–364.

Nörr, Dieter. 1994. "Innovare." *Index*, 22: 61–86.
Ober, Josiah. 2001. *Political Dissent in Democratic Athens: Intellectual Critics of Popular Rule*. Princeton: Princeton University Press.
Olivelle, Patrick. 1993. *The Āśrama System. The History and Hermeneutics of a Religious Institution*. Oxford: Oxford University Press.
Ost, François. 2009. *Traduire: défense et illustration du multilinguisme*. Paris: Fayard.
Ostwald, Martin. 1969. *Nomos and the Beginnings of Athenian Democracy*. Oxford: Clarendon Press.
Ostwald, Martin. 1986. *From Popular Sovereignty to the Sovereignty of Law*. Berkeley: University of California Press.
Pangle, Lorraine Smith. 2014. *Virtue is Knowledge*. Chicago: University of Chicago Press.
Parker, Robert. 2005. "Law and Religion." In Michael Gagarin and David Cohen (eds.), *The Cambridge Companion to Ancient Greek Law*. New York: Cambridge University Press.
Paul, Shalom M. 1970. *Studies in the Book of the Covenant in the Light of Cuneiform and Biblical Law*. Leiden: Brill.
Pearson, Lionel. 1976. *The Art of Demosthenes*. Meisenheim am Glan: Anton Hain Verlag.
Pfau, Thomas. 2013. *Minding the Modern: Human Agency, Intellectual Traditions and Responsible Knowledge*. Indiana: University of Notre Dame Press.
Piccinelli, Ferdinando. 1980. *Studi e ricerche intorno alla definizione: Dominium est ius utendi et abutendi re sua, quatenus iuris ratio patitur*. Naples: Jovene.
Pitkin, Hanna. 1987. "The Idea of a Constitution." *Journal of Legal Education*, 37: 167–169.
Plato. 1980. *The Laws of Plato*. Translated by Thomas Pangle. New York: Basic Books.
Plato. 1997. "Republic." In John M. Cooper and D.S. Hutchinson (eds.), *Complete Works*. Indianapolis and Cambridge: Hackett Publishing.
Plato. 2013. *The Republic*. Translated by Tom Griffith and edited by G. R. F. Ferrari. New York: Cambridge University Press.
Plutarch. 1998. *Greek Lives*. Translated by Robin Waterfield. Oxford: Oxford University Press.
Pollock, Frederick. 1906. Notes to Maine, *Ancient Law: Its Connection with the Early History of Society and its Relation to Modern Ideas*. London: John Murray.
Polybius. 1962. *The Histories of Polybius*. Translate by Evelyn Shuckburgh. Bloomington: Indiana University Press.
Popper, Karl. [1944] 2013. *The Open Society and its Enemies*. Princeton: Princeton University Press.
Pradeau, Jean-François. 2005. "L'irréalisable vérité de la *République* platonicienne: Remarques sur le statut et sur le contenu de la *politeia* de la *République*." In Mogens Hansen (ed.), *The Imaginary Polis*. Copenhagen: The Royal Danish Academy of Sciences and Letters.
Press, Gerald A. 2007. *Plato: Guide for the Perplexed*. New York: Bloomsbury.
Prodi, Paolo. 2000. *Una storia della giustizia. Dal pluralismo dei fori al moderno dualismo tra coscienza e diritto*. Bologna: Il Mulino.
Pugliese, Giovanni. 1941. *Studi sull "iniuria."* Milan: Giuffrè.
Pugliese, Giovanni. 1962. *Il processo civile romano, I: Le legis actiones*. Rome: Edizioni Ricerche.
Raber, Fritz. 1969. *Grundlagen klassischer Injurienansprüche*. Vienna, Cologne and Graz: Böhlau.
Rawson, Elizabeth. 1983. *Cicero: A Portrait*. Bristol: Bristol Classical Press.
Renger, Johannes. 2002. "Royal Edicts of the Old Babylonian Period—Structural Background." In Michael Hudson and Marc Van De Mieroop (eds.), *Debt and Economic Renewal in the Ancient Near East*. Bethesda: CDL Press.

Resnik, Judith and Dennis Curtis. 2011. *Representing Justice: Invention, Controversy, and Rights in City-States and Democratic Courtrooms*. New Haven: Yale University Press.

Rhodes, P. J. 2009. "Civic Ideology and Citizenship." In Ryan Balot (ed.), *A Companion to Greek and Roman Political Thought*. Chichester: Wiley-Blackwell.

Richardson, John S. 1983. "The *Tabula Contrebiensis*: Roman Law in Spain in the Early First Century B.C." *The Journal of Roman Studies*, 73: 33–41.

Robson, Elenor. 2007. "Gendered Literacy and Numeracy in the Sumerian Literary Corpus." In G. Cunningham and J. Ebeling (eds.), *Analysing Literary Sumerian: Corpus-Based Approaches*. London: Equinox.

Romm, James. 2014. *Dying Every Day: Seneca at the Court of Nero*. New York: Knopf.

Rosen, Lawrence. 2006. *Law as Culture: An Invitation*. Princeton: Princeton University Press.

Rosenwein, Barbara H. 2010. "Problems and Methods in the History of Emotions." *Passions in Context: International Journal of the History and Theory of Emotions*, 1: 1–32.

Rosen-Zvi, I. 2008. *ha-Ṭekes she-lo hayah: miḳdash, midrash u-migdar be-Masekhet Soṭah*. Jerusalem: Magnes.

Roth, Martha T. 1995. "Mesopotamian Legal Traditions and the Laws of Hammurabi." *Chicago-Kent Law Review*, 71: 13–39.

Roth, Martha T. 1997. *Law Collections from Mesopotamia and Asia Minor*. 2nd edn. Atlanta, GA: Scholars Press.

Rowe, Christopher. 2010. "The Relationship of the *Laws* to Other Dialogues: A Proposal." In Christopher Bobonich (ed.), *Plato's Laws: A Critical Guide*. New York: Cambridge University Press.

Rubinstein, Lene. 2005. "Main Litigants and Witnesses in the Athenian Courts: Procedural Variations." In Michael Gagarin and Robert Wallace (eds.), *Symposion 2001, Vorträge zur griechischen und hellenistischen Rechtsgeschichte* (Evanston, September 5–8, 2001). Vienna: Verlag der Österreichischen Akademie der Wissenschaften.

Rupprecht, Hans A. 2005. "Greek Law in Foreign Surroundings: Continuity and Development." In Michael Gagarin and David Cohen (eds.), *The Cambridge Companion to Ancient Greek Law*. New York: Cambridge University Press.

Ruschenbusch, Eberhard. 1965. "ΥΒΡΕΩΣ ΓΡΑΦΗ. Ein Fremdkörper im athenischen Recht des 4. Jahrhunderts v. Ch." *Zeitschrift der Savigny-Stiftung für Rechtsgeschichte: Romanistische Abteilung*, 82: 302–309.

Ruschenbusch, Eberhard. 2010. *Solon: das Gesetzeswerk-Fragmente*. Stuttgart: Steiner.

Ruskola, Teemu. 2012. "The East Asian Legal Tradition." In Mauro Bussani and Ugo Mattei (eds.), *The Cambridge Companion to Comparative Law*. New York: Cambridge University Press.

Sabbatucci, Dario. 1981. "Il peccato cosmico." In *Le délit religieux dans la cité antique (Actes Rome 1978)*. Rome: École Française de Rome.

Sacco, Rodolfo. 1991. "Legal Formants: Dynamic Approach to Comparative Law." *The American Journal of Comparative Law*, 39: 1–34 (instalment I) and 343–401 (instalment II).

Santucci, Gianni. 2014a. "*Legum inopia* e diritto privato. Riflessioni intorno ad un recente contributo." *Studia et documenta historiae et iuris*, 80: 373–393.

Santucci, Gianni. 2014b. "Die *rei vindicatio* im klassischen römischen Recht – ein überblick." *Fundamina : A Journal of Legal History*, 2: 833–846.

Scafuro, Adele. 1994. "Witnessing and False-Witnessing: Proving Citizenship and Kin Identity in Fourth-Century Athens." In Allan L. Boegehold and A.C. Scafuro (eds.), *Athenian Identity and Civic Ideology*. Baltimore: Johns Hopkins University Press.

Scheid, John. 1981. "Le délit religieux dans la Rome tardo-républicaine." In *Le délit religieux dans la cité antique (Actes Rome 1978)*. Rome: École Française de Rome.

Scheid, John. 2001. *La religione a Roma*. Rome and Bari: Laterza.

Scheid, John. 2013. *Les dieux, l'État et l'individu. Réflexions sur la religion civique à Rome*. Paris: Seuil.

Schiappa, Edward. 1991. *The Beginnings of Rhetorical Theory in Classical Greece*. New Haven: Yale University Press.

Schiffman, Lawrence H. 2010. *Qumran and Jerusalem: Studies in the Dead Sea Scrolls and the History of Judaism*. Grand Rapids: William B. Eerdmans.

Schiller, A. Arthur. 1971. "Jurist's Law." In A. Arthur Schiller (ed.), *An American Experience in Roman Law*. Gottingen: Vandenhoeck & Ruprecht.

Schmähling, Eberhard. 1938. *Die Sittenaufsicht der Censoren*. Stuttgart: Kohlhammer.

Schneewind, Jerome B. 1998. *The Invention of Autonomy: A History of Modern Moral Philosophy*. Cambridge: Cambridge University Press.

Schofield, Malcolm. 1996. "Sharing in the Constitution." *Review of Metaphysics*, 49(4): 831–858.

Schofield, Malcolm. 1999. *Saving the City: Philosopher-Kings and Other Classical Paradigms*. London and New York: Routledge.

Schofield, Malcolm. 2006. *Plato: Political Philosophy*. Oxford: Clarendon Press.

Schofield, Malcolm. 2010. "The *Laws*' Two Projects." In Christopher Bobonich (ed.), *Plato's Laws: A Critical Guide*. New York: Cambridge University Press.

Schrage, Eltjo. 2003. "Het proces Jezus." *Ars Aequi*, 52(5): 355–364.

Schulz, Fritz. 1946. *History of Roman Legal Science*. Oxford: Clarendon Press.

Schulz, Fritz. 1951. *Classical Roman Law*. Oxford: Oxford University Press.

Schulz, Fritz. 1953. *History of Roman Legal Science*. 2nd edn. Oxford: Clarendon Press.

Schulz, Fritz. 1954. *Prinzipien des römischen Rechts*. Berlin: Duncker & Humblot.

Schulz, Fritz. 1963. *History of Roman Legal Science*. Reprint 2nd edn. Oxford: Clarendon Press.

Scott, Joan. 1986. "Gender: A Useful Category of Historical Analysis." *American Historical Review*, 91(5): 1053–1075.

Scurlock, JoAnn. 1995. "Death and Afterlife in Ancient Mesopotamian Thought." In Jack Sasson (ed.), *Civilizations of the Ancient Near East*, vol. 3. New York: Charles Scribners' Sons.

Sealey, Raphael. 1994. *The Justice of the Greeks*. Ann Arbor: University of Michigan Press.

Serrao, Feliciano. 1973. "Legge (diritto romano)." In *Enciclopedia del diritto*, vol. 23. Milan: Giuffrè, 794–850.

Serrao, Feliciano. 1974. *Classi partiti e legge nella repubblica romana*. Pisa: Pacini.

Serrao, Feliciano. 2006. *Diritto privato economia e società nella storia di Roma*, vol. 1. 3rd edn. Naples: Jovene.

Shaw, Brent D. 2015. "The Myth of the Neronian Persecution." *Journal of Roman Studies*, 105: 73–100.

Simon-Shoshan, Moshe. 2012. *Stories of the Law: Narrative Discourse and the Construction of Authority in the Mishnah*. New York: Oxford University Press.

Slanski, Kathryn E. 2003a. *The Babylonian Entitlement Narus (Kudurrus): A Study in their Form and Function*. Boston: American Schools of Oriental Research.

Slanski, Kathryn E. 2003b. "Representation of the Divine on the Babylonian Entitlement Monuments (Kudurrus)," *Archiv für Orientforschung*, 50: 308–320.

Slanski, Kathryn E. 2007. "The Mesopotamian 'Rod and Ring': Icon of Righteous Kingship and Balance of Power between Palace and Temple." In Harriet Crawford (ed.), *Regime Change in the Ancient Near East and Egypt: From Sargon or Agade to Saddam Hussein*. New York: Oxford University Press.

Slanski, Kathryn E. 2012. "The Law of Hammurabi and Its Audience." *Yale Journal of Law & the Humanities*, 24(1): 97–110.

Sommerstein, Alan H. and Andrew J. Bayliss. 2013. *Oath and State in Ancient Greece*. Berlin: De Gruyter.

Sophocles. 1991. *Antigone*. Translated by David Grene. In David Grene and Richard Lattimore, (eds.), *The Complete Greek Tragedies*, vol. 2. Chicago: University of Chicago Press.

Stackert, Jeffrey. 2014. *A Prophet like Moses: Prophecy, Law, and Israelite Religion*. Oxford and New York: Oxford University Press.

Stein, Peter. 1966. *Regulae Iuris: From Juristic Rules to Legal Maxims*. Edinburgh: Edinburgh University Press.

Stern, David. 1996. *Midrash and Theory: Ancient Jewish Exegesis and Contemporary Literary Studies*. Evanston: Northwestern University Press.

Stern, David. 1998. "The Captive Woman: Hellenization, Greco-Roman Erotic Narrative, and Rabbinic Literature." *Poetics Today*, 19: 91–127.

Sternberg, Meir. 1985. *The Poetics of Biblical Narrative: Ideological Literature and the Drama of Reading*. Bloomington: Indiana University Press.

Suolahti, Jaakko. 1963. *The Roman Censors: A Study on Social Structures*. Helsinki: Suomalainen tiedeakatemia.

Surkis, Judith. 2014. "Of Scandals and Supplements: Relating Intellectual and Cultural History." In Darrin McMahon and Samuel Moyn (eds.), *Rethinking Modern European Intellectual History*. Oxford and New York: Oxford University Press.

Talamanca, Mario. 1990. *Istituzioni di diritto romano*. Milan: Giuffrè.

Talamanca, Mario. 1997. "*Lex* ed *interpretatio* in Lab. 4 *post. a Iav. epit.* D, 19, 1, 50." In *Nozione formazione e interpretazione del diritto dall'età romana alle esperienze moderne. Ricerche F. Gallo*, vol. 4. Naples: Jovene.

Taylor, Charles. 1971. "Interpretation and the Sciences of Man." *The Review of Metaphysics*, 25(1): 3–51.

Tellegen-Couperus, Olga and Jan W. Tellegen. 2013. "*Artes Urbanae*: Roman Law and Rhetoric." In Paul Du Plessis (ed.), *New Frontiers. Law and Society in the Roman World*. Edinburgh: Edinburgh University Press.

Teubner, Günther and Andreas Fischer-Lescano. 2004. "Regime Collisions: The Vain Search for Legal Unity in the Fragmentation of Global Law." *Michigan Journal of International Law*, 25(4): 999–1046.

Thalheim, Theodor. 1916. "Ὕβρεως γραφή." In Wilhelm Kroll (ed.), *Paulys Realencyclopädie der classischen Altertumswissenschaft (RE) 17, Band IX,1*. Stuttgart: Metzler.

Thomas, Rosalind. 2005. "Writing, Law, and Written Law." In Michael Gagarin and David Cohen (eds.), *The Cambridge Companion to Ancient Greek Law*. New York: Cambridge University Press.

Thucydides. 1972. *A History of the Peloponnesian War*. Rev. edn. Translated by Rex Warner; Introduction by M.I. Finley. New York: Penguin Classics.

Thucydides. 1996. *History of the Peloponnesian War*. Translated by Richard Crawley. In Robert Strassler (ed.), *The Landmark Thucydides: A Comprehensive Guide to the Peloponnesian War*. New York: Touchstone.

Thür, Gerhard. 1977. *Beweisführung vor den Schwurgerichtshöfen Athens: Die Proklêsis zur Basanos*. Vienna: Verlag der Österreichischen Akademie der Wissenschaften.

Tierney, Brian. 1997. *The Idea of Natural Rights: Studies on Natural Rights, Natural Law and Church law 1150-1625*. Atlanta: Scholars Press.

Tigay, Jeffrey H. 1996. *Deuteronomy = [Devarim]: The Traditional Hebrew Text with the New JPS Translation*. Philadelphia: Jewish Publication Society.

Todd, Stephen. 1991. "The Purpose of Evidence in Athenian Courts." In Paul Cartledge, Paul Millett, and Stephen Todd (eds.), *Nomos: Essays in Athenian Law, Politics and Society*. Cambridge: Cambridge University Press.

Todd, Stephen. 1993. *The Shape of Athenian Law*. Oxford: Oxford University Press.

Tuori, K. 2007. *Ancient Roman Lawyers and Modern Legal Ideals: Studies on the Impact of Contemporary Concerns in the Interpretation of Ancient Roman Legal History*. Frankfurt am Main: Klostermann.

Turner, Victor. 1982. *From Ritual to Theatre: The Human Seriousness of Play*. New York: PAJ Publications.

Twining, William. 2006. "Glenn on Tradition: An Overview." *Journal of Comparative Law*, 1(1): 107–115.

Twining, William. 2009. *General Jurisprudence: Understanding Law from a Global Perspective*. New York: Cambridge University Press.

Van De Mieroop, Mark. 2002. "A History of Near Eastern Debt?" In Michael Hudson and Marc Van De Mieroop (eds.), *Debt and Economic Renewal in the Ancient Near East*. Bethesda: CDL Press.

Vandendriessche, Sarah. 2006. *Possessio und Dominium im postklassischen römischen Recht: eine Überprüfung von Levy's Vulgarrechtstheorie anhand der Quellen des Codex Theodosianus und der Posttheodosianischen Novellen*. Hamburg: Kovac.

Vegetti, Mario. 2013. "How and Why Did the *Republic* Become Unpolitical?" In Noburu Notomi and Luc Brisson (eds.), *Dialogues on Plato's Politeia (Republic): Selected Papers from the Ninth Symposium Platonicum*. Sankt Augustin: Academia Verlag.

Veldhuis, Niek. 2011. "Levels of Literacy." In Eleanor Robson and Karin Radner (eds.), *The Oxford Handbook of Cuneiform Culture*. Oxford: Oxford University Press.

Vendryes, Joseph. 1918. "Les correspondances de vocabulaire entre l'indo-iranien et l'italo-celtique." *Mémoires de la Société Linguistique de Paris*, 20: 265–285.

Vermeule, Emily. 1966. "The Boston Oresteia Krater." *American Journal of Archaeology*, 70(1): 1–22.

Vernant, Jean-Pierre and Pierre Vidal-Naquet. 1988. *Myth and Tragedy in Ancient Greece*. Translated by Janet Lloyd. New York: Zone Books.

Veyne, Paul 1984. *Writing History: Essay on Epistemology*. Translated by Mina Moore-Rinvolucri. Middletown, CT: Wesleyan University Press.

Volkmann, Hans. 1969. *Zur Rechtssprechung im Principat des Augustus*. Munich: C. H. Beck.

von Benda-Beckmann, F. and Keebet von Benda-Beckmann. 2010. "Why Not Legal Culture?" *The Journal of Comparative Law*, 5(2): 104–117.

von Savigny, Friedrich Carl. 1840. *System des heutigen römischen Rechts*, vol. 1. Berlin: Veit und Comp.

Waterfield, Robin. 2009. *Why Socrates Died: Dispelling the Myths*. London: Faber & Faber.

Watson, Alan. 1968. *The Law of Property in the Later Roman Republic*. Oxford: Clarendon Press.

Watson, Alan. 1974. *Legal Transplants: An Approach to Comparative Law*. Edinburgh: Scottish Academic Press.

Watson, Alan. 1983a. "Legal Change: Sources of Law and Legal Culture." *Scholarly Works*. Available online at http://digitalcommons.law.uga.edu/fac_artchop/534.

Watson, Alan. 1983b. "Roman Slave Law and Romanist Ideology." *Phoenix*, 37(1): 53–65.
Watson, Alan. 1993. *International Law in Archaic Rome: War and Religion*. Baltimore: Johns Hopkins University Press.
Watson, Alan. 1998. *Ancient Law and Modern Understanding*. Athens, GA: University of Georgia.
Watson, Alan et al. 1985. *The Digest of Justinian. English translation with the Latin text edited by Theodor Mommsen with the aid of Paul Krueger*. Philadelphia: University of Pennsylvania Press.
Watt, Gary. 2013. *Dress, Law and Naked Truth: A Cultural History of Fashion and Form*. London: Bloomsbury.
Webber, Jeremy. 2004. "Culture, Legal Culture, and Legal Reasoning: A Comment on Nelken." *Australian Journal of Legal Philosophy*, 29: 27–36.
Weil, Simone. [1940–1] 2003. *The Iliad or the Poem of Force: A Critical Edition*. Edited by James P. Holoka. New York: Peter Lang.
Weiss, Roslyn. 2012. *Philosophers in the Republic: Plato's Two Paradigms*. Ithaca: Cornell University Press.
Wells, Bruce and F. Rachel Magdalene, eds. 2009. *Law from the Tigris to the Tiber: The Writings of Raymond Westbrook*, 2 vols. Winona Lake: Eisenbrauns.
Westbrook, Raymond. 1988. *Studies in Biblical and Cuneiform Law*. Cahiers de la Revue Biblique 26. Paris: Gabalda.
Westbrook, Raymond. 2003a. "Introduction: The Character of Ancient Near Eastern Law." In Raymond Westbrook (ed.), *A History of Ancient Near Eastern Law*, 2 vols. Leiden and Boston: Brill.
Westbrook, Raymond. 2003b. "Old Babylonian." In Raymond Westbrook (ed.), *A History of Ancient Near Eastern Law*, vol. 1. Leiden: Brill.
Westbrook, Raymond. [1985] 2009a. "Biblical and Cuneiform Law Codes." In Wells, Bruce and F. Rachel Magdalene (eds.), *Law from the Tigris to the Tiber: The Writings of Raymond Westbrook*. Winona Lake: Eisenbrauns.
Westbrook, Raymond. [1989] 2009b. "Cuneiform Law Codes and the Origins of Legislation." In Bruce Wells and F. Rachel Magdalene (eds.), *Law from the Tigris to the Tiber: The Writings of Raymond Westbrook*. Winona Lake: Eisenbrauns.
Westbrook, Raymond. [1995] 2009c. "Social Justice in the Ancient Near East." In Bruce Wells and F. Rachel Magdalene (eds.), *Law from the Tigris to the Tiber: The Writings of Raymond Westbrook*. Winona Lake: Eisenbrauns.
Westbrook, Raymond. 2009d. *Law from the Tigris to the Tiber: The Writings of Raymond Westbrook*, 2 vols. Edited by Bruce Wells and F. Rachel Magdalene. Winona Lake: Eisenbrauns.
Westbrook, Raymond. 2015. *Ex oriente lex: Near Eastern Influences on Ancient Greek and Roman Law*. Edited by Deborah Lyons and Kurt Raaflaub. Baltimore: The Johns Hopkins University Press.
White, Hayden. 1973a. *Metahistory: The Historical Imagination in Nineteenth-Century Europe*. Baltimore and London: The Johns Hopkins University Press.
White, James Boyd. 1973b. *The Legal Imagination: Studies in the Nature of Legal Thought and Expression*. Boston: Little, Brown & Co.
White, James Boyd. 1984. *When Words Lose Their Meaning: Constitutions and Reconstitutions of Language, Character, and Community*. Chicago: The University of Chicago Press.
White, James Boyd. 1985. *Heracles' Bow: Essays on the Rhetoric and Poetics of Law*. Madison: The University of Wisconsin Press.

White, James Boyd. 1990. *Justice as Translation: An Essay in Cultural and Legal Criticism*. Chicago: The University of Chicago Press.

Wieacker, Franz. 1973. "*Contractus* und *obligatio* im Naturrecht zwischen Spätscholastik und Aufklärung." In P. Grossi (ed.), *La Seconda Scolastica nella formazione del diritto privato moderno*. Milan: Giuffrè.

Willets, Ronald F. 1967. *The Law Code of Gortyn*. Berlin: de Gruyter.

Williams, Raymond. 1976. *Keywords: A Vocabulary of Culture and Society*. New York: Oxford University Press.

Wimpfheimer, Barry S. 2011. *Narrating the Law: A Poetics of Talmudic Legal Stories*. Philadelphia: University of Pennsylvania Press.

Wimsatt, William K. 1954. *The Verbal Icon: Studies in the Meaning of Poetry*. Lexington: University of Kentucky Press.

Winter, Irene J. 1992. "Idols of the King." *Journal of Ritual Studies*, 6(1): 13–42.

Winter, Irene J. 1996. "Sex, Rhetoric, and the Public Monument: The Alluring Body of Naram-Sîn of Agade." In Natalie Boymel Kampen (ed.), *Sexuality in Ancient Art: Near East, Egypt, Greece, and Italy*. Cambridge: Cambridge University Press.

Wittmann, Roland. 1974. "Die Entwicklungslinien der klassischen Injurienklage." *Zeitschrift der Savigny-Stiftung für Rechtsgeschichte: Romanistische Abteilung*, 91: 285–359.

Wohl, Victoria. 2002. *Love among the Ruins: The Erotics of Democracy in Classical Athens*. Princeton: Princeton University Press.

Wolf, Joseph Georg. 2015. "Documents in Roman Practice." In David Johnston (ed.), *The Cambridge Companion to Roman Law*. New York: Cambridge University Press.

Wright, David. 2009. *Inventing God's Law: How the Covenant Code of the Bible Used and Revised the Laws of Hammurabi*. Oxford: Oxford University Press.

Xenophon. 1925. *Constitution of the Lacedaemonians*. Cambridge, MA: Harvard University Press.

Yadin-Israel, Azzan. 2004. *Scripture as Logos: Rabbi Ishmael and the Origins of Midrash*. Philadelphia: University of Pennsylvania Press.

Yadin-Israel, Azzan. 2014. *Scripture and Tradition: Rabbi Akiva and the Triumph of Midrash*. Philadelphia: University of Pennsylvania Press.

Zimmermann, Reinhard. 1996. *The Law of Obligations: Roman Foundations of the Civilian Tradition*. Oxford: Oxford University Press.

Zuckert, Catherine. 2009. *Plato's Philosophers: The Coherence of the Dialogues*. Chicago: University of Chicago Press.

Zumbansen, Peer. 2010 "Transnational Legal Pluralism." *Transnational Legal Theory*, 1(2): 141–189.

Zumbansen, Peer. 2014. "Law & Society and the Politics of Relevance: Facts and Field Boundaries in 'Transnational Legal Theory in Context'." *No Foundations: An Interdisciplinary Journal of Law and Justice*, 11: 1–37.

Zweigert, Konrad and Hein Kötz. 1998. *An Introduction to Comparative Law*. 3rd edn. Translated by Tony Weir. Oxford: Oxford University Press.

INDEX

abuse
    moral transgressions 135–7, 138, 139, 141
    transgressions of cultural norms 132, 134
Achilles 6, 7, 107
adultery 14
    moral transgressions 135, 138, 139, 141
    transgressions of cultural norms 133–4, 134–5
advocates 143, 145
Aeschines 91, 95
Aeschylus 23, 32
    Oresteia 34–8, 41, 44
Agennius Urbicus 123
ager publicus 115
agrarianism 79, 112
agreements
    archaic Roman law 79–84
    classical Roman law 84–9
    late Roman law 89–90
    modern subjectivism 75–7
    Roman law and society 77–9
Akkadian language 21–2
Allen, Danielle 163
Ambrose of Milan 137
amicitia 144–9
Anaximenes 92, 95, 101
Ando, Clifford 143, 159
Andrews, Malcolm xiii
Antiquity
    legal documents and other materials 1
    questions of meaning 1–2
    time and space 1
Aquillus Gallus 146
Ara Pacis 6, 9
Arcangeli, Alessandro 109
argumentation
    Athenian democracy 92–5
    based on challenges 99–100
    based on oaths 103–4
    based on torture 102–4, 105–6
    based on wills 99
    concerning violence 106–7
    documentary evidence 92–5

ex tempore 100
false testimony 101–2
just and beneficial laws 95–6
legal technicalities 104–6
litigiousness 107
speech writing 91–2 (*see also* Demosthenes)
witness testimony 92, 90–9, 100
Aristophanes 44, 91, 92
Aristotle 55, 77, 93
    Constitution of Athens 132
    Nichomachean Ethics 50
    Politics 42–3, 44, 45, 46, 48, 54, 56
    Rhetoric 95, 96, 99, 101, 167
artifacts 5, 6, 18
assault 106
atechnoi pisteis 93, 94, 99
Athenian Decrees 4, 56
Athenian democracy 92–5
Athenian Law-Court speeches 1, 14. See also Demosthenes
Athenian plague 159
Atkison, Larissa M. 163
Auerbach, Erich 17
Augustus 89, 130, 131, 134, 135
Augustus coin 8
Augustus, law of 134, 135, 138, 139, 141
Austin, John 11, 12

Bahrani, Zainab 162
Bartor, Assnat 165
Bauman, Richard A. 144, 169
Benda-Beckmann, F. von 110
Bentham, Jeremy 11, 12
Berkowitz, Beth A. 165
Berman, Joshua 160
Bhagavadgītā 78
Biblical law. *See* Hebrew Bible
Binder, Guyora 164
bona fides 88
Bonner, Robert J. 167
Bottéro, Jean 158
Bowersock, G. W. 158

Bruner, Jerome 165
Bryen, Ari 10
Budick, Sanford 165
Burckhardt, Jacob 3, 5, 18, 159

canon law 76
Capito, C. Ateius 144, 153, 154
Capogrossi Colognesi, Luigi 168, 169
Carandini, Andrea 168
Carey, Chris 93, 167, 168
Cascio, Elio Lo 169
Cascione, Cosimo 166
Cassius Dio 138
casuistic presentations 66, 67, 70
Catalano, Pierangelo 166
census 134
Chavel, Simeon 165
Chiba, Masaji 11, 159
Christianity 16, 75–6, 89, 90, 123, 137, 158
   trial of Jesus Christ 125, 126, 128, 129, 131, 139, 141
Cicero, Marcus Tullius 43, 45, 88, 116–18
   bust 147
   De oratore 146
   descriptions of Quintus Mucius 149–52
   political-criminal trials 127–8, 129, 131, 134, 139, 140
   Topica 147
civil law 76
clientela 151
Code of Hammurabi. *See Law Stele of Hammurabi*
codes. *See* legal codes
Cohen, David 132–4, 168, 170
command theory 11
communis opinio 152
comparative law 13–16
Connor, W. Robert 163
Constantine 123
Constitutio Antoniniana 123
constitutionalism
   constitutional rule 55–7
   democracy 43–4, 45
   established rule, custom, or way of life 41, 42, 43
   extra-constitutional rule 47–51
   kallipolis 47–52, 54–5
   participation 44–5
   politeia 46, 47–50, 55, 56
   rule by governing body 41, 42, 43
   rule of law 45–6
   tyranny 42, 44, 45
   willing acquiescence 51–4

context 17–19, 65
continuity 11
contracts. *See* agreements
Cooper, Jerrold S. 161
Corbo, Chiara 169
Cornell, Tim 166
cosmic order 78
Cotterrell, Roger 110–11
covenant 75–6
Cover, Robert 6, 10, 164
Crawford, Michael H. 168
criminal law 125
   abuse 132, 134, 139, 141
   adultery 133–4, 134–5, 138, 139, 141
   famous trials 125–31, 138–9, 141
   moral transgressions 135–9, 141
   popular and private claims 129, 130, 131, 140–1
   transgression of cultural norms 132–5
critical-hermeneutic method 17–19
cultural approach to law 3–10
cultural artifacts 5, 6, 18
cultural history xii–xiii, 109
cultural norms 132–5
cuneiform 25, 61
Curtis, Dennis 162
custom 77

De Martino, Francesco 166
Dead Sea Scrolls 61, 63, 165
debts 31
Delian League 4
democracy 43–4, 45, 92–5
Demosthenes 91–5
   Against Aphobus 96–104
   Against Conon 99, 106–7
   Against Onetor 99, 104–6
   Against Stephanus 94–5
   political-criminal trials 126–7, 128, 129, 132, 139, 140, 141
Deuteronomic Code 61, 69–70, 71, 72, 73
Diacon, Paul 166
dignitas 81, 89
dike 22, 33
Diocletian 124
Diósdi, György 168
divinely ordered universe 23, 27–8, 31, 68
documentary evidence 92–5
dominium 120
Donnelly, John Jr xii
Dover, Kenneth James 167
Draco 14, 62, 128

Egypt 158
entechnoi pisteis 96
ethics 77, 88
Etxabe, Julen 7, 13
eunomia 45–6
Euripides 32, 42, 92
evidence
  atechnoi pisteis 93, 94, 99
  entechnoi pisteis 96
  false testimony 101–2
  given on oath 103–4
  given under torture 92, 96, 100, 101, 102–4, 105–6
  wills 99
  witness testimony 92, 96–9, 100
ex tempore arguments 100
exemplum 135

false testimony 101–2
fides 80, 87–8
Finkelstein, J. J. 165
Finley, Moses 3, 159
Fiori, Roberto 166
Fish, Stanley E. 164
form criticism 67
formalism 14
formulae 85, 86, 113
Forsythe, Gary 168
Forum Romanum 127, 129, 156, 157
Frank, Jill 163
Friedman, Lawrence 110
friendships 144–9
functionalism 14–15

Gagarin, Michael 168
Gaius 89, 121
  Digesta 171
  Institutes 6, 63, 86, 154, 171
Gaon, Sherira 66
gentiles 80, 84
Germanic customary law 124
Gernet, Louis 159
Glenn, Patrick 12, 13, 159
globalization 10
Gordley, James 166
Gortyn Code 62, 65, 66
gravitas 78
Greek legal tradition 3, 13, 62
  Athenian Decrees 4, 56
  Athenian democracy 92–5
  Athenian Law-Court speeches 1, 14 (*see also* Demosthenes)
  dike 22
  documentary evidence 92–5
  geography of Greece 1, 3
  Gortyn Code 62, 65, 66
  Homeric society 10
  litigiousness 107
  popular and private claims 129, 130, 140–1
  speech writing 91–2 (*see also* Demosthenes)
  wrongs (*see* criminal law)
Greek tragedies 18, 32, 92
  Antigone 41, 42, 44
  Oresteia 34–8, 41, 44
Greenidge, Abel Henry Jones 170
Guettel Cole, Susan 170

Hagemann, Matthias 170, 171
Halbertal, Moshe 165
Halliwell, Stephen 49
Hammurabi 161
Hammurabi Code. *See Law Code of Hammurabi*
Hansen, M. H. 107
Harper, Kyle 169
Harris, Edward M. 167, 169
Hart, H. L. A. 12, 159
Hebrew Bible 1, 17, 69
  comparison with *Law Stele of Hammurabi* 27
  Covenant Code 61, 67
  Dead Sea Scrolls 61, 63
  Deuteronomic Code 61, 69–70, 71, 72, 73
  Deuteronomy 17, 18, 27, 71, 160
  Exodus 17, 18, 27, 67, 160
  Holiness Code 61
  Leviticus 27
  midrashic exegesis 17, 69–74
  mishpat 22
  Priestly Code 61
  Torah 66, 70, 71, 73
  tsedeq 22
Heidegger, Martin 18
Heitland, William Emerton 168
hermeneutics 17–19
Herodotus 41, 42, 92
Hesiod 22, 23, 32
  Works and Days 33–4
Hiltebeitel, Alf 166
historical context 17–19, 65
historical-critical method 18
historical jurisprudence 10–13
historical narratives 159
Hitzig, Hermann Ferdinand 170, 171

Homer 6, 10, 23, 33
    Iliad 7, 32, 34, 107
    Odyssey 7, 32, 34
homicide 67
honestas 78
Honig, Bonnie 163
hospitality 7, 34
Humbert, Michel 168
Humphreys, Sally 97
Hurowitz, Victor 165
Husa, Jaakko 160

Ibbetson, David J. 171
Indo-European peoples 78, 88
international relationships 84, 88–9
Irish law 78
Isaeus 96
Ishtar Gate 6, 8
Isocrates 91, 107
Israelite/Jewish culture 61–2. *See also* Hebrew Bible)
ius civile 3, 11, 79, 118, 120
ius commercii 120
ius gentium 3, 11, 79, 118, 120
ius Quiritium 84, 85, 86
ius respondendi 153

Jacobsen, Thorkild 162
Jaeger, Werner 167
Jakab, Eva 116, 124, 169
Jesus Christ 125, 126, 128, 129, 131, 139, 141
John, King of England xi, xii
Julius Caesar 134–5
juries 128, 143
jurisprudence 10–13
jurists 146
justice
    dike 22, 33
    divine origin 23, 27–8, 31
    Hammurabi Code (*see Law Stele of Hammurabi*)
    misharu 21–2, 28
    mishpat 22
    retribution and restoration 31, 32–7
    social justice 31
    tsedeq 22
Justinian 90, 118, 124
    Corpus Juris Civilis 1, 63, 76
    Digest 16, 68, 137, 151, 152, 154, 155

Kahn, Paul W. 164
kallipolis 47–51, 54–5

Kant, Immanuel 76
Kaser, Max 113, 119, 166, 167, 169
Kelsen, Hans 12
Klepsydra 97
Knox, B. 162
kosmiotes 54
kosmos 33
Krause, Jens-Uwe 170
Krygier, Martin 12–13
Kunkel, Wolfgang 144, 170

Labeo, M. Antisius 119, 134, 144, 153, 154
LaCapra, Dominick 18, 19, 160
Lamberton, R. 162
land surveyors 116, 117, 12, 123
Lane, Melissa 47, 164
Launaro, Alessandro 169
Law Stele of Hammurabi 1, 6, 21, 23, 61, 67
    cultural context 25–6
    divine mandate 27–8, 31, 68
    earlier law collections 161
    inscription 26–7
    perfomative quality 29–31
    relief sculpture 27–9
    social foundations 24–5
Lebow, Richard Ned 159
legal agreements. *See* agreements
legal arguments. *See* argumentation
legal codes 59–60. *See also Law Stele of Hammurabi*; Roman law
    context and purpose 65–6
    Israelite/Jewish culture 61–2
    just and beneficial laws 95–6
    Mesopotamia 60
    modern resonance 64–6
    poetics 66–9
legal culture 110
legal diversity 123–4
legal professionals 143–4
    Capito 144, 153, 154
    imperial lawyers 154–6
    Labeo 119, 134, 144, 153, 154
    Quintus Mucius 149–52, 155, 156
    respondere cavere agree 144
legal relationship 75, 77
legal representation 143, 151, 157
legal traditions 12–13
legal training 152
legis actiones 84, 85, 86, 113
Legrand, Pierre xii, 15–16
Lentz, Tony 167
Levinson, Bernard 17, 160
Levy, Ernst 167, 169

lex agraria 116
Lintott, Andrew William 116
Locke, Hew xi–xii
Lycurgus 46, 56
Lysias 14, 96

McGinn, Thomas, A. J. 135, 138, 171
Magna Carta xi, xii
Maine, Henry Sumner 10–12, 159
mancipatio 80, 111, 112, 118, 120
manslaughter 130
Maresch, Klaus 169
marriage 81, 82, 89, 139
Masi Doria, C. 166
medieval jurists 76
"Melian Dialogue" 32, 38–9
Menn, Stephen 163
mentalité 16
merchants 84, 85
Mesopotamia 1–2, 21, 60, 67. *See also Law Stele of Hammurabi*
Meyer, Elizabeth A. 159
Mezey, Naomi 164
Michaels, Ralf 15
Michalowski, Piotr 161
midrashic exegesis 17, 69–74
Minos 46
Mirhady, David C. 167, 168
misharu 21–2, 28
Mishnah 61, 66
mishpat 22
Mitteis, Ludwig 129
Mommsen, Theodor 170
moral transgressions 135–9, 141
mores 77
Mucii Scaevolae 144, 149
Mucius Scaevola, Quintus 149–52, 155, 156

Nails, Debra 163
Natural law 75, 76, 79
Nature 76
Nelken, David 159
Neo, Terentius 148
Nerva 119
Niebuhr, B. J. 159
Nietzsche, Friedrich 3
Nightingale, Andrea 164
"normative universes" 13
Nörr, Dieter 169

oaths 100, 103–4
obligations 87
Olivelle, Paatrick 166

oral traditions 12–13
orators 128. *See also* Cicero, Marcus Tullius; Demosthenes
ownership. *See* property

pacisci 84, 166
Pangle, Smith 164
Papinian 136
Papirius, Publius 148
Parthenon 5, 6
pater familias 79, 86, 87, 139
patria potestas 80, 112
Paul (Roman jurist) 119
pax deorum 78, 84
Peloponnesian War 38, 44, 93
Pilate, Pontius 126
Pitkin, Hanna 57
Plato
    Crito 53
    Laws 43, 45–50, 52, 53, 56
    Republic 21, 39, 43, 44, 46–50, 54–5
Plautus 145
plebs 84
Plutarch 56
poetics 66–9
politeia 46, 47–50, 55, 56
Polybius 45, 163
Pomponius 147–8, 149, 153, 155
positivism 77
precepts 66–7
private law 75, 77, 78
Prodi, Paolo 166
professionalization debate 144
property 109–11
    archaic Roman law 111–12
    Roman Empire 118–24
    Roman Republic 112–18
prostitution 138
pseudo-Agennius Urbicus 121, 123
public land 115–16
Pudicitia 83
Pugliese, Giovanni 170, 171

rabbinic exegesis 17, 69–74
rabbinic legal codes 61–2
Raber, Fritz 171
Ranke, Leopold von 159
Rashi 70–1, 165
Rechtsgeschäft 75, 77
Rechtsverhältnis 75
"religious land" 123
res mancipi 80, 112, 118, 120
Resnik, Judith 162

respondere cavere agree 144
restoration 31
retribution 31, 32–7
rhetoric 143
Rhodes, P. J. 44
Richardson, John S. 116
Roman citizenship 113, 115, 120, 131, 134, 135, 154
Roman law 6, 63. *See also* Justinian
   ager publicus 115
   agrarianism 79, 112
   amicitia 144–9
   archaic law 79–84, 111–12
   census 134
   Christian theology and 16
   civil trials 82, 84
   classical Roman law 84–9, 118
   clientship 80
   colonate 124
   communis opinio 152
   Constitutio Antoniniana 123
   dignitas 81, 89
   disputes 82
   dominium 120
   empire 118–24, 154–6
   exemplum 135
   fides 80, 87–8
   formulae 85, 86, 113
   gentiles 80, 84
   Germanic customary law and 124
   Hellenistic influence 88
   international relationships 84, 88–9
   ius civile 3, 11, 79, 118, 120
   ius commercii 120
   ius gentium 11, 79, 118, 120
   ius Quintium 84, 85, 86
   ius respondendi 155
   jurisdiction of Roman governors 126, 129
   jurists 146 (*see also* Gaius; Labeo, M. Antisius; Paul (Roman jurist); Ulpian)
   land records 121, 122, 123
   land surveyors 116, 117, 121, 123
   late Roman law 89–90
   law of Augustus 134, 135, 138, 139, 141
   legal diversity 123–4
   legis actiones 84, 85, 86, 113
   lex agraria 116
   mancipatio 80, 111, 112, 118, 120
   marriage 81, 82, 89
   mores 77
   Nerva 119
   nobilitas 85
   obligations 87
   ownership and possession 109–24
   pacisci 84, 166
   pater familias 79, 86, 87, 139
   patria potestas 112
   pax deorum 78, 84
   plebs 84
   professionals (*see* legal professionals)
   republic 112–18, 145–6, 154, 156
   res mancipii 80, 112, 118, 120
   ritual acts 80–1
   social bonds 82, 86
   sodalitas 80
   sources of law 146
   sponsio 80
   Sullan laws 130, 131
   Tabula Contrebiensis 116
   taxes 123, 124
   traditio 118, 120
   Twelve Tables 1, 63, 111, 112, 134
   war veterans 113, 114
   wrongs (*see* criminal law)
Roman roads 9
Roman virtues 78
Rosen, Lawrence xii, 164
Rosen-Zvi, I. 165
Roth, Martha 1–2, 17, 161
Rubinstein, Lene 168
rule of law 45–6

Sacco, Rodolfo 11
Santucci, Gianni 166
Savigny, Friedrich Carl von 75, 159, 165
Scheid, John 166
Schiappa, Edward 167
Schiffman, Lawrence H. 164, 165
Schiller, A. Arthur 146
Schneewind, Jerome B. 166
Schofield, Malcolm 51
Schulz, Fritz 135, 153, 166
Scipio Nasica, Gaius 148
Seneca 137, 138
Serrao, Feliciano 166
Servius Sulpicius 152
sexual conduct 70–1, 73
sexual transgressions 132–3, 137, 139, 141. *See also* adultery; rape
Shakespeare, William xi
Shaw, Brent 158
Simon-Shoshan, Moshe 165
sin 76
slaves 31, 123

abuse of 131, 132, 135–8, 139
revolt 116
torture of 92, 96, 100, 101, 102, 105–6
social imaginary 143
social justice 31
social status 145
Socrates 21, 34, 43, 44, 48, 49, 50, 53–5
trial 125–6, 128, 129, 138
Solon 45–6, 56, 62, 95, 128, 132
Sophocles 32
Antigone 41, 42, 44
sovereignty 10
Spartacus 116
speech writing 91–2. *See also* Demosthenes
Spinoza, Baruch 17
sponsio 80
Stackert, Jeffrey 160, 165
Stern, David 165
Sternberg, Meir 17
subjectivism 75–7, 128
Sulla, Cornelius 134
Sullan laws 130, 131, 138
Surkis, Judith 160

Tabula Contrebiensis 116
Tacitus 154
Talamanca, Mario 166
Talmuds 62, 64
Tarpeian Rock 82
Taylor, Charles 143
taxes 123, 124
Tellegen, Jan W. 144
Tellegen-Couperus, Olga 144
Thalheim, Theodor 170
Thomas, Rosalind 159, 168
Thucydides 7, 23, 41, 42, 43, 92, 159
"Melian Dialogue" 32, 38–9
Todd, Stephen 97
Torah 66, 70, 71, 73
torture 92, 96, 100, 101, 102–4, 105–6
Tosefta 61–2
traditio 118, 120
treaties 84
trial scenes 125–31, 138–9, 141

tsedeq 22
Twelve Tables 1, 63, 66, 111, 112, 134
Twining, William 159
tyranny 42, 44, 45

Ulpian 87, 136–7, 155, 170, 171
usus 111

Valerius Maximus 138
Vandendriessche, Sarah 169
Vegetti, Mario 48
Veldhuis, Niek 161
Vermeule, Emily 163
Verres 129, 130
Veyne, Paul 5
violence 106–7
virtues 78

war veterans 113, 114
warrior culture 7
waterclocks 97
Waterfield, Robin 169
Watson, Alan 113, 166, 168
Weisberg, Robert 164
Westbrook, Raymond 64, 158, 159, 161, 162, 164, 168
White, Hayden 5
White, James Boyd 10, 16, 19
wills 99
Wimpfheimer, Barry S. 164, 165
Wimsatt, William K. 165
Winter, Irene J. 162
witness testimony 92, 96–9, 100
Wittmann, Roland 170, 171
Wolf, Joseph Georg 159
women's rights 103, 132
wrongs. *See* criminal law

Xenophon 44

Yadin-Israel, Azzan 165

Zimmermann, Reinhard 170, 171